JFK
in the
SENATE

Center Point
Large Print

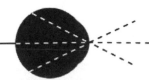

**This Large Print Book carries the
Seal of Approval of N.A.V.H.**

JFK
in the
SENATE

Pathway to the Presidency

John T. Shaw

CENTER POINT LARGE PRINT
THORNDIKE, MAINE

This Center Point Large Print edition is published
in the year 2013 by arrangement with
St. Martin's Press.

The text of this Large Print edition is unabridged.
In other aspects, this book may vary
from the original edition.
Printed in the United States of America
on permanent paper.
Set in 16-point Times New Roman type.

ISBN: 978-1-61173-947-3

Library of Congress Cataloging-in-Publication Data

Shaw, John, 1957–
JFK in the senate : pathway to the presidency / John T. Shaw.—
    Large print edition.
pages cm
Originally published: New York City : Palgrave Macmillan, 2013.
ISBN 978-1-61173-947-3 (library binding : alk. paper)
1. Kennedy, John F. (John Fitzgerald), 1917–1963.
    2. Legislators—United States—Biography.
    3. United States—Politics and government—1953–1961.
    4. United States. Congress. Senate—Biography.
    5. Presidents—United States—Biography. I. Title.
E842.S43 2013b
973.922092—dc23
[B]
                                                2013032799

For Mindy

For of those to whom much is given, much is required. And when at some future date the High Court of History sits in judgment on each one of us—recording whether in our brief span of service we fulfilled our responsibilities to the state—our success or failure, in whatever office we hold, will be measured by the answers to four questions:

First, were we truly men of courage—with the courage to stand up to one's enemies—and the courage to stand up, when necessary, to one's own associates—the courage to resist public pressure as well as private greed?

Secondly, were we truly men of judgment—with perceptive judgment of the future as well as the past—of our own mistakes as well as the mistakes of others—with enough wisdom to know what we did not know, and enough candor to admit it?

Third, were we truly men of integrity—men who never ran out on either the principles in which we believed or the people who believed in us—men whom neither financial gain nor political ambition could ever divert from the fulfillment of our sacred trust?

Finally, were we truly men of dedication—

with an honor mortgaged to no single individual or group and compromised by no private obligation or aim, but devoted solely to serving the public good and the national interest?

John F. Kennedy,
Farewell Address to the
Massachusetts State Legislature,
January 9, 1961

Contents

Acknowledgments

JFK in the Senate would not be bound between these two covers without the assistance of many people.

The excellent staff in the U.S. Senate Library helped me track down books and articles about the Senate in general and John F. Kennedy in particular. Thanks to reference librarians Annie Cobleigh, Meghan Dunn, Melanie Srivisal, Sarah Gilliland, and Natalie Sager. Special thanks to Brian McLaughlin, Zoe Davis, Nancy Kervin, and Tamara Elliot, who graciously accommodated my seemingly endless requests without making me feel like I was an imposition. Thanks also to those at the library's front desk: Kara Baer, Rachel Donelson, Beverly Forrest, and Robert Nix, and to Leona Faust, the Senate librarian.

I'm greatly indebted to the staff of the Senate Historical Office. Don Ritchie, the Senate historian, initially directed me to Kennedy's work on the Kennedy Committee and sparked my broader interest in JFK's Senate career. Betty Koed, the assistant Senate historian, has been incredibly helpful throughout this project. She reviewed my manuscript with both rigor and kindness and offered dozens of detailed suggestions. Richard Baker, the Senate Historian emeritus, also read my manuscript with care and offered excellent suggestions on how to fine-tune the text. Special thanks to Heather Moore, the manager of the Historical Office's photographic collection. Heather displayed her collection of photos about John F. Kennedy's Senate years for me to review and provided critical background information.

The staff at the Senate Press Gallery has also been very helpful to me over many years. I would like to especially thank Beth Crowley, Laura Eckhart, and Amy Gross for their help on this project.

My gratitude extends to the staff at the John F. Kennedy Presidential Library in Boston. Stacey Chandler responded to my many questions with cheerful, prompt, and carefully researched emails. Stacey and Stephen Plotkin graciously helped me navigate the Kennedy Library's archives during my visit in August of 2012. Maryrose Grossman from the Library's audiovisual archives section kindly tracked down dozens of photos from JFK's Senate years for me to review.

This entire project would not have happened without the inspiring and inspired work of my agent Sam Fleishman of Literary Artists. All authors should have the good fortune to have an agent as wise, supportive, and enthusiastic as Sam. He calmly and skillfully guided me through the many challenges an author confronts.

Market News International (MNI) has been a wonderful place to work for more than 20 years. Heather Scott, the Washington bureau chief, has been unfailingly encouraging and enthusiastic about the book. Thanks also to Denny Gulino, the former Washington bureau chief; Mike Connor, the CEO of MNI; Tony Mace, the New York bureau chief; and John Carter, the global managing editor of MNI.

For the past 15 years I've been a contributing writer to the *Washington Diplomat* magazine and would like to thank Victor Shiblie, the publisher, and Anna Gawel, the managing editor, for the opportunity to write for their fine magazine.

I feel very fortunate to have collaborated with Palgrave Macmillan on this book. Special thanks go to Luba Ostashevsky, who was an energetic supporter of this book from the beginning. I would also like to thank Laura Lancaster, Carla Benton, and Alan Bradshaw who helped bring the book to fruition, and Christine Catarino for her creative marketing.

I'm grateful to the Hoover Institution at Stanford University for offering me several media fellowships. These week-long fellowships allowed me to conduct research, draft chapters, and meet with Hoover fellows. Special thanks to Dave Brady and Mandy MacCalla in Palo Alto and to Christie Parell in Washington.

My aunt, Ann Eagan, and her daughter, Maureen

Eagan, were wonderful hosts when my wife and I visited Boston to work at the Kennedy Library in the summer of 2012. We enjoyed a number of delightful evenings with Ann, Maureen, and many of the Boston Shaws.

The idea for this book was born during a vacation on Tilghman Island, on the Eastern Shore of Maryland. My wife and I are indebted to our Tilghman neighbors, Ray and Jane Mayfield, for their friendship and for sharing their breathtaking views of the Chesapeake Bay.

I'm convinced that I won life's lottery with my family: my parents, Joe and Terri Shaw; my brothers, Dave and Tim; my sisters, Susan, Pam, and Marybeth; and my in-laws, Dan Mueller, Harry Sheehan, Cathy Shaw, Patrick Bachler, and Ishara Kassirer.

Finally, my deepest appreciation goes to my wife, Mindy Steinman. Every author should have a spouse as intelligent, supportive, witty, and just plain fun as Mindy. She is also a great writer, superb editor, and intrepid problem solver. She makes every day a joy.

One
The Unveiling

I

On the afternoon of March 19, 1959, most of the 98 U.S. senators and about 50 of their invited guests jammed into the ornate Senate Reception Room for a ceremony. In one respect this early spring event was your standard Senate occasion. The Senate's chaplain offered a patriotic prayer and Democratic and Republican leaders spoke, as did the vice president in his capacity as president of the Senate. But this occasion was unusual, both because of the participants and because of the purpose of the ceremony.

Senator Carl Hayden of Arizona, who was the Senate president pro tempore, the Senate's most senior Democrat, presided over the event. He was a bald, terse, and crusty man who was rarely without a cigar. He made the necessary introductions and kept the program moving along. Holding forth with great flourish was the Senate's Republican leader, Everett Dirksen of Illinois, invoking Old Testament scripture and uttering lofty pronouncements about the Senate and the flow of American history. "What an amazing and moving pageant this Republic is," he intoned as he prepared to paraphrase the Book of Revelation and suggest a Hollywood movie about the life of Joshua.[1]

The three featured speakers at the ceremony were tucked into one corner of the reception room: Vice President Richard Nixon, Senate Majority Leader Lyndon Johnson of Texas, and John F. Kennedy, the junior senator from Massachusetts. They and their guests had gathered to celebrate the unveiling of portraits of five of the greatest senators in American history—the Famous Five, as they were known—as determined by a special committee that Kennedy chaired.

The remarks made by Nixon, Johnson, and Kennedy highlighted their different relationships with the Senate, their distinctive political personalities, and the way their careers had overlapped. As they joined together on this March afternoon to celebrate senators of the past, all three hoped to win the presidency the following year and put behind them their direct association with the Senate.

Nixon, lean and black-haired, said the ceremony would be remembered as one of the proudest days in the history of the Senate because it honored not only five historic figures who served in the upper chamber but also "hundreds of others throughout the years who have borne the proud title of U.S.

Senator." The vice president, who had been in his second year of Senate service when he was elected vice president on a ticket with Dwight Eisenhower in 1952, noted the ceremony was the culmination of an effort that began nearly nine decades earlier in 1870 when Senator Justin Smith Morrill of Vermont wrote to the architect of the Capitol suggesting that artists be commissioned to paint portraits of leading senators in the reception room. "No action was taken. Or should I say that the Senate acted in its usual, very deliberate way," Nixon quipped.[2]

Johnson, the majority leader and the widely recognized powerhouse of the Senate, used his remarks to make it clear that the project to identify the five Senate greats had been his idea from the start. He recalled that in the summer of 1955, as he was recovering in the hospital from a heart attack, he was visited by then Republican leader William Knowland and Earle Clements, Johnson's Senate deputy. At Johnson's suggestion, they discussed filling five panels on the walls of the Senate Reception Room with paintings of the leading senators in American history. Shortly thereafter, Knowland and Clements introduced a resolution in Johnson's name creating a special committee to determine the five Senate greats. Johnson recalled that he had initially been designated to lead the project, but because of health reasons he was forced to pass on the assignment to the "very able and gifted" Kennedy.[3]

Although the ceremony was to honor the five former senators, Johnson noted that "in a real sense we have met here to honor the institution of the Senate, which all of us love so much, for what it is, and for what it has always been in our system: the testing place for the character of the living generations of Americans." Borrowing from Lincoln's Gettysburg Address, Johnson said, "Our recognition here can add little to the stature and esteem already so securely theirs. Yet by this action we remind ourselves—and perhaps remind the entire Nation—of some of the most enduring values. History has not had to seek out these men, to give them their due. They were honored in their own times, even though they were frequently criticized. . . . But the greatness that emerges from each of them and towers high is the greatness of character." Then he made a veiled allusion to the fact that these five senators had each dreamed of residing in the White House but never quite made it there. Johnson said the Senate's Famous Five "aspired, at times, for other roles. Most of them, in fact, found less than complete fulfillment of their aims and of their convictions."[4]

But the clear star of the event was Kennedy, a rising force in American politics who was already actively running for the 1960 Democratic presidential nomination. Slender, youthful, and confident, he shifted smoothly from lofty to playful. Blending serious reflections and humorous stories, Kennedy made the Senate event his own.

Kennedy described the five men who were chosen for the Senate's so-called Hall of Fame. First was Henry Clay of Kentucky, whom Kennedy called "probably the most gifted parliamentary figure in the history of the Congress, whose tireless devotion to the Union demonstrated that intelligent compromise required both courage and conviction." Kennedy noted that Clay served in the Senate on four separate occasions between 1806 and 1852 and was deeply skilled "in the art of the possible." During his long career, Clay served as Speaker of the House and secretary of state and ran for the presidency three times. Next was Daniel Webster of Massachusetts, whom Kennedy described as "the eloquent and articulate champion of 'Liberty and Union, now and forever, one and inseparable.' " Webster served from 1827 to 1841 and from 1845 to 1850 and used his legendary oratorical skills to dominate the Senate of his time. "His splendid dignity and decorum elevated the status and prestige of the Senate," Kennedy proclaimed. The third choice was John Calhoun of South Carolina. Also a senator from pre–Civil War days, Calhoun served in the upper chamber from 1832 to 1843 and from 1845 to

1850. Kennedy described Calhoun as a forceful champion of state sovereignty, a masterful defender of the rights of political minorities, and the author of a penetrating and original theory about government. Kennedy called Calhoun "the intellectual leader and logician of those defending the rights of a political minority against the dangers of an unchecked majority."[5]

Moving to the twentieth century, Kennedy's committee selected two accomplished senators who represented the progressive and conservative traditions in modern America. Robert M. LaFollette Sr. of Wisconsin was, according to Kennedy, "a ceaseless battler for the under-privileged in an age of special privilege, a courageous independent in an age of conformity, who fought memorably against tremendous odds and stifling inertia for the social and economic reforms which ultimately proved essential to American progress in the 20th century." LaFollette served in the Senate from 1906 to 1925 and was at the forefront of most of the major economic and foreign policy debates of his time, often on the losing side. The committee's final choice was Robert Taft of Ohio, whom Kennedy saw as "the conscience of the conservative movement and its most constructive leader, whose high integrity transcended partisan-ship and whose analytical mind candidly and courageously put principle above ambition." Taft served in the Senate from 1939 to 1953 and demonstrated, Kennedy argued, the importance of balanced and forceful opposition in an age of powerful governments.[6]

Kennedy acknowledged that the choice of these five was not without dissent. Contemporary Americans were more familiar with the controversies surrounding Taft and LaFollette, but he said that Clay, Webster, and Calhoun also had their detractors. "Let us also remember that it was said of Henry Clay that 'he prefers the specious to the solid, and the plausible to the true. He is a bad man, an imposter, a creator of wicked schemes.' Those words were spoken by John C. Calhoun," Kennedy said as the audience broke into laughter. "On the other hand, who was it who said that Calhoun was a rigid fanatic, ambitious, selfishly partisan and a sectional 'turncoat' with 'too much genius and too little common sense,' who would die a traitor or a madman? Henry Clay, of course," Kennedy said, to more laughter. He then recalled that John Quincy Adams had once remarked on the "gigantic intellect, the envious temper, the ravenous ambition, and the rotten heart of Daniel Webster."[7]

Kennedy said his panel's effort to identify five of the most outstanding U.S. senators was also an opportunity to call attention to the high traditions of the Senate and its significant role in American history. "This Nation, I know, will honor for all time to come these men and all those who seek to follow in their hard path."[8]

When the speeches were concluded, the senators and their guests watched as brown drapes were removed from each of the five paintings. As the likenesses of Clay, Webster, Calhoun, LaFollette, and Taft were unveiled, they were met with great applause. Among those in the audience were several descendants of the Famous Five: Henrietta Clay, great-granddaughter of Henry Clay; John Calhoun, the great-grandson of John Calhoun; Allston Calhoun, the great-great-nephew of John Calhoun; Fola and Mary LaFollette, the daughter and sister of Robert LaFollette; and William Taft III, the son of Robert Taft.

II

In addition to marking the culmination of his committee's four years of work, the Senate Reception Room ceremony was both a "coming of age" and a "preparing to leave" event for Kennedy.

John F. Kennedy had served in the Senate since January 1953 and had been a compelling yet quiet presence for nearly eight years. A national celebrity because of his famous family, celebrated war record, and impressive literary prowess, Kennedy struggled to find a role in the upper chamber that was commensurate with his ambition and promise. As he stood before the full Senate in the reception room, next to Vice President Nixon and Senate Majority Leader Johnson, discussing this Senate project, Kennedy was at the zenith of his career in the Senate. He almost seemed to be one of the club.

But he was not spending a lot of time around the Senate that spring because his presidential campaign was in full swing. In March 1959 alone, Kennedy campaigned in Utah, Oregon, Montana, Rhode Island, and Florida and spent time away from the Capitol to give major speeches on nuclear deterrence and urban challenges to policy groups in Washington, D.C. The day before the Senate Reception Room ceremony, he traveled to Milwaukee and gave a soaring speech on the challenges confronting America. "The next year, the next decade, in all likelihood the next generation, will require more bravery and wisdom on our part than any other period in our history," Kennedy said. "We will be face to face, every day, in every part of our lives and times, with the real issue of our age—the issue of survival."[9]

During his Senate years Kennedy displayed considerable talent and unmistakable star quality, but also a reluctance to immerse himself in the drudgery of legislative affairs. One observer likened him to a charming young man who dazzles a dinner party but then skips out and leaves others to clean the dishes.[10] During his eight years in the Senate, Kennedy filled out physically, deepened intellectually, sharpened his writing skills, became a polished and effective speaker, and mastered the nuances of American politics. He matured in a striking way. "In all my life, I never saw anybody grow the way Jack did," House Speaker Tip O'Neill wrote. "He turned into a great personality and a beautiful talker. But until he was in the Senate you just couldn't imagine that he was really going anywhere."[11]

Kennedy participated actively and sometimes boldly in the central policy debates of his time: the challenges posed by China and the Soviet Union, the icy armistice in Korea, France's faltering military interventions in Vietnam and Algeria, the appropriate defense posture for America during the Cold War, and the politically charged attempt to rein in corrupt labor unions. However, critics accused Kennedy of giving headline-producing speeches on controversial topics and then leaving the gritty work of producing legislation to his Senate colleagues.

Kennedy was not a Senate leader and tried to avoid several controversial matters, such as the debate on civil rights legislation and the condemnation of Senator Joseph McCarthy of Wisconsin. Had he stayed in the Senate, it would have taken Kennedy decades to become a committee chairman. The other path to Senate influence, a party leadership position, was dominated by Lyndon Johnson. The powerful Senate Democratic leader controlled his party's, and his chamber's, substantive agenda and legislative schedule. And Johnson was not inclined to share power, especially with a cool, sometimes remote, Harvard-educated man who seemed to look upon Johnson's beloved Senate with detachment, if not disdain.

John Kennedy never envisioned a career in the Senate as an end unto itself. He didn't seek out mentors, or build a network of kindred spirits, or plunge into causes, or analyze how he could become a better senator. Kennedy was not interested in slowly honing his legislative skills and patiently waiting for opportunities to nudge legislation forward. He was not drawn to the day-to-day challenge of writing bills that might eventually become law. He found the Senate a frustrating place in which years of work could be wiped away by a brief presidential statement or veto threat.[12]

Kennedy aspired to be president even before he was elected to the Senate in 1952. He was fully aware that the Senate was not necessarily the best political base for a presidential bid. While it gave him a national platform, it also required him to cast difficult votes and declare his position on controversial issues. He knew history demonstrated that the Senate was not a congenial place for senators who wanted to travel immediately to the White House. Before Kennedy's election as president in 1960, only one other sitting senator—Warren G. Harding of Ohio—went directly from the Senate to the White House, and that was in 1920.

However, Kennedy shrewdly used the upper chamber as a policy and political training ground. Through study, travel, briefings with experts, and debates with his colleagues, he learned about domestic and foreign policy. Kennedy became an expert in labor law and was an impressive contributor to debates on Algeria, Indochina, Eastern Europe, and the competing forces of nationalism and colonialism. Some of his Senate speeches were strikingly impressive; they were well written, historically literate, informative, coherent, and forward leaning.

During his eight years in the Senate, John Kennedy learned how to frame issues, delve into problems, and craft compromises. He transformed himself into a man of substance and probity. Kennedy also forged his political identity during his Senate years. He learned how to project himself as a future-oriented politician who was keenly focused on the challenges of the coming decade—the 1960s—while also steeped in America's past. His love of history helped Kennedy offset his relative youth, which worried some voters; it allowed him to project himself as a young man with depth, even gravitas. As the author of several books, including *Profiles in Courage*, and a slew of newspaper, magazine, and journal articles, Kennedy sought to be seen as a statesman-scholar. He was more interested in becoming an Abraham Lincoln or Winston Churchill than a Robert Taft or Richard Russell, two Senate lions of the legislative process. Statecraft elevated by scholarship stirred him far more than did the mechanics of muscling legislation through the Senate.

The conventional criticism of Kennedy's Senate years has been that he used them simply as a stepping-stone to the presidency, but I'd like to offer a different, more nuanced view. Though Kennedy was not a legislative powerhouse or a master of the Senate, he did make important contributions to public policy and the national debate, especially in what he called "the high realm of foreign affairs," and in some domestic areas such as labor, housing, and education. He worked on legislation, gave strong and sometimes prescient speeches, and asked tough and well-informed questions as a member of various Senate committees. Additionally, Kennedy, through his writings and work on special projects such as the special committee to identify the Senate's five greats, contributed to the institution of the Senate.

Perhaps even more significantly, the Senate had

a major effect on Kennedy. He entered the upper chamber in January 1953 as a callow, lightly regarded former House member and emerged eight years later as a compelling political figure who became only the second sitting senator to win the White House. During his Senate years, Kennedy matured, forged a distinctive political identity, and crafted a personal and policy narrative that captivated the nation and would propel him to the presidency. He found a way to the White House that eluded dozens of other senators, including the five great ones Kennedy's committee selected: Webster, Clay, Calhoun, Taft, and LaFollette. This pathway from the Senate to the presidency remained untraveled again for nearly a half century, until a junior senator from Illinois, Barack Obama, discovered it for himself in 2008.

Two
Congressman Kennedy

I

On the morning of January 3, 1947, John F. Kennedy's first day as a member of the U.S. House of Representatives, he met several of his aides at the Statler-Hilton Hotel in downtown Washington. He had just arrived in D.C. from a vacation at his family's home in Palm Beach, Florida. As they headed to breakfast, one of his aides said that House Minority Whip John McCormack of Massachusetts was trying to get in touch with him. Kennedy said he'd go to the Capitol to see him after he finished his breakfast. When pressed by an aide to go immediately, Kennedy said that McCormack had been in Washington for a long time and could wait. "He can get along without me for another 15 minutes. Let's go into the drugstore and get some eggs."[1]

For those inclined to like Kennedy, this response displayed admirable qualities of calmness, self-confidence, and independence. For those inclined to be critical of Kennedy, the quip indicated arrogance, a sense of entitlement, and a reluctance

29

to be a team player. In actuality Kennedy displayed all those attributes during his three terms in the House of Representatives, which ended in January 1953.

Kennedy's road to Congress was circuitous. Born on May 29, 1917, in Brookline, Massachusetts, Kennedy was the second son in a family of nine children. His mother, Rose Fitzgerald Kennedy, was a pious, devout, tightly wound woman from a prominent political family in Boston. Her father, John Fitzgerald, known as "Honey Fitz," had served as the mayor of Boston and in the U.S. House of Representatives. Kennedy's father, Joseph Kennedy, was a hard-charging, successful, and abrasive businessman who dreamed that one of his sons would go into politics and ascend to the presidency. In addition to his stellar business career, Joe Kennedy Sr. served as the first chairman of the Securities and Exchange Commission, the head of the U.S. Maritime Commission, and as America's ambassador to the United Kingdom. Joe Sr. focused his hopes for a successful political career on his oldest son, Joseph Jr. An extroverted and exuberant young man, Joe Jr. was killed in a World War II bombing mission, shattering his father's dreams for him and his career. After his son's death, Joseph Kennedy wrote to a friend, "You know how much I had tied my whole life up to his and what great things I saw in the future for him. Now it's all over."[2]

Young John Kennedy was bookish, witty, reserved, disorganized, and sickly. An indifferent student at Brookline and suburban New York City public schools as well as at the private Canterbury and Choate schools, the boy whom his family and friends called Jack was a charming underachiever. But as war loomed in Europe and Asia, and as his father took the high-profile ambassadorial post, Jack's interest in current events intensified. He had loved history since he was a small boy. Always a serious reader, he devoured history books and began subscribing to the *New York Times* at age 14. William Carleton, a family acquaintance and political science professor, recalls visiting the Kennedys in Palm Beach and participating in an hours-long family discussion of history and politics. His conversation with the young Kennedy extended into the early hours of the morning. "It was clear to me that John had a far better historical and political mind than his father or elder brother; indeed that John's capacity for seeing current events in historical perspective and for projecting historical trends into the future was unusual," Carleton wrote.[3]

Kennedy's academic interests were ignited relatively late in his college career. There were intellectual stirrings in his sophomore year at Harvard University that blossomed during his junior year. In his final year at Harvard, he wrote his senior thesis on British appeasement of Germany in the 1930s. "Appeasement in Munich" earned Kennedy magna cum laude honors and became the foundation for his best-selling book *Why England Slept*, which was published in 1940.

Following his graduation from Harvard that year, Kennedy briefly attended Stanford Business School but did not find the experience satisfying. He then took an extensive trip to Latin America. Still searching for a career and a professional niche, in October 1941, Kennedy joined the navy. He worked in naval intelligence in Washington, D.C., and South Carolina, and then won an assignment in the South Pacific on motor torpedo boats, known as PT boats. The boat that Kennedy commanded, the *PT 109*, was on patrol near New Georgia in the Solomon Islands when it was sliced in half by a Japanese destroyer in the early morning of August 2, 1943. Kennedy and his crew were lost for more than a week before being rescued. Whatever may be said of Kennedy's boat-piloting skills, few questioned his bravery in the South Pacific as he helped rescue the ten other surviving members of his crew. His heroics were chronicled in articles in the *New York Times* and the *Boston Globe* and in a major essay by John Hersey in the *New Yorker* that was later abridged by *Reader's Digest*. Kennedy publicly down-played his heroics but did not object when others extolled his bravery. He sometimes reacted to the growing legend about his war heroism ironically and even profanely. "My story about the collision is getting better all the time," he once quipped. "Now I've got a Jew and Nigger in the story and with me being a Catholic, that's great."[4] But Kennedy's bravery in the South Pacific became integral to his political career and gave him an unusual prominence. A television show later dramatized Kennedy's World War II heroics. When Kennedy was running for president, Robert Donovan's best-selling book about the *PT 109* drama was read across the nation and became the basis for a popular movie.[5]

Sick from his war injuries and other ailments, Kennedy retired from the navy on March 1, 1945, and was uncertain what he wanted to do next. He tried journalism, working as a correspondent for the *Chicago Herald American* and then the International News Service; he covered the founding conference of the United Nations in San Francisco, the Potsdam conference, and Prime Minister Winston Churchill's losing 1945 campaign in Great Britain. Kennedy's journalistic output was solid but unremarkable, and he decided that reporting wasn't for him. He found it too reactive; he wanted to make decisions, not write about those made by others.

In 1946, Congressman James Michael Curley decided not to seek reelection in Massachusetts's 11th Congressional District, which was composed of Cambridge; Charlestown; the North, South, and West Ends of Boston; and parts of Brighton and Somerville. It remains unclear how actively Kennedy's father worked to encourage Curley to retire. Several historians have argued that Joseph Kennedy paid many of Curley's debts and took other steps to induce him to retire, leaving an open congressional seat for his son to pursue.[6] Until then, John Kennedy had never envisioned a career in politics. "I was at loose ends at the end of the war," he later recalled. "I was reluctant to begin law school again. I was not very interested in following a business career. I was vitally interested in national and international life. . . . But I never thought at school and college that I would ever run for office myself. One politician was enough in the family and my brother Joe was obviously going to be that politician. I hadn't considered myself a political type and he filled all the requirements for success."[7]

But Joe's death and the open congressional seat prompted him to seriously consider entering the race. "Suddenly, the time, the occasion and I all met. I moved into the Bellevue Hotel with my grandfather and began to run," Kennedy recalled. He acknowledged several disadvantages he faced as a candidate. The 11th district was blue collar and ethnically diverse and was dominated by Irish and Italian communities. Kennedy was an outsider who had only briefly lived in the district.

"My family roots were there but I had lived in New York for ten years and on top of that I had gone to Harvard, not a particularly popular institution at that time in the 11th congressional district."[8]

Preparing to run for the seat, Kennedy filed his candidacy papers from the Bellevue, which gave him a residential address in the district. He later rented an apartment at 122 Bowdoin Street, which remained his legal address for the rest of his political career and was printed on his driver's license even when he was in the White House.

Kennedy began actively running for the House seat in January 1946. He formally announced for the Democratic nomination in April and became part of a sprawling ten-person primary that June. Kennedy's campaign literature portrayed him as a war hero and a tough-minded veteran with deep roots in the district. One brochure noted that his grandfather Patrick was from East Boston while his grandfather, Honey Fitz, was from the North End. "It was from his grandfathers, perhaps, that Kennedy inherited his interest in public affairs and his desire to serve the people of this district in the halls of Congress," the brochure read.[9]

Kennedy's campaign slogan was simple: "The New Generation Offers A Leader." Only 29 years old at the time, he padded his resume. He claimed to have been his father's secretary at the U.S. embassy in London, whereas he was actually taking a break from Harvard to do research. He said that it was at the suggestion of President Franklin Roosevelt that he wrote his book *Why England Slept*, which was a creative interpretation of how he came to write his senior thesis at Harvard. His campaign hyperbolically described his "world-wide experience" as a newspaper correspondent.[10]

Kennedy's congressional platform statement was stark, grim, and challenging. "The people of the United States and the world stand at the crossroads. What we do now will shape the history of civilization for many years to come. We have a weary world trying to bind up the wounds of a fierce struggle. That is dire enough. What is infinitely far worse is that we now have a world which has unleashed the terrible powers of atomic energy. We have a world capable of atomic warfare. We have a world capable of destroying itself. The days which lie ahead are most difficult ones." Kennedy pledged that if he were elected to the House, he would work relentlessly for peace. "Above all, day and night, with every ounce of ingenuity and industry we possess, we must work for peace. We must not have another war."[11]

Kennedy pledged to work on housing, especially for veterans. He vowed to fight for national health care and ensure protections for organized labor such as a higher minimum wage, reasonable work hours, a healthy workplace, the right to organize, collective bargaining, and the right to strike. In the foreign policy realm, Kennedy said that the United Nations was the best hope for world peace and lamented that the United States had acceded to Soviet demands to weaken the United Nations by giving a veto power to members of the Security Council. He even envisioned a scenario in which the atomic bomb might be turned over to the United Nations.

Kennedy, along with the other Democratic candidates, realized that the primary was not going to be determined by the most compelling policy prescriptions but by reaching out to the various constituencies that dominated the 11th District. The 1946 primary was, according to one analyst, "a confrontation of neighborhoods, ethnic groups and personalities."[12] Kennedy's leading opponents were Mike Neville, a former state representative and former mayor of Cambridge, and John Cotter of Charlestown, a former aide to Congressman Curley. Kennedy pushed himself relentlessly in advance of the June primary. Though not an extrovert or a glad-hander by nature, he forced himself to approach voters and request their support. He worked from early morning until late at night, sometimes 18 hours a day. He shook hands at factory gates, waterfront docks, taverns, barbershops, and voters' homes. According to one aide, he was "aggressively shy."[13] And as he plunged into the rough-and-tumble of Boston politics, he also kept his sense of humor. Speaking near the end of a lengthy candidates' forum in which all the participants emphasized their modest starts in life, Kennedy deadpanned, "I seem to be the only person here who didn't come up the hard way."[14] Kennedy enlisted much of his family to help in the campaign; his mother and his sisters Jean, Pat, and Eunice hosted house parties for women voters that became an important Kennedy campaign technique. His younger brother Robert, who had recently been discharged from the navy, organized three wards in East Cambridge. Robert later joked that his job was to minimize his older brother's losses there.[15]

Kennedy's father was determined to spare no expense for his son's congressional race. It has been estimated that he spent between $250,000 and $300,000 of his own money on the campaign, a massive sum at that time and more than the total expenditures of his son's opponents combined. Money was spent in many areas of publicity: billboards, newspaper ads, radio broadcasts, national magazine ads, and newsreels. There were also allegations of bribes and the use of creative accounting techniques to disguise the flow of funds. "The Kennedy strategy," said his opponent Mike Neville, was to "buy them out or blast them out."[16] Joe Sr. arranged for 100,000 copies of the *Reader's Digest* article about

John's heroism in World War II to be distributed throughout the district. "We're going to sell Jack like soap flakes," his father reportedly said. "With the money I spent, I could have elected my chauffeur," he later proclaimed, an assertion his son presumably did not welcome.[17] Kennedy's financial war chest was so lavish that it triggered considerable resentment from his opponents and others studying the race. A mock ad from one opponent captures this resentment: "Congress seat for sale—No experience necessary—Applicant must live in New York or Florida—Only million-aires need apply."[18]

There were also allegations of hardball tactics. One of Kennedy's opponents was an Italian American named Joe Russo, a popular undertaker in the district. Fearful that he might capture the Italian vote, the Kennedy campaign recruited another Joe Russo, a 27-year-old janitor from Boston's West End, to join the race and dilute the Italian vote.[19] The second Mr. Russo was given an undisclosed compensation. The Kennedy campaign's decision to recruit a second Russo was considered unusual at the time and just within the boundary of tough political combat.

On June 18, Kennedy won the primary with 42 percent of the vote. He received 22,183 votes to Neville's 11,341 and Cotter's 6,671. Since the district was overwhelmingly Democratic, Kennedy's victory in the June primary assured his election to Congress in November 1946. He relaxed in Los Angeles for a few weeks after the primary, spent part of the summer in Hyannis Port, and then coasted in the fall to a decisive November victory. Describing himself as a "fighting conservative," Kennedy defeated his Republican opponent, Lester Brown, by 69,093 votes to 26,007.[20]

His first political victory became the prototype for future Kennedy campaigns: a disciplined organization, a hard-working candidate, active family support, and a campaign war chest flush with resources.

II

When Congressman John Kennedy moved to Washington in January 1947, he was a minor celebrity. Not yet 30, Kennedy's well-publicized war record, best-selling book, famous family, and controversial father ensured that he would not be just another House freshman. "He was the glamorous young bachelor, the most enticing new figure on Capitol Hill in many years," wrote historian Herbert Parmet.[21] Kennedy moved into a home in the upscale Georgetown neighborhood of D.C. His house at 1528 Thirty-First Street NW became known as the Hollywood Hotel because of frequent parties and occasional visits from movie starlets. Kennedy lived a pampered life with a housekeeper, Margaret Ambrose, and a valet, George Thomas, who drove him to work and brought home-cooked meals to his office. Informal and sometimes sloppily dressed, Kennedy became known for his love of sports, movies, and beautiful women. His life was fast and scattered, with frequent travel between Washington, Boston, Hyannis Port, Palm Beach, and Europe. "He was considered," said one of his aides, "offbeat by congressional standards."[22]

The Congress that Kennedy joined in January 1947 was dominated by Republicans. They held the majority in the House by 245 to 188. The GOP's winning 1946 midterm campaign slogan was "Had Enough?" and it had tapped into the public's frustration with the Democratic Party to secure control of both chambers of Congress. Republicans offered sharp criticism of President Harry Truman, congressional Democrats, organized labor, and Communists—both those in the Soviet Union and those who had allegedly infiltrated the American government.

Kennedy joined two House committees: the Education and Labor Committee and the District of Columbia Committee. On the domestic front, Kennedy worked on housing issues, which had been prominent during his campaign. He was focused on the narrow issue of veterans housing and the broader issue of housing supply after

World War II. Following the war, there was a housing shortage of nearly 5 million units in the United States. Desperate for shelter, people lived in chicken coops, attics, basements, and even boxcars. Between 20 and 30 percent of all Americans lived in substandard housing.[23] Just months after joining the House, Kennedy gave a passionate speech to the National Public Housing Council in Chicago. "Veterans need homes and they need them quickly. . . . Any veteran who watched the American supplies pouring ashore on the Normandy beaches; who saw the Pacific Islands cleared and our air landing strips rolled out in four or five days; who saw the endless waste of war and the seemingly never ending productivity that replaced that waste; is it any wonder that the veteran cannot understand why he is not housed?"[24]

The Senate, spurred by Republican Robert Taft of Ohio and Democrats Robert Wagner of New York and Allen Ellender of Louisiana, crafted a bipartisan bill that set a goal of 1.25 million new urban housing units per year for the next ten years. They also supported federal grants for slum clearance, easier-to-obtain Federal Housing Administration loans for aspiring homeowners, and long-term low-interest loans for the construction of 500,000 public housing units along with government subsidies for their maintenance. The bill passed the Senate on

April 15, 1947, on a voice vote, but House Republicans blocked the measure. A conservative coalition in the House Banking Committee refused to even hold hearings on the bill for many months. In July, just as Congress was about to adjourn for the year, the committee refused to report the bill to the floor.

Congressman Kennedy was convinced that the nation needed a long-term housing program along the lines of the Taft-Wagner-Ellender bill. With the House set to adjourn without acting on housing legislation, a furious Kennedy went to the House floor and expressed his frustration. He argued that the House was preparing to leave Washington without acting on "the most pressing problem with which this country is now confronted —the severe ever-growing shortage of housing which faces our veterans and others of moderate income." Kennedy observed that while there was a need for up to 1.25 million new urban housing units a year, far fewer than that were being built. He lashed out at the House Banking Committee for being too busy to hold hearings on the only housing bill that offered hope to the homeless and veterans of World War II who were crammed into crowded quarters. The congressman noted that in Boston, as of July 1946, more than 40 percent of the city's married veterans lived in rented rooms or doubled up with other families. "Their need is drastic," he said.[25]

Kennedy hammered Republicans for proposing to launch a study of the problem, saying the essence of the crisis was well known and that the GOP proposal for additional study was a "fraud." Republicans, he charged, had been captured by lobbyists from the real estate industry and from building associations. Kennedy concluded his remarks with scathing words. "I was sent to this Congress by the people of my district to help solve the most pressing problem facing this country—the housing crisis. I am going to have to go back to my district Saturday, a district that probably sent more boys per family into this last war than any in the country, and when they ask me if I was able to get them any homes, I will have to answer, 'not a one—not a single one.' "[26]

Kennedy's frustration with the housing impasse in the House of Representatives continued for several more years. During the protracted housing debate, Kennedy sharply criticized those who were blocking the legislation, including the American Legion, which, he said, was acting as a stooge for the real estate lobby. "The leadership of the American Legion has not had a constructive thought for the benefit of the country since 1918," he snapped. He later wondered if this criticism of the powerful veterans group might end his political career. But it didn't, and he learned that sometimes unvarnished candor pays off.[27]

When the House narrowly approved a major

housing bill in 1949, Kennedy viewed the passage of the legislation as bittersweet. The vote represented an accomplishment, but he lamented the time that had been wasted and the people who had suffered needlessly. "For over four years now the Congress of the United States has been studying and investigating the housing shortage in the country. The facts are plain," he said, adding that the delay had caused misery for veterans and those living in slums.[28] Kennedy's fight for housing for veterans and others of modest incomes was both good public policy and a moral imperative. He believed it was both necessary and the right thing to do.

In addition to waging the housing battle, Congressman Kennedy plunged into debates over labor policy. As Kennedy entered the House, the nation was reeling from industrial unrest and a succession of major strikes that threatened to paralyze the American economy. The number of man-days lost in strikes ranged between 3 and 6 million a month in late 1946. Congressional Republicans saw this as but one more indication that the power of labor unions needed to be curtailed. The Republican Congress was determined to curb what many viewed as the out-of-control power of "Big Labor." Even President Truman supported labor legislation that placed some restrictions on organized labor, such as measures to prohibit some secondary boycotts and to help solve disputes under existing collective bargaining agreements.[29]

But House Republicans dismissed Truman's proposals as too little, too late. The House Education and Labor Committee, under the leadership of Republican Fred Hartley from New Jersey, drafted and passed a tough anti-labor bill in April 1947. Some of its most controversial provisions included making unions liable for damage suits for violations of contract; banning jurisdictional strikes, secondary boycotts, and mass picketing; outlawing closed shops; prohibiting industry-wide bargaining, in which large nationwide unions were thought to have too much power; identifying and banning unfair union practices; denying recognition by the National Labor Relations Board to unions whose officers refused to swear they were not Communists; and authorizing the president to proclaim cooling-off periods and halt strike votes by employees before walkouts. It was a sharp departure from the approach created by the New Deal–era Wagner Act, which guaranteed a worker's right to organize and required companies to bargain with duly recognized union representatives. The Wagner Act also empowered the National Labor Relations Board to supervise elections in which unions might choose their own representatives.[30]

Congressman Kennedy took a middle ground in the labor debate; he was more critical of organized labor and more open to reforms than were most Democrats, but his idea of what constituted appropriate changes to labor law was more moderate than that of most Republicans. During the House debate on labor legislation, Kennedy issued his own report rather than sign on to either the Republican majority report or the Democratic dissent. Kennedy took to the floor and urged a more cautious and careful response than the Hartley bill called for. He acknowledged that in the dozen years since the passage of the landmark Wagner Act, there had been considerable turbulence and unrest in the labor movement. Unions had grown too powerful in their relations with members, business, and government. He acknowledged there was a real problem and legislation was needed, but argued that the Hartley bill went too far. "This bill would in its present form strike down in one devastating blow the union shop, industry-wide bargaining, and so strangle collective bargaining with restraints and limitations as to make it ineffectual." Those supporting the Hartley bill were moving into dangerous territory. "In seeking to destroy what is bad, they are also destroying what is good," he charged.[31]

He said the legislation would "bring not peace but labor war—a war bitter and dangerous." The bill in its present form, Kennedy said, played "into the hands of the radicals in our unions, who preach the doctrine of the class struggle. If this bill is passed, this Congress will have fired the opening shot."[32] The House passed the Hartley bill while the Senate passed more moderate legislation proposed by Robert Taft. A compromise package cleared the Congress in the spring of 1947 over President Truman's veto. Kennedy opposed both the Hartley bill and the final compromise, which became known as the Taft-Hartley law. He remained active in labor issues for the rest of his congressional career and participated in debates to either modify or repeal Taft-Hartley.

Interestingly, while this battle over labor legislation continued on the House floor, Kennedy traveled to Pennsylvania to debate another young congressman who was also a junior member of the House Labor Committee, Richard Nixon of California. Kennedy and Nixon squared off over labor issues at a forum hosted by Democratic congressman Frank Buchanan in McKeesport, near Pittsburgh. The two congressmen sparred politely for more than an hour, went out for a meal after the debate, and shared a compartment on the Capital Limited overnight train that brought them back to Washington.[33] This exchange by two junior congressmen in a district that neither represented was unusual for the time, but it illustrates the importance of labor issues to the nation. It was also the first known public debate between two men whose later debates for the presidency would become defining events in twentieth-century American politics.

Congressman Kennedy also participated in a high-profile probe into labor unrest at the Allis-Chalmers machinery manufacturing plant in Wisconsin. He called for a perjury charge against Harold Christoffel, former president of United Auto Workers Local 248, for his account of the 1941 Communist-inspired strike against the plant. Kennedy pursued the Christoffel controversy relentlessly, and his aggressive role in this probe prompted a colleague, Republican congressman Charles Kersten of Wisconsin, to call his actions one of the first shots against American Communism in this country.[34]

Another of Congressman Kennedy's interests was education. Though he believed that federal assistance for schools was important, he proceeded cautiously in the debate regarding federal support for parochial schools. He was concerned that direct public support for parochial schools would violate the First Amendment. Kennedy drafted an amendment that would allow parochial schools to receive aid for noneducational services such as buses, books, and health services. In 1949, he supported a bill that authorized $300 million annually in federal grants to states to assist elementary and secondary schools with some assistance for nonpublic schools.

A member of the House District of Columbia Committee, Kennedy took an interest in the capital's financial and governance challenges. He opposed a sales tax for Washington and supported Home Rule for the district. On March 3, 1950, he placed a memo in the Congressional Record titled *The Case for Home Rule for Washington.* The congressman also headed a probe into the profits and rising fares of the Capital Transit Company.[35] He introduced legislation that would give parking privileges in Washington to disabled veterans, permit the city of Washington to borrow funds for capital projects, and allow insurance companies in the District to invest funds in World Bank financial instruments.

Kennedy's interest in foreign policy was evident throughout his congressional career. He was a strong supporter of the emerging containment doctrine that sought to prevent the Soviet Union from making advances in the world. He backed Truman's 1947 request for aid to Turkey and Greece. He also praised the administration for developing the Marshall Plan and creating the North Atlantic Treaty Organization; he felt both were integral to European political and economic stability. But he blamed the Truman administration for the stalemate in Korea in 1950. And earlier, when Communists won control of China in 1949, Kennedy tore into the administration. He blasted the State Department, individual

American diplomats, and even the revered George Marshall for the United States' inability to stop the Communist takeover of China.

Speaking in Salem, Massachusetts, on January 30, 1949, Kennedy unleashed a blistering attack on the Truman administration's policies. "Our relationship with China since the end of the Second World War has been a tragic one, and it is of the utmost importance that we search out and spotlight those who bear the responsibility for our present predicament," he said. Kennedy charged that the administration failed to adequately support the Nationalist government but instead had pressed it to accept a coalition government with the Chinese Communists. "Our policy in China has reaped the whirlwind. The continued insistence that aid would not be forthcoming unless a coalition government with the Communists was formed was a crippling blow to the national government. So concerned were our diplomats and their advisers . . . with the imperfections of the diplomatic system in China after 20 years of war, and the tales of corruption in high places, that they lost sight of the tremendous stake in a non-Communist China," he charged. "This is the tragic story of China whose freedom we once fought to preserve. What our young men had saved, our diplomats and our President have frittered away."[36]

Several days later Kennedy largely repeated his

speech on the House floor, attacking the administration's China policy. He said that Americans were just learning the extent of the political upheaval that had befallen China, and it was clear that the responsibility for the American foreign policy setback in the Far East rested squarely with the White House and the State Department. He attacked John Fairbank and Owen Lattimore, two prominent American scholars who were sharply critical of the Nationalist government. The House must assume, Kennedy declared, the responsibility for preventing the "onrushing tide of communism from engulfing all of Asia."[37]

Although he was not a member of the House's national security committees, Kennedy was fascinated by foreign policy and frequently traveled overseas, even while Congress was in session. Kennedy was a regular visitor to Europe, including a 1947 trip to examine how Marshall Plan programs were being designed. In 1951 he took a seven-week trip to Asia and the Middle East to round out his travel experiences. During this trip alone, Kennedy visited Hong Kong, India, Indochina, Iran, Israel, Japan, Korea, Malaya, Pakistan, Thailand, and Yugoslavia.[38] He used these trips to meet with international leaders, learn about specific issues, and bolster his foreign policy credentials, often using family funds to finance them.

III

Looking at John F. Kennedy's three terms in the House, several broad themes are striking. First, Kennedy was a loyal Democrat with a pronounced independent streak that he seemed to relish displaying. He was a traditional liberal on many domestic issues such as housing, Social Security, the minimum wage, taxes, regulation, and education. But he was harder to label on national security issues. He was sharply critical of many aspects of the Truman administration's foreign policy, especially as it concerned China and Korea. "I never had the feeling that I needed Truman," he once said, apparently meaning that he did not believe his political fate was linked to the electoral strength of this Democratic president.[39] Kennedy also displayed independence from Democratic leaders in Massachusetts. He was the only member of the Massachusetts delegation who declined to sign a petition for clemency for his predecessor, James Michael Curley, when he was about to be sentenced for mail fraud. Tip O'Neill, who would succeed Kennedy as the 11th District's representative, said Kennedy was a different kind of politician. "It was said that Jack Kennedy was the only pol in Boston who never went to a wake unless he had known the deceased. He played by his own rules."[40]

Second, Kennedy's serious health problems

affected his effectiveness in the House. He had colon, stomach, and back problems as well as Addison's disease, which had been diagnosed in 1947.[41] He was frequently absent because of these illnesses, and when he was at work, he was often lethargic, listless, and distracted. He was razor thin and haggard; one staffer, Mark Dalton, said he looked like a "skeleton."[42] Democratic congressman Richard Bolling of Missouri described him as a "frail, sick, hollow man."[43] George Smathers, a Democratic congressman from Florida, said Kennedy's health was a major factor in his uninspired House performance, as were his conflicted feelings about political life. "In those days he was a rather sickly fellow," Smathers recalled. "In addition to his bad back he was constantly plagued with colds and one thing after another—constantly laid up. If you had to pick a member of that freshman class who would probably wind up as president, Kennedy was probably the least likely. He was so shy he could hardly tell you his name. One of the shyest fellows I'd ever seen."[44]

Third, there was an unmistakably restless quality about Kennedy during his service in the House. Mary Davis, then his secretary, said Kennedy never felt at home in the lower chamber. He was detached from the daily operations of his own office and delegated as much to others as he could, including meeting with constituents.[45]

William Douglas, a family friend and later a Supreme Court justice, said John Kennedy was disinterested and bored by the House. "He was sort of drifting," Douglas said, adding that Kennedy failed to find issues that excited him while a congressman.[46] Although he was an adequate lawmaker, Kennedy's House career was not distinguished. Although several issues piqued his interest, his follow-through was episodic. Talented and intelligent, Kennedy was known for initiating, rather than completing, projects. House members, he felt, were regarded as "worms" to whom no one paid attention.[47] Kennedy later acknowledged that his years in the House were frustrating because "you are one of 435 members. You have to be there many, many years before you get to the hub of influence, or have an opportunity to play any role on substantive matters."[48]

Three
The 1952 Campaign

I

Even before his first term in the House of Representatives concluded, John Kennedy began looking for a way to move on. Perpetually restless, Kennedy never envisioned his service in the House as anything more than a passing stop on a more ambitious political journey. Kennedy's aides and colleagues said he was frustrated and bored in the House. He never sought out mentors or learned its rhythms or committed himself to working diligently in its committees. He never sought a role that gave him more influence or put him on a path to future power in the House. Kennedy was "a fish out of water" in the House, Tip O'Neill once said. "He didn't get along with the leadership, and they resented his frequent absences and his political independence. Jack was never one to do his homework. He preferred to travel, and he was always being invited to speak around the state."[1]

Kennedy briefly considered running for the Senate in 1948 against Republican incumbent

Leverett Saltonstall but decided it was too soon for him to mount a statewide race. He also believed, perhaps wrongly, that 1948 would not be a good political year for Democrats given President Truman's lagging popularity. But he was determined to lay the foundation for a statewide race and had his staff schedule appearances for him throughout Massachusetts. David Powers, an aide in his 1946 House race, tacked a state housing authority map of Massachusetts on the bedroom wall of Kennedy's Bowdoin Street apartment. They placed a colored pin on each city and town that the congressman visited on a political trip. Their goal was to blanket the map. Once this was accomplished, Kennedy said he would be ready for a statewide race.

Kennedy began a nearly four-year quest to visit each of Massachusetts's 39 cities and 312 towns, many of which he traveled to more than once. Based in Washington during the congressional workweek, Kennedy typically flew to Boston on Thursday evening for a full weekend of political events that kept him busy until Sunday evening, when he took an overnight train back to Washington. His schedule was very different from that of most House members of this time, who usually returned to their home districts only a few times a year.

Over these four years, while winning reelection

to his House seat in 1948 and 1950, Congressman Kennedy addressed countless civic, fraternal, political, and veterans groups across the state. He was a fixture at Catholic communion breakfasts and Protestant church socials. "Jack told me to let everybody know he was available as a speaker on weekends and I talked Kennedy to the local Elks, VFWs, Amvets, Holy Name Societies and volunteer fire departments wherever I went," Powers recalls. "I became his booking agent. No town was too small or too Republican for him. He was willing to go anywhere, and every group was glad to have him, not only because he was an interesting political figure and a well-known war hero but because he never charged a dime for expenses."[2]

Kennedy's traveling entourage usually included aides Powers, Bob Morey (who did the driving), John Galvin, and Frank Morrissey. As they crisscrossed Massachusetts, the congressman and his aides stayed at whatever accommodations were available. Powers recalls dingy, poorly lit hotels with a bathtub at the end of the hall. Always on the go and nearly always running late, Kennedy was fueled by hamburgers and milk shakes that were gulped down during ten-minute lunch and dinner stops. Galvin recalls once seeing Kennedy shaving in the men's room of a bowling alley between events.[3]

During his travels Kennedy was often in

excruciating back pain. He put on a brave face during public events but sometimes used crutches to get from the car to the engagement. While being driven to the next event, Kennedy would lean back on the seat and close his eyes in pain, Powers recalls. At night he often soaked in a bath for an hour and then slept with a wooden board under his mattress, or placed the mattress on the floor, for more support.[4]

During these speaking tours across Massachusetts, Kennedy took note of energetic and impressive people who might be helpful in a future campaign. He jotted down names on slips of paper and gave them to Grace Burke, the secretary in his Boston office, who typed the information onto index cards and filed them for future reference. While Kennedy geared his speeches to his audiences, the substantive portion of his remarks often touched on two themes: the United States was engaged in a life-or-death struggle with Communism, and the ailing Massachusetts economy needed to be revived by new laws and more forceful representation in Washington.

Kennedy's political engagements accelerated in 1951, when he spoke in more than 70 communities. Looking ahead to 1952, he saw two enticing statewide contests: a gubernatorial race and a Senate race. Democratic governor Paul Dever spent months agonizing over whether he should run for reelection in 1952 or challenge incumbent Republican senator Henry Cabot Lodge. For practical reasons Kennedy decided he would run for whichever office the governor did not choose. While Lodge was an extremely formidable opponent and any race against him would be daunting, Kennedy was far more interested in a Senate race than a bid for the governorship. He found the range and types of issues that a senator dealt with far more interesting than those that a governor confronted. Looking out at the state capitol once during a meeting, Kennedy told his aide, Lawrence O'Brien, "I don't look forward to sitting over there in the governor's office and dealing with sewer contracts."[5] But he told his aides that he would run for either of the two offices. "I would rather run for Governor or the Senate and lose and take the shot than go back and serve another term as a Congressman," he said.[6] He was envious of two of his 1946 House classmates, Richard Nixon of California and George Smathers of Florida, who had won Senate races in 1950. In January 1951, he told then state representative Tip O'Neill that he was going to be leaving the House, and if O'Neill wanted to run for his House seat, he should begin preparations to do so quietly.[7]

During the first few months of 1952, Kennedy waited impatiently for Dever to make his choice. A deeply frustrated Kennedy remarked that he was eager for the governor to stop equivocating and make a decision. Finally, on April 6, 1952, Palm Sunday, Dever told Kennedy he was going to run for reelection, freeing Kennedy to jump into the Senate race against Lodge. He checked with Archbishop Richard Cushing to be sure it was appropriate to announce his candidacy during Holy Week. Assured that there were no liturgical reasons to delay, Kennedy was ready to move forward.[8]

II

Kennedy announced his candidacy for the Senate the next day. His one-page written statement summarized the central policy points he had been making during his four years of travel throughout Massachusetts. He said the United States faced grave dangers in its battle with Communism and had to respond forcefully, and that Massachusetts faced a serious crisis of industrial decline that must be reversed. He noted that Washington's preoccupation with international problems was understandable because foreign policy was a matter of national survival. "We must be consistent and sincere and ever opposed to vacillation, political expediency and the easy compromise," he said.[9]

Referring to the economic crisis battering

Massachusetts, Kennedy said that the state's industrial and manufacturing base had been weakened, compared to other states, and that unemployment, particularly in textile and shoe sectors, was rising. "For entirely too long the representatives of Massachusetts in the United States Senate have stood by helplessly while our industries and jobs disappear. Because of this, thousands of families today are denied the opportunity for successful and decent living," he said. Other states had vigorous leaders in the Senate who forcefully defended the interests of their constituencies. "Massachusetts has need of such leadership," he declared. "I, therefore, am opposing Henry Cabot Lodge Jr., for the office of the United States Senator from Massachusetts."[10]

In his accompanying biographical statement, Kennedy made a more affirmative case for his candidacy. He noted that he was elected to the House in 1946 in his "first try" for any political office and easily won reelection in 1948 and 1950. As a member of the House Education and Labor Committee and the House District of Columbia Committee, he claimed significant experience and policy successes on important domestic issues. According to Kennedy's narrative, he had led the battle for desperately needed veterans housing, fought to extend rent and price controls, and was the first member of Congress to call attention to the "shocking state of civil defense" and the need for an adequate program to protect citizens in the event of bombing at home. Kennedy reminded voters of his support for civil rights legislation and his introduction in the House of a national minimum wage law that would protect the workers and industries of Massachusetts and New England by eliminating the wage differential between North and South. The congressman depicted himself as a strong supporter of a powerful air force, adding that he voted against tax cuts in 1947 and 1948 because he wanted the money preserved to build planes for American defenses.[11]

In the foreign policy realm, Kennedy emphasized his support for assistance to Italy, Greece, and Turkey as well as the Marshall Plan to help revive war-torn Europe. He touted his hard-line stance toward China, boasting about his tough speech on the House floor criticizing the Truman administration for not aggressively supporting the Chinese Nationalist government. He also cited legislation he supported to ban the shipment of war materials to "Red China" either directly or indirectly through Hong Kong.[12]

In a curious reference, Kennedy's biographical statement also included an assessment made about him during the 1950 debate on defense legislation by Congressman Clare Hoffman, a Republican from Michigan, who tepidly praised Kennedy as "a man of more than average ability and integrity." In other campaign statements and brochures, the Kennedy campaign depicted the congressman as a resolute, straight-talking leader who thought clearly, spoke frankly, acted courageously, led fearlessly, and served faithfully.[13]

In contrast, Kennedy portrayed Lodge as a polished, even slick, politician. "Lodge unquestionably is the shrewdest and smoothest politician in the Republican party. If Senator Robert A. Taft was as deft and clever a politician as Lodge, he probably would have the GOP Presidential nomination sewed up and in his pocket right now," a Kennedy campaign paper read. It continued, "If the Republican Party has a '100 per cent politician' in the entire country, it's the junior Massachusetts Senator [Lodge] who is commanding national attention as the Eisenhower campaign manager. He's a skilled craftsman at the art of politics, a master of political finesse."[14]

Not surprisingly, the Kennedy campaign depicted its candidate as a serious-minded man who was well known for "his candor and directness on even the most controversial questions. There is rarely any doubt where he stands. That trait is not characteristic of Lodge who has been on both sides of numerous issues and can shift and reverse his field in bewildering fashion."[15]

The Kennedy campaign sought all possible angles to hit Lodge. They hammered him for his absences in the current legislative session while serving as Dwight Eisenhower's presidential campaign manager. They scorched him for shifting positions on scores of issues and assembled a 162-page document called "Lodge's Dodges" that cited dozens of apparent policy shifts. They attacked him from the left on domestic issues, accusing the senator of opposing key housing and labor legislation. They blasted Lodge from the right on foreign policy, calling him too supportive of President Truman's foreign policy and too timid in opposing Communism. They attacked Lodge for vaguely suggesting he had a plan that would allow for the withdrawal of American troops from Korea. Kennedy argued that American withdrawal from Korea would allow Communist advances to sweep through Asia and even imperil Alaska. "That would be a prelude to the Third World War, and this is the danger that Mr. Lodge is asking us to run."[16]

At the core of Lodge's deficiencies, Kennedy charged, were character flaws. "A lack of integrity is a serious thing. I should have preferred to have met my opponent flatly on the issues of the day," the congressman said in a speech. Observing that the problems of the day were "grim, serious, tragic," Kennedy said he preferred that the nation's challenges were less demanding. "I wish devoutly that they were less fearful than they are. But neither you nor I can change them. But we can change the manner in which we will meet them—

either face to face or slinkingly and slyly with hypocrisy," he said, taking a swipe at his opponent. "Lodge shifts his stand on almost every issue in an effort to win the votes of the different groups he is addressing. . . . Mr. Lodge has shown great skill in making claims. Distortion, exaggeration and evasion form the basis of his political campaign, but when the screen is removed, his official record of years of neglect for the interests of Massachusetts is exposed."[17]

Though Kennedy traveled frequently as a congressman, including two extensive foreign trips in 1951, he audaciously blasted Lodge for being more interested in global affairs than matters that directly affected his state. He charged that the senator was so enamored with international affairs that he had little time to deal with the prosaic concerns of the people of Massachusetts. "When one looks at a globe of the world, and my opponent now enjoys the reputation of being a globe watcher, Massachusetts is hardly discernible. But to the four and a half million people who live in the state, it is the most important part of the globe. One cannot have his thoughts on the outskirts of Paris and be thinking of the thousands who work in Massachusetts' industrial plants. When Mr. Lodge voted for this Taft-Hartley law, he could not have been thinking of the working men and women of our state," Kennedy said.[18] The mention of Paris was a reference to Lodge's well-publicized trip to NATO headquarters in September 1951 to urge Eisenhower to leave his job as Supreme Allied Commander and run for president on the Republican ticket.

III

Kennedy had developed a clear message over his four years of speaking to audiences throughout Massachusetts. He was fairly well known, especially in political circles. However, after his early April announcement, his official campaign got off to a lackluster start. His campaign manager, Mark Dalton, had not been given any clear marching orders from Kennedy on how to build an organization. Kennedy said he was surprised that little progress had been made on the organizational front, but even his close aides felt he was being disingenuous on this score. "Jack knew very well that no organizing had been done because he had given nobody the authority to do it," recalled Ken O'Donnell, a top Kennedy aide.[19]

In a late May meeting, Joseph Kennedy sought a status report from Dalton on the campaign and was not happy with what he heard. He forced the resignation of Dalton and installed Robert, John's 26-year-old brother and a recent law school graduate working for the Justice Department, as the new campaign chief. A campaign neophyte who had few political contacts in Boston, Robert Kennedy plunged into the assignment. He was brash, tough, hard-working, well organized, and had the respect of his brother and father. Working with campaign strategist Lawrence O'Brien, they built a formidable political operation. From the outset they were determined to circumvent the Massachusetts Democratic Party, which was largely focused on Dever's gubernatorial reelection bid. Drawing on John Kennedy's years of contacts, the campaign developed extensive files of community leaders who would become the organizational foundation of the campaign. The Kennedy team built its operation city by city, town by town, appointing nearly 300 people to serve as campaign secretaries to organize and monitor the campaign effort in their communities.[20]

O'Brien believed a strong organization could affect between 3 percent and 5 percent of the total vote, a critical margin in a closely contested election. He was convinced that since the two candidates did not have major ideological disagreements, the campaign would be won on organizational superiority. O'Brien believed the key to Kennedy's success was his network of 300 secretaries and nearly 21,000 volunteers. The campaign sought out people who were active in the community but new to politics. This allowed the campaign to stay clear of intraparty battles and turf struggles while focusing on promoting Kennedy and attacking Lodge. An early example of the strength of the organization came in late June when the campaign submitted Kennedy's candidacy petition papers with 232,324 signatures. Only 2,500 were required by the state. The campaign then went a step further and sent thank you notes to each person who signed the petition. It was a good start for Kennedy and an ominous sign for Lodge.[21]

IV

The battle between Kennedy and Lodge was one of the most closely watched contests in the autumn of 1952. The *New York Times* devoted a long feature to the riveting race. It observed that with Democrats holding a precarious two-seat majority in the Senate, the outcome of this race could help tip the power balance in the upper chamber. The race had an "out-sized importance" because Democrats viewed Lodge, a key adviser to Eisenhower, as a "symbol" who would be "particularly pleasing to strike down." For Republicans, Kennedy was seen as a strong supporter of Truman's Fair Deal and "would be a particularly desirable casualty for a Republican crusade" built on the theme of the necessity for change.[22]

The contest between Kennedy and Lodge was intriguing on many levels. Both candidates were inheritors of prominent names and considerable wealth. Both were honors graduates from Harvard who had worked in journalism and published books as young men about the need for democracies to be better prepared militarily. Both volunteered for combat duty during World War II and were decorated for their bravery. The lives of the two families intersected in both cooperative and competitive ways. Lodge's grandfather, Henry Cabot Lodge, defeated a challenge by Kennedy's grandfather, John "Honey Fitz" Fitzgerald, and retained his Senate seat in 1916.[23]

Senator Lodge, the incumbent, was 15 years older than Congressman Kennedy and was something of a role model for the younger man. Kennedy once told columnist Arthur Krock that Lodge had been his "ideal" public servant when he was a student at Harvard and Lodge was a first-term senator. Lodge praised Kennedy's war heroics in a July 1943 speech that was placed in the *Congressional Record* and wrote Kennedy a note of sympathy when his sister, Kathleen, was killed in a plane crash. Kennedy and Lodge had a cordial relationship. While they served in different chambers of Congress and came from different political parties, Kennedy and Lodge bumped into each other from time to time in Washington and Massachusetts. At a Boston black-tie dinner in 1947, a photo shows Kennedy and Lodge sitting at a table joking with Republican senators Leverett Saltonstall of Massachusetts and Joseph McCarthy of Wisconsin.

In 1952, Lodge was a prominent Republican in the Senate, a respected member of the Senate Foreign Relations Committee, and a political force in Massachusetts. Defeating him would be a huge victory for Kennedy and would be certain to attract national attention. His father told him that defeating Lodge would be hard but noteworthy: "When you've beaten him, you've beaten the best. Why try for something less?"[24]

Lodge was a political heavyweight. After graduating from Harvard, he began a career in journalism but soon gravitated toward the family business of politics and public service. After a stint in the Massachusetts legislature, Lodge ran for the Senate in 1936 and defeated James Michael Curley, then the Democratic governor of Massachusetts. Lodge was viewed as moderate to liberal on domestic issues such as housing, labor, and Social Security. On foreign policy, he was initially very wary of American overseas engagement. In 1939, he said the United States should stay neutral even as Hitler invaded Poland. "The fight in Europe is not our fight, it's theirs," he declared. But like many others, the Japanese attack on Pearl Harbor in December 1941 drove Lodge toward a more internationalist perspective. "I was 100 percent wrong that we could stay out of the Second World War," Lodge would later say.[25]

During World War II, Lodge took a leave of absence in 1942 to serve in the army in Libya. He requested a second leave from the Senate for military service in 1944, but this was rejected when the secretary of war barred current members of Congress from active military service. Lodge resigned his seat in the Senate in February 1944, becoming the first senator since the Civil War to leave the Senate to serve on active duty in the military. He fought in France and Italy with distinction and then returned home and ran for and won a Senate seat in 1946, defeating Senator David Walsh, a five-term Democratic incumbent.

Lodge returned to the Senate as a passionate internationalist. He was a determined champion of the Marshall Plan and supported the creation of NATO. He portrayed himself as a stern foe of Communism but discouraged others from depicting the rivalry as a holy war rather than a struggle between two opposing systems of government. "It is not a holy war," he said in 1947. "I hope it never becomes a holy war, because so long as you can keep it on the ground of national interest you can modify your course in accordance with the requirements of the situation. The minute it becomes a holy war, then you are in to the death and nothing can stop you."[26]

Lodge remained progressive on domestic issues such as increasing the minimum wage and federal aid for education. Within Republican circles, he pushed the GOP to "modernize" and adopt moderate stances on health care and housing, end racial discrimination, and expand Social Security coverage. "I'm a different sort of Republican," Lodge said. "If there is a good proposition and a Democrat offers it, I'm for it; if it's lousy and a Republican offers it, I'm against it." Conservative Republicans, led by Senator Robert Taft, had little time for him. Taft defeated Lodge's bid in 1949 to become the head of the Senate Republican Policy Committee, an important group among Senate Republicans.[27]

When Lodge led the effort to persuade Eisenhower to seek the GOP's presidential nomination, he warned the general that if he didn't go after the nomination, Taft would likely win it and would easily be defeated by the Democratic candidate in 1952. Lodge spent considerable time and energy throughout 1951 and the first half of 1952 persuading Eisenhower to run for president and then organizing what became a bitter battle with Taft for the GOP nomination. At the party's July convention in Chicago, Eisenhower won the Republican nomination and launched his general election campaign against the Democratic candidate, Adlai Stevenson.

It was not until Labor Day that Lodge turned his complete attention to his own campaign, with the election only two months away. Some of his supporters worried that his immersion in the Eisenhower campaign would come back to haunt him. "He neglected his campaign outrageously," a Republican official said. "He just paid no attention to his race up here." One political adviser said Lodge's work on the Eisenhower campaign had been both distracting and exhausting. "Cabot had been in the Ike business for a year. He was very tired and this took a great deal of spark out of him." Not only had his involvement in Eisenhower's campaign worn him down, it angered many in the Taft wing of the Republican Party, some of whom were from Massachusetts.[28]

As his reelection campaign geared up, Lodge pledged to the people of Massachusetts that if they returned him to the Senate, he would devote his time and energy to help create jobs and work for a more peaceful world. He vowed to go after more defense contracts for Massachusetts, protect and advance Massachusetts industries, cut waste, lower taxes, control prices, and work for medical aid, housing, and old age security "without socialism." He promised to fight for equality of civil and economic rights, press for more defense spending, especially for the air force, promote effective alliances in Europe and Asia, and support a plan to end the bloody stalemate in Korea.[29]

V

By the time that Lodge focused on the race in a forceful way, Kennedy had a well-honed message and a smoothly functioning political machine focused on winning over important groups such as labor, Catholics, Jews, and women. The Kennedy campaign organized receptions or teas to reach out to women voters. The candidate and his family had hosted house parties during his first congressional campaign in 1946, and they expanded the concept during his 1952 Senate race. With the help of his mother, Rose; his sisters Pat, Eunice, and Jean; and his cousin Polly Fitzgerald, the Kennedy campaign hosted more than 30 teas across the state. Typically, invitations were sent to Democratic women in the area by the local Kennedy campaign secretary. Sometimes an advertisement was placed in the local paper the day before a reception. Attendance at Kennedy teas ranged from a few hundred women to several thousand. Both the candidate and his mother spoke briefly after being introduced by a local leader. During the tea the Kennedy family formed a receiving line and met each woman as she filed by. The attendees were asked to sign a guest book and later received a thank you note from Kennedy and a request that she volunteer. These volunteers made phone calls, sent out campaign literature, went door to door distributing the campaign's tabloid newspaper, and helped register voters. In total, about 75,000 women attended these teas. Lodge initially dismissed the tea parties with sarcasm. "I am told they are quite pleasant affairs and I am sure they are not too fattening."[30] The Kennedy campaign also organized two televised *Coffee with the Kennedys* morning shows in which Rose talked about her family and her son's good qualities. The campaign helped organize about 5,000 house parties across the state to watch the shows.

Perhaps sensing that momentum was on Kennedy's side, Lodge challenged him to a series of debates across Massachusetts on both state and national issues. Two face-to-face encounters took place. The first was on September 16, when the candidates squared off at South Junior High School in Waltham before an overflow crowd of more than 1,000, with hundreds of others listening to the debate on loudspeakers outside the gym. The announced topic was "Issues Facing the Democratic and Republican Parties in the Coming Election," but it became a wide-ranging exchange. The debate was largely a draw, with one reporter calling it a "genteel political duel" that was "polite enough to do credit to a Boston dining room." Another account described it as a "gentlemanly tranquil forum." But Kennedy took a more forceful and aggressive approach than many anticipated. He blasted Lodge for being the Republican Party's "number one" supporter of Truman's foreign policy. Curiously, he also accused Republicans of being too partisan. "To claim our successes were bipartisan, our failures Democratic is good politics perhaps, but not good sense," Kennedy said. Lodge tried to stay above the partisan fray and was even willing to criticize his own party, saying it tended to look backward and not ahead: "If you send me back to the Senate, I will continue to work with men of good will regardless of party on all propositions that have merit." As the two men jousted, Kennedy's father sat in the balcony and sent notes to his son, which were delivered by two runners.[31]

The two candidates also appeared together in October on a national public affairs TV program called *Keep Posted*, which was broadcast live from New York City and simulcast by a Boston TV station. The topic was "Who will do more for the country, Eisenhower or Stevenson?" so the exchange was ostensibly about the presidential race. To many viewers, Lodge appeared uncomfortable with the medium of TV, whereas Kennedy seemed calm and relaxed.

Though Kennedy's campaign was picking up steam, it also had its stumbles. One self-inflicted wound had its genesis in 1950, when Kennedy spoke candidly in what he thought was an off-the-record conversation with a class at Harvard. A teaching fellow, John Mallan, wrote an account of Kennedy's comments that was published in the *New Republic* in October 1952. In the article, he recalled Kennedy saying he was not sure why Americans were still fighting in Korea, that he supported the controversial McCarran Act to register Communist organizations, that Joseph McCarthy might be "on to something" in his quest to root out Communists from the U.S. government, that he was underwhelmed by Dean Acheson as secretary of state, and that he was glad Nixon won a Senate seat in 1950. The article generated a furor, especially in liberal circles, and Kennedy issued an angry statement that did not dispute the substance of the article. The entire matter was an unneeded distraction and caused some liberals to reassess their support of Kennedy.[32]

But Lodge had his stumbles as well. He struggled with how to use Republican senator Joseph McCarthy to promote his candidacy. In 1952 McCarthy was still a popular, albeit controversial, figure in the Republican Party. McCarthy also had strong support among the 750,000 members of the Irish Catholic community in

Massachusetts, many of whom usually supported Democrats. Lodge had a cool relationship with McCarthy based on fundamental differences over issues and strikingly different backgrounds. McCarthy, though friendly with Kennedy, was willing to come to Massachusetts to help Lodge in the interests of party loyalty. But McCarthy insisted that Lodge publicly request the visit. Lodge wavered, and McCarthy never personally appeared in Massachusetts to campaign for him but did send a telegram of support.

The two candidates sought the editorial support of the state's major newspapers. Five of the state's six largest daily newspapers endorsed Lodge for reelection: the *Boston Herald*, *Berkshire Eagle*, *Lowell Sun*, *Springfield Union*, and *Worcester Evening Gazette*. The *Boston Globe* maintained its tradition of not endorsing any candidate. The *Lowell Sun* offered glowing praise of the Republican senator: "Henry Cabot Lodge is certainly one of the few truly great statesmen and never was more deserving of election to the Senate than he is this year." But in a critical development, the politically conservative *Boston Post* endorsed Kennedy, a move Lodge thought cost him thousands of votes. John Fox, publisher of the *Post*, cited Kennedy's strong anti-Communist stance as a major reason for the paper's editorial support. However, it came out later that Joseph Kennedy loaned Fox $500,000 in the late fall of 1952 as his paper struggled with financial problems.[33]

As in John Kennedy's first House race, his father poured vast sums into his son's Senate race. While the Kennedy campaign officially spent $350,000 for the 1952 campaign, most analysts think that vastly understates the actual amount. Some have estimated that Joe Kennedy alone spent more than $1 million on the race.[34]

While Kennedy's financial resources were an important asset to his campaign, the candidate himself grew to be a formidable challenger. He became a confident campaigner and an effective speaker, forcing himself outside his comfort zone as he made the case for his candidacy. "He could not be called a natural politician; he was too reserved, too private a person by nature," said Lawrence O'Brien. "But he knew what he wanted and he would force himself to do whatever was necessary to achieve it."[35]

As the election neared, John Kennedy told aides he felt he had run the best campaign possible. He said there was nothing else he could have done. On November 4, 1952, Eisenhower swept the nation and easily won Massachusetts by 208,000 votes over Stevenson. The Senate election was a nail-biter, and it wasn't until early on November 5 that it became clear Kennedy had won by about 70,000 votes. When the final tally was counted, Kennedy won with 51.5 percent of the vote. The final vote was 1,211,984 for Kennedy and 1,141,247 for Lodge. On the morning after the election, Lodge sent a terse wire of congratulations to Kennedy. "I extend congratulations and express the hope that you will derive from your term in the Senate all the satisfaction which comes from courageous, sincere and effective public service." Lodge's disappointment may have been eased by a kind note he received from George Marshall, one of the nation's most revered military and political figures: "I am terribly sorry that the electorate failed you in your state. They made a great error for you were among the most conspicuous statesmen in public office."[36]

Many political experts believe that only Kennedy could have beaten Lodge. "The Kennedy campaign in 1952 was the most nearly perfect political campaign I've even seen," said O'Brien. "It was a model campaign because it had to be. Jack Kennedy was the only man in Massachusetts who had the remotest chance of beating Henry Cabot Lodge that year and Kennedy couldn't have won without an exceptional political effort."[37]

VI

The Sunday following his election, Kennedy appeared on NBC's *Meet the Press*. The host, Lawrence Spivak, began the interview by remarking on Kennedy's "sensational victory" in Massachusetts at the same time that Eisenhower was sweeping the nation. Spivak said Kennedy's victory "has brought him to national attention as the most important Democratic figure in New England." When asked to discuss his campaign against Lodge, Kennedy offered a simple explanation for his victory: "I worked a lot harder in Massachusetts than did Senator Lodge. He was working for General Eisenhower and I think that he felt that would take care of his Massachusetts position." During the interview he was also asked to opine on the important issues of the day, such as education funding, French struggles in Indochina, the stalemated war in Korea, the impact of the Taft-Hartley law, and the future of the Democratic Party.[38] With his Senate victory, Kennedy had arrived as a major political figure on the national scene.

In the waning weeks of 1952, as he was winding down his service in the House, Kennedy bumped into his successor as the congressman of the 11th District, Tip O'Neill. He urged O'Neill to take a different approach than the one he had taken, suggesting that O'Neill develop a close relationship with House Majority Leader John McCormack and prepare for a consequential House career. "Whatever you do, don't make the mistake I did. Be nice to John McCormack," O'Neill recalled Kennedy saying.[39]

But Kennedy did not regret the path he had taken. He was ready to move on to the Senate. During the 1952 campaign, Kennedy never specified what he hoped to accomplish in the upper chamber. He had harshly criticized Lodge for spending too much time working on foreign policy, which was the part of the job that was most interesting to Kennedy. While Kennedy was determined to become active in foreign policy, he knew that he must first tackle the most critical issue to Massachusetts voters by crafting a plan to revive the Massachusetts and New England economies. That would be his first job as the junior senator from Massachusetts.

Four
The Senate of the 1950s

I

When John Kennedy was sworn in as a United States senator from Massachusetts on January 3, 1953, a long period of Democratic control of the presidency was ending, and Republicans were poised to run the White House and both chambers of Congress. The 20-year run of Franklin Roosevelt and Harry Truman was over, and the era of Dwight Eisenhower was about to begin.

Eisenhower was elected to the presidency on November 4, 1952. Though the new Congress, including Kennedy, was sworn in 17 days before Eisenhower, the new president had already begun to shape the political landscape and impose a quiet dominance that would extend for eight years and profoundly affect Kennedy's Senate career. As his longer-term political ambitions took shape, Kennedy would come to define his political agenda in stark contrast, even in opposition, to the president's.

Eisenhower entered the presidency with high expectations—from both the admiring American public and himself. Born in Denison, Texas, in October 1890 and raised in Abilene, Kansas, Eisenhower attended the U.S. Military Academy at West Point and was a member of the fabled class of 1915—"the class the stars fell on"—that produced 64 generals from its 164 graduates. Eisenhower rose to the rank of lieutenant colonel by the end of World War I, after which he served as a loyal and respected staffer to Generals Fox Connor, John J. Pershing, and Douglas MacArthur, all of whom trained the young soldier. "This is the best officer in the U.S. Army," MacArthur wrote in an evaluation of Eisenhower. "When the next war comes, move him right to the top."[1] When World War II broke out, General George Marshall did just that, summoning Eisenhower to Washington to run the War Plans Division. His job was to devise a strategy for the war. He detailed how the United States could first concentrate most of its resources to defeat Germany and then turn to the Pacific to defeat Japan. In 1942, Eisenhower was selected to head the European theater of operations. As a four-star general, he commanded the historic D-Day landings in Normandy in June 1944 and became revered in America and across the world as the general who defeated Adolf Hitler. Eisenhower was a skilled manager and administrator who was adept at establishing clear goals with the resources available.[2]

After his World War II success, Eisenhower

became president of Columbia University in 1948 and then the first Supreme Allied Commander for NATO in Europe in 1951. Throughout his military career, Eisenhower kept his distance from partisan politics and never declared himself a member of either political party. President Truman signaled he would support Eisenhower in 1948 if he chose to run for the presidency as a Democrat. Eisenhower declined but was far more interested when a group of moderate Republicans approached him in 1951 about becoming the 1952 GOP presidential nominee. They appealed to him by saying he was needed to rescue his country from two unacceptable alternatives: the weary and corrupt Democratic Party, and a Republican Party led by arch-conservative Senator Robert Taft, a committed isolationist.

In January 1952, Eisenhower resigned his NATO command and returned to the United States for what became a brutal primary battle with Taft. He narrowly defeated Taft at the Republican Party convention in July. The general election that fall proved easier for Eisenhower as he hammered Democrats for their alleged corruption and failures in Korea, China, and against global Communism. Eisenhower easily defeated the Democratic nominee, Adlai Stevenson, winning 55 percent of the vote.

Eisenhower drove the nation's political agenda for eight years, although his quiet leadership was not always apparent to his contemporaries. He was, according to one biographer, "the most misunderstood of the modern presidents."[3] His political strength was rooted in a simple reality. The American people liked him. During his two terms as president, Eisenhower's approval rating averaged 66 percent and only once dipped below 50 percent. *New York Times* columnist James Reston wrote that the president's popularity was "a national phenomenon, like baseball." Reston believed Eisenhower was popular because "he was in tune with the worldwide spirit of the age. He was a good man in a wicked time; a consolidator in a world crying for innovation."[4]

Sworn in as president when he was 62, Eisenhower projected health, vitality, simplicity, and self-confidence. In fact he was more crafty, ambitious, and egotistical than most realized. Warm and friendly in public, he could be acerbic in private and had a ferocious temper. He was a rambling, syntax-challenged, extemporaneous speaker but an incisive and precise writer who examined public policy issues with rigor and discipline. He exuded the sensibilities of Middle America, unapologetically enjoying bridge, golf, fishing, and camping. He once described an intellectual as "a man who takes more words than are necessary to tell more than he knows."[5]

On the domestic front, Eisenhower was a fiscal conservative who believed that balanced budgets, partly achieved by restrained defense spending, would provide the foundation for American economic prosperity. This prosperity would be enjoyed by the public and help the United States eventually prevail in the Cold War. He thought it was politically foolish and economically unnecessary to try to repeal New Deal social programs such as Social Security and unemployment insurance, but felt it was necessary to keep them from expanding beyond the ability of the nation to pay for them. Still, he did launch the massively expensive interstate highway system and supported building the St. Lawrence Seaway. Eisenhower was an institutional innovator who shaped the modern presidency by appointing the first chief of staff, congressional liaison, and national security adviser. He also worked to build what he called a "modern" Republican Party that would look to the future rather than refight battles from the New Deal era.[6]

Perhaps the most consequential decision of his presidency was to name California Governor Earl Warren to the Supreme Court as the chief justice in 1953. In Warren's first year, he drafted and pushed through the Supreme Court by a unanimous vote the *Brown v. Board of Education* ruling that overturned the "separate but equal" doctrine, legally ending school segregation. The historic ruling, which has been called the "Second

Emancipation Proclamation," accelerated the civil rights movement.[7] While Eisenhower had significant misgivings about the Supreme Court decision, he insisted on enforcing it. He also instructed his attorney general, Herbert Brownell, to draft a major civil rights bill in 1956 that was approved by Congress in a scaled-back form in 1957.

In foreign policy, Eisenhower's most consequential action came early in his presidency, when he concluded an armistice in Korea in July 1953. This gave the American public an armed truce that it could live with rather than a stalemated war it would not accept. Eisenhower defeated the isolationist wing of the Republican Party and spent eight years fortifying and defending robust internationalism under American leadership. After intense analysis and careful debate within the administration, Eisenhower established a new national security doctrine, dubbed the "New Look," which envisioned a smaller conventional force, reduced defense expenditures, and a larger nuclear force. In the last few years of his presidency, America's nuclear arsenal jumped from 6,000 to 18,000 nuclear weapons.[8] As international crises occurred in Europe and Asia during his two terms, Eisenhower seriously contemplated the use of nuclear weapons several times. His defense strategy led a number of Democrats, including

John Kennedy, to argue the administration was not spending enough for the military and caused a missile gap to arise between the Soviet Union and the United States.

Eisenhower presided over a vigorous but restrained rivalry with the Soviet Union. He met Soviet leaders and offered a series of arms control proposals that they ultimately rejected, but the American initiatives signaled to the world that the United States was acting in good faith and sought an accommodation with its chief rival. He brushed aside Soviet warnings that the United States and its Western allies should leave West Berlin. During his eight years as president, Eisenhower strengthened American alliances in Europe and Asia. He also launched a number of covert American operations that toppled governments in Iran and Guatemala. As he was leaving office, he started plans for an American-supported effort to oust Cuban leader Fidel Castro that ultimately resulted in the 1961 Bay of Pigs debacle.

Eisenhower also continued America's involvement in Indochina. He opposed sending American ground troops to save beleaguered French forces in the spring of 1954, saying, "This war in Indochina would absorb our troops by the legions." But he did commit the American government to support South Vietnam in the aftermath of the 1954 Geneva Accords, which divided Vietnam into northern and southern regimes. He supported approximately $1 billion in assistance between 1955 and 1961 for South Vietnam and authorized the deployment of about 1,000 American military advisers to bolster the government of Ngo Dinh Diem in South Vietnam. Like many of his contemporaries, Eisenhower viewed the deeply flawed government of Diem as preferable to the Communist alternative.[9]

Democrats, including Kennedy, often derided Eisenhower as an absentee president who failed to deliver the kind of vigorous and aggressive leadership the nation needed. They accused Eisenhower of delegating foreign policy to Secretary of State John Foster Dulles and domestic policy to White House Chief of Staff Sherman Adams. Democrats criticized the Eisenhower years as a time of complacency, when the United States gazed "down the long green fairways of indifference."[10]

John Kennedy eventually defined his Senate career and his political agenda in opposition to Eisenhower. While he sometimes supported the president, he dismissed the administration as a slow-moving, backward-looking government that failed to keep the United States moving forward as the world unfolded with breakneck speed. On several important foreign policy matters, he positioned himself to the right of Eisenhower, arguing that more funds for the military were needed. Senator Kennedy also developed a fuller appreciation for the power of the presidency during the Eisenhower years, learning that legislation and initiatives that he worked on for years in the Senate could be killed by a simple statement or warning from Eisenhower.[11]

II

If Eisenhower was the dominant political force in the United States for most of the 1950s, Democratic Senator Lyndon Johnson of Texas was the most powerful person in the Senate during this decade and shaped John Kennedy's Senate career in important ways.

Born in the Texas hill country in August 1908, Johnson graduated from Southwest Texas State Teachers College, taught high school for a year in Houston, and then joined the Washington staff of Democratic congressman Richard Kleberg in 1931. Johnson was appointed the Texas state director of the National Youth Administration in 1935 and was first elected to the U.S. House of Representatives in a 1937 special election in which he ran as a staunch supporter of the New Deal. He narrowly lost a Senate race in 1941 and continued serving in the House until 1949. In 1948 he was elected to the Senate, winning by a mere 87 votes.[12]

A member of the impressive class of 1948, Johnson entered the Senate with Hubert

Humphrey of Minnesota, Paul Douglas of Illinois, Robert Kerr of Oklahoma, Estes Kefauver of Tennessee, and Margaret Chase Smith of Maine. Humphrey and Douglas were liberal stalwarts; Kerr was a skilled legislative operator; Kefauver had a shrewd eye for the limelight and dogged investigative skills; and Smith was known for her principle and courage. With large ambitions and an instinct for where power resided, Johnson sought out Georgia senator Richard Russell as a mentor and plotted his ascent up the leadership hierarchy. Helped by the electoral defeats of a succession of Senate Democratic leaders, Johnson was elected the Senate Democratic whip in 1951 and the Senate Democratic leader in 1953 when he was only 44. Since Republicans then had a narrow majority in the Senate, Johnson served as minority leader, but when Democrats won back control in the 1954 elections, Johnson became the Senate majority leader in January of 1955.

Johnson was, by all accounts, a force of nature. Democratic senator George Smathers of Florida described Johnson's presence as a "great, overpowering thunderstorm that consumed you as it closed in around you."[13] Johnson was also shrewd and purposeful, thrusting himself into the leadership of the Democratic Party in the Senate. He served simultaneously as the Senate Democratic leader and the chairman of the Senate Democratic Policy Committee, the Senate Democratic Steering

Committee, and the Senate Democratic Campaign Committee. The Policy Committee developed party positions on important legislation and established overall strategy. The Steering Committee assigned Democratic senators to the Senate's committees, and the Campaign Committee allocated campaign funds to individual senators for their campaigns. Additionally, Johnson served as the chairman of the Defense Preparedness Subcommittee, the chairman of a subcommittee of the Senate Appropriations Committee, and, late in his Senate career, as the chairman of the Senate Committee on Aeronautical and Space Sciences. With his hands on so many levers of power and with a keen instinct on how to move legislation through the Senate, he became the undisputed master of the Senate. He once said, "I do understand power whatever else may be said about me."[14]

Johnson worked with men he saw as peers, such as House Speaker Sam Rayburn, senators Richard Russell and Robert Taft, and with Senate colleagues he viewed as lieutenants, such as Earle Clements, Hubert Humphrey, and Mike Mansfield. He skillfully navigated the various factions of the Democratic Party, dealing separately with conservative senators from the South, the border states, and Southwest, and with liberals from the North and West. While shrewd and aggressive about building an impressive power base for himself, Johnson also was careful to allow his colleagues a piece of the action. In 1953, Johnson introduced what became known as the Johnson rule, which stipulated that all Democratic senators would get one major committee assignment before any senator would get a second. This ensured that all of his Democratic members would sit on at least one major committee and allow younger senators to move into important positions earlier in their careers. He developed an intuitive feel for the Senate, and many said his most important skill was the ability to read people, especially his fellow senators. He could paint vivid political portraits of everyone in the Senate, describing their strengths, weaknesses, and long-term goals. He could be cocky and swaggering when that approach was needed, and quiet and nuanced when that was more appropriate. "For Johnson understood that the most important decision each Senator made, often obscurely, was what kind of Senator he wanted to be; whether he wanted to be a national leader in education, a regional leader in civil rights, a social magnate in Washington, an agent of the oil industry, a wheel horse of the party, a President of the United States," wrote Johnson biographer Doris Kearns.[15]

Johnson's dominance of the Senate was under-stood by all, respected by most, and resented by some. Paul Douglas, the liberal Democratic senator from Illinois who often clashed with Johnson for being too cautious, compared the Senate under Johnson to a Greek tragedy. "All the action takes place offstage, before the play begins. Nothing is left to open and spontaneous debate, nothing is left for the participants but the enactment of their prescribed roles."[16] Despite pressures from Paul Butler, the head of the Democratic National Committee, and other liberal leaders and activists, Johnson resisted pleas to offer a comprehensive alternative Democratic agenda to underscore the party's differences with Eisenhower. Johnson opted for a different approach: he decided to hold back, see what the president proposed, and then work with Eisenhower in those areas where he could and fight with the president where he must. Above all, he wanted Democrats to be seen by the public as constructive, conciliatory, and willing to help the president when he faced challenges from his strident right wing. "The American people are tired of wrecking crews. They want builders— people who can construct," Johnson said.[17] He preferred to pass modest legislation that became law and make incremental progress rather than wage symbolic fights that achieved little. He would rather help build houses than fight a losing battle over housing policy. When he did offer his own policy agenda in 1956, it was modest and practical rather than soaring and ideologically compelling. It called for a modest expansion of Social Security, tax cuts, medical research and hospital construction, school construction, highway construction, a housing program, water resources projects, assistance to depressed areas, a constitutional amendment to eliminate the poll tax, immigration law reforms, and deregulation of the oil and gas industry.[18]

One of Johnson's great accomplishments as the Senate majority leader was driving a civil rights bill through the Senate in 1957, the first civil rights legislation since 1875. Taking legislation that Eisenhower proposed and the House largely endorsed, Johnson rewrote it so it could pass in a deeply divided Senate and overcome a filibuster by southern Democrats. Some criticized his decision to turn a broad civil rights bill into a narrower voting rights bill as cynical and self-serving. But it was a skillful display of legislating.[19]

At the heart of Johnson's approach to running the Senate was an intense pragmatism that focused on achieving what was possible and then looking for other opportunities in the future. "There were no trumpets, the pennons never flew; the model was not Henry at Agincourt but Metternich at Vienna. The 'art of the possible' was a middlebrow art, practical, successful and in the end rather dull," wrote Harry McPherson, a Johnson aide. His boss, McPherson observed, was not interested in "failing proudly."[20]

III

The Senate that John Kennedy entered in January 1953 had a clear hierarchy influenced by seniority, committee chairmanships, committee assignments, leadership positions, and reputation. McPherson described the Senate as divided into whales and minnows. Whales were those senators who either chaired important committees or were senior members of these panels. They had deep policy expertise and considerable experience; they were accomplished legislators who confronted difficult problems, made tough decisions, and fought hard to prevail in legislative battles. They also, critics said, fought tenaciously to protect their turf and often resisted forward-leaning legislation. Minnows were those who entered and left the Senate leaving little trace—either because of their limited skills or because they had few opportunities to make their marks.

On the Democratic side of the aisle, Richard Russell of Georgia was viewed as a statesman of the first order. Courtly and polite, he was deeply read in history and an expert on the rules of the Senate and on national security and agricultural issues. Russell was also an avowed segregationist who battled for decades to kill civil rights legislation. Robert Kerr of Oklahoma, a former governor and a wealthy businessman, possessed the Senate's most formidable mind and sharpest tongue. McPherson called him "incomparably the Senate's most powerful and effective debater."[21] Rowland Evans and Robert Novak, two journalists who covered the Senate, described Kerr as "perhaps the greatest vote trader the Senate has ever seen." They continued, "Kerr was merciless in debate, reckless in promoting the interests of his state and blessed with an uncanny faculty for digesting and retaining whole huge doses of complex information."[22] Kerr seemed destined for greatness, but his career stalled due to shady financial transactions and his parochial focus on the oil and gas industry. Earle Clements of Kentucky, the assistant Democratic leader and acting Democratic leader when Johnson was ill, was a skilled backroom operator who helped keep the Senate running. He deferred to Johnson and was willing to do thankless tasks for the leader and even cast difficult votes, several of which led to his defeat. The Senate of the 1950s included a number of impressive southern and western Democrats including Lister Hill and John Sparkman of Alabama, Walter George of Georgia, Carl Hayden of Arizona, John Stennis of Mississippi, and Allen Ellender of Louisiana. The Democratic Party also had a stable of promising young liberal senators including Hubert Humphrey of Minnesota, William Fulbright of Arkansas, Mike Mansfield of Montana, and Henry "Scoop" Jackson of Washington.

In January 1953, Robert Taft was the Senate majority leader and had been the most dominant Republican for more than a decade. It was once said that Congress consisted of the House, the Senate, and Bob Taft. Taft became Eisenhower's chief advocate in the Senate despite their bruising primary battle the previous year. But just a few months into the new year, he grew ill, was diagnosed with cancer, and died that summer. Taft was replaced as majority leader by William Knowland of California, a hard-line conservative who lacked Taft's experience. He had little legislative finesse and was only mildly effective. He decided not to run for reelection in 1958 and instead ran for governor of California and was defeated by Edmund Brown Sr. In 1959 Everett Dirksen of Illinois became the Senate Republican leader, a position he held for a decade. Flamboyant, even theatrical, Dirksen became a dominant figure on Capitol Hill and was a darling of the media, but he was often difficult to pin down on issues. During his tenure as party leader, Dirksen helped assemble critical bipartisan coalitions, including several on civil rights legislation.

Following Taft's death, Styles Bridges of New Hampshire became the most influential Republican in the Senate in the 1950s. Conservative but flexible, he was able to deal with the various factions and personalities of his caucus. Although he expounded a combative conservative philosophy, he was also the quintessential dealmaker. He and Johnson worked well together and crafted many agreements behind closed doors, over whiskey and soda.

Eugene Millikin of Colorado was the Republican leader on tax policy and a senior member of the Finance Committee. A 1950 *Time* magazine article described him: "Witty and popular and the Republicans' best cloakroom statesman, he commands great respect among his colleagues."[23] Kennedy's colleague, the senior senator from Massachusetts, Leverett Saltonstall, was the Republican majority whip in 1953 and an expert on national security issues. He was also chairman of the Senate Armed Services Committee. Kennedy and Saltonstall enjoyed a friendly, respectful, and cooperative relationship, even though Kennedy was about the age of Saltonstall's oldest son. Kennedy called Saltonstall "Senator" at all times and sometimes asked his advice on Massachusetts matters.

The Senate Republican caucus included other personalities through the 1950s who had a great impact on American political life. Joseph McCarthy of Wisconsin was the chairman of the Government Operations Committee in 1953 and 1954 and became first famous and then infamous for his pursuit of Communists who allegedly infiltrated the U.S. government. McCarthy was a powerful voice in the early 1950s but then overreached, and his career unraveled in 1954 when the Senate voted to condemn him. He died a broken man in 1957. Barry Goldwater of Arizona, a former Phoenix businessman, entered the Senate in 1953 and eventually became the leader of the conservative movement within the Republican Party. He and Kennedy disagreed on almost all issues but enjoyed an easy, jocular relationship. On one occasion, Kennedy was serving as the temporary president of the Senate and was presiding over a session that extended into the evening. Kennedy was eager to leave for a social event. Goldwater was speaking on the Senate floor and, apparently sensing Kennedy's impatience, intentionally droned on. Kennedy scrawled a brief, pungent note to Goldwater that was delivered by a page. "Why are you always such a shit?" he asked Goldwater, who broke into laughter.[24]

IV

The Senate that Kennedy entered had traditions and norms that profoundly affected how senators approached their jobs. Most of the Senate's important work began in its committees, the dominant institutions in the upper chamber. The five most prestigious committees were Appropriations, Foreign Relations, Finance, Judiciary, and Armed Services. By most accounts, membership on Appropriations and Foreign Relations were the most coveted. Those on the Appropriations Committee funded the government and could funnel money to their own states and the states and districts of their allies in Congress. A seat on the Foreign Relations Committee increased the profile of the senator and gave him the necessary credentials for national leadership and a potential presidential campaign. A cut below the Big Five committees in terms of prestige were four that had jurisdiction over important aspects of the economy: the Agriculture, Banking, Commerce, and Labor committees. The next rung on the committee hierarchy were three panels sometimes referred to as the pork committees: Interior, Post Office, and Public Works. The least prestigious panels were often referred to as duty committees because they specialized in thankless, politically unrewarding tasks. They were Rules, Government Operations, and the District of Columbia committees.[25]

Most of the major Senate committees were dominated by southerners. Coming from states run by Democrats in which Republicans rarely even appeared on the ballot, once a senator from the South was elected he could often stay in the Senate for decades as long as he avoided a primary opponent. He often acquired enough seniority to eventually become a committee chairman. In 1957, for example, senators from the Deep South chaired seven of the nine most important committees. "The Senate might be described without too much violence to fact as the South's unending revenge upon the North for Gettysburg," William White wrote in his 1957 best-selling book about the Senate, *Citadel.* The Senate, according to White, was "the only place in the country where the South did not lose the war."[26]

White also discussed what he called the Inner Club, an informal, bipartisan directorate that led the Senate. "At the core of the Inner Club stand the Southerners, who with rare exceptions automatically assume membership almost with the taking of the oath of office." The Inner Club was dominated by southern Democrats and conservative Republicans (often from the Midwest), who tended to see the Senate as the final destination of their careers. These senators were devoted to the institution and took the time and attention to develop their legislative skills and policy expertise. "The long custom of the place impels him, if he is at all wise, to walk with a soft foot and to speak with a soft voice and infrequently," White wrote. "All the newcomer needs, if he is able and strong, is the passage of time—but this he needs indispensably, save in those rare cases where the authentic geniuses among Senate types are involved." In White's view, Richard Russell was the current embodiment of the Senate type.[27]

The Senate Kennedy entered in 1953 was influenced by informal expectations that shaped how senators viewed their overall careers and their daily activities. The first was apprenticeship, the willingness for a newly arrived senator to defer to the leadership of the Senate and do the unglamorous but necessary work of the body, such as presiding in the chair. Second was a commitment to delve into the detailed, dull, and often politically unrewarding work of the Senate. A good senator should be a workhorse, not a show horse. Third was the emphasis on specialization, in which senators focused on legislative work in their committees and developed a specific policy expertise in agriculture, taxes, foreign policy, labor, or other issues. There were customs that pertained to treating colleagues with courtesy, helping others, and publicly defending the Senate as an institution. Senators who adhered to these folkways would likely become respected and effective legislators. But this institutional loyalty might undermine other political ambitions. "As a general rule, it seems that a man who entirely adheres to the Senate folkways has little chance of ever becoming President of the United States," wrote Donald Matthews, a political scientist who studied the Senate of the 1950s.[28] The typical senator of the 1950s was a man who was either elderly or in late middle age. He was a white Protestant and a college-educated lawyer who was an inveterate joiner of clubs and organizations. Despite campaign finance rules that limited to $25,000 what a candidate could officially spend to run for the Senate in the general election, analysts said the minimum cost of a Senate race was $100,000, the average cost was $500,000, and a closely contested race might cost over $1 million. Campaign finance laws were to be evaded, not followed, and evasion was easy.[29]

A bastion of men, the Senate had an active Senate Ladies Club composed of the wives of the senators and presided over by the wife of the vice president. Their informal motto was, "Once a Senate wife, always a Senate wife." During Kennedy's time in the Senate, the presiding officer of the Senate Ladies Club was Pat Nixon, who dutifully led meetings every Tuesday and joined the other Senate wives in wearing white Red Cross uniforms and making bandages and clothes for the troops. The ladies brought sack lunches, sipped from mugs with their names on them, worked on their projects, and talked. Occasionally, Senator Kennedy's wife, Jackie, attended the Tuesday meetings. It was here that she met Mrs. Nixon.[30]

In the Senate that Kennedy joined in January 1953, a typical legislative session ran from

January to August. Senators had a staff of about a dozen who were packed into a three- or four-room office suite. Senators were paid $12,500 a year, had a $2,500 tax-free expense fund, and were basically subsidized for one round trip each session between Washington and their home. A 1952 *New York Times* survey found that the average senator and congressman had out-of-pocket office expenses that exceeded his salary by more than $3,000 each year.[31] Some law-makers had family wealth to draw upon while others worked part time for law firms or businesses to supplement their incomes. The more academically inclined senators wrote books and joined the lecture circuit.

Many senators of the 1950s commented on the difficulties caused by the heavy influx of constituent mail that sometimes reached several hundred letters a day. About two-thirds of the letters dealt with legislative matters, while the rest were constituent requests for assistance. Dwight Griswold, a Republican senator from Nebraska who entered the Senate with Kennedy, wrote an essay a few months into his tenure in which he lamented the frantic pace. "It is doubtful if a Senator has enough time to be a statesman. He is so busy with normal office work that he does not have sufficient time to study the important legislation that is presented." Griswold continued, "The plain fact is that no Senator can visit or lunch with friends, take his wife out to dinner, dictate or even sign letters and study legislation as he should."[32] Richard Neuberger, a Democratic senator from Oregon, wrote a similar essay in 1956, saying, "In the hurly burly of the Senate, considered judgments are a rare luxury. I expected deliberation. Instead, I have found haste and even a certain amount of frenzy."[33]

Despite the personal grind and the financial demands, politicians from around the country eagerly sought a Senate seat. Once elected, senators usually didn't want to leave. One senator told Donald Matthews he didn't know why anyone would want the job of a senator, but then added, "Don't quote me on that, I'm running for reelection."[34]

A seat in the Senate conferred power, prestige, and influence. It also provided an opportunity to study important issues and grow professionally. As Senator Paul Douglas of Illinois said, "Men learn more, faster in the Senate than any other time in their lives, after the age of five."[35] On this point, Senator Kennedy would probably have agreed, at least until 1961—his first year as president.

Five
Senator Kennedy and the Home Front

I

John F. Kennedy was passionate about foreign policy. It engaged his deepest interests and summoned his most creative thinking, political imagination, and love of historical analogy and example. Kennedy approached domestic issues more as a dutiful student. As a senator from an industrial state, he had no choice but to get involved in domestic matters. But he was cautious, selective, and tentative in his approach. While Kennedy took on labor reform, education, and housing, he stayed relatively clear of several of the major issues that dominated American politics throughout his nearly eight years in the Senate. During the important debate over civil rights, Kennedy was tactical and even timid. He supported the first major civil rights bill in 1957 but was not a central figure in the deliberations that brought it to fruition. Several colleagues, including Illinois's Paul Douglas, said Kennedy declined invitations to help lead the legislative effort and vigorously fight for new civil rights laws.[1]

His reticence appeared to be largely the result of political considerations; he wanted to retain strong support in the South without antagonizing liberals for whom civil rights legislation was a passionate cause. Kennedy supported a central feature of an early draft of the bill that authorized the attorney general to use injunctive power to enforce school desegregation and other civil rights. But this provision was removed by a coalition of conservative Democrats and some Republicans. Kennedy also supported a controversial jury trial amendment favored by conservatives. As Kennedy walked the civil rights political tightrope, he was very cautious and seemed determined not to antagonize either northern liberals or southern conservatives.[2]

Kennedy's approach to the Senate's censure of Joseph McCarthy was also very careful, even confusing, and caused him considerable political anguish later in his political career. McCarthy's fierce attacks on his political opponents and sweeping charges of Communist allegiance and infiltration polarized American politics for the first half of the 1950s. Kennedy largely stayed clear of McCarthy, who was a friend of his father's and was his brother Robert's onetime boss.

The Senate's deliberations and eventual 67 to 22

vote condemning McCarthy occurred while Kennedy was recovering in a hospital from back surgery in December 1954. All Senate Democrats, except Kennedy, who was ill and not in Washington, voted to condemn McCarthy. Senate Republicans were deeply divided on the question. All members of the Senate Republican leadership, except for Saltonstall of Massachusetts, voted against the motion. Kennedy and his top aides said at the time that his illness prevented him from voting on the McCarthy resolution. But Ted Sorensen, a senior Kennedy aide, acknowledged in his 2008 memoir that he had the distinct impression Kennedy did not want to vote on the McCarthy condemnation motion. Sorensen wrote, "There was no point in my trying to reach him on an issue he wanted to duck." He added, "My guess is that, if he had truly wanted to reach me from the hospital, he could have. I was—and remain—disappointed by his inaction. . . . JFK showed no courage on that vote. Neither did I."[3]

Some domestic issues did seize Kennedy's attention. He worked actively and impressively to defeat a 1956 proposal to overhaul the Electoral College, saying it would be worse than the current situation and would weaken Massachusetts's role in national elections. He studied the issue carefully, participated actively in the Senate debate, and won praise for his nuanced and impressive critique of the various proposals. The question of changing the Electoral College engaged Kennedy's intellectual interests as well as his instinct to protect his home state.

Kennedy was also very interested in the reforms proposed by the Hoover Commission, chaired by former president Herbert Hoover, which sought to promote greater government efficiency. As the chairman of the Senate Subcommittee on Reorganization, Kennedy held more than two dozen hearings on the Hoover Commission proposals in 1956 and helped win Senate passage of nearly a dozen of them. He held extensive hearings on the commission's proposal to create an administrative vice president to ease the administrative burdens of the president.

Kennedy also held extensive hearings on legislation to broaden the coverage of the minimum wage law and introduced legislation to create a national unemployment compensation system with benefits up to 39 weeks. He was also involved in a curious assortment of other issues: advocating for lobbying reform, repealing the loyalty oath, lowering the voting age to 18, pushing for a national library of medicine, creating new budget systems, and establishing the Cape Cod National Seashore Park.

II

John F. Kennedy based much of his 1952 campaign against incumbent senator Henry Cabot Lodge on the promise that he would be less interested in global statesmanship and more determined to help advance his economically lagging region and struggling state. In the waning weeks of the 1952 campaign, Kennedy told a labor group that he wanted to help revive Massachusetts and the six states of New England—and implied this task was apparently too prosaic to interest his opponent, Senator Lodge. "It is a good and fine thing for members of the Senate to engage as statesmen in the high realm of foreign affairs. It is even, perhaps, a good thing for a Senator to devote himself to the fine art of president-making . . . even if that activity is based on a rather desperate effort to help himself," Kennedy charged, referring to Lodge's leadership of Dwight Eisenhower's presidential campaign. "But I say to you that it is a gross betrayal of a Senator's own constituents, when he has his head so high in the clouds that he has neither the will nor the time to look after problems that cry for solution in his own back yard."[4]

Kennedy said important industries were failing across New England, but the region's representatives in Washington were not working cooperatively to solve critical problems. Steps were needed to improve the competitive position of those industries and better integrate New England's economy with that of the nation. Kennedy implored New England lawmakers to set aside their political differences and work for the good of the region, adding that if he were elected to the Senate, he would help forge a strong bloc of New England lawmakers to craft solutions.[5]

After his election to the Senate, Kennedy was determined to construct and present a plan for New England's economic revival. He instructed his staff to interview economic experts, review a raft of studies on the topic, and write a plan for him to present to the Senate. On May 18, 1953, Kennedy gave the first of three Senate speeches on his New England economic plan. Each lasted for more than two hours and was dense with details on how to ignite the region's economic revitalization. Kennedy emphasized that he wanted to help New England in a way that was also good for the nation. "As a senator's responsibility is not only to his State but to his Nation, I think that it's proper to point out that even though many of the recommendations I have made are of special importance to New England, nevertheless, none is contrary to the national interest, but rather would, if enacted, be of benefit to all of the people wherever they may live." But Kennedy did acknowledge that much of New England's loss of industry had been to the South.

While not seeking to penalize those states, Kennedy said the South, more than any other region, had benefited from the assistance of the federal government as well as the free market.[6]

Kennedy argued that while New England was still relatively prosperous, key industries such as textiles and fishing were faltering, and some communities, such as Lawrence, Massachusetts, were struggling badly. The primary answer to New England's economic woes was not new programs, special favors, or large expenditures by the federal government, he said. There was an urgent need for strong state and local action in New England along with private-sector initiatives. Business leaders in New England had to modernize and expand their manufacturing plants in order to increase the region's prosperity.[7]

New England, he said, had become too dependent on outmoded methods and customs. Its principal natural resources, such as fisheries and forests, were being depleted. People were moving away. Fast-growing industries were relocating to states that were closer to their markets and had ample natural resources. Many communities had relied heavily on one or two industries that were now in rapid decline. "Machinery is old; management is old; methods are old. Too often government, management and labor have resisted new ideas and local initiative," he said in a stern acknowledgment of the region's self-created problems. He noted that in the past seven years in Massachusetts alone, 70 textile mills had either closed down or moved to other states. Those business liquidations and migration had led to the loss of more than 28,000 jobs. A crisis was at hand.[8]

Kennedy's New England economic program had four elements: first, to help diversify and expand commercial and industrial activity in problem areas; second, to prevent further business decline and relocation; third, to try to ease the hardships caused by unemployment and recession; and finally, to identify the larger national challenges that needed to be tackled in tandem with his regional agenda. Kennedy said the federal government's role in the revitalization of New England was limited but important.[9]

In that speech and the two subsequent ones later that month, Kennedy presented his agenda in considerable detail. Part of its appeal was the sheer number of ideas he proposed. The Kennedy program called for creating regional industrial and development corporations; curtailing tax provisions that hurt New England firms and workers; creating job retraining and technical assistance programs; developing low-cost power options; earmarking funds for the fishing industry; increasing the minimum wage from 75 cents to $1 an hour; updating and enforcing laws pertaining to child labor; revising the Taft-

Hartley labor law to prevent unfair restrictions on unionizing in competing areas such as the South; setting minimum standards in unemployment compensation programs; eliminating tax breaks that some companies used to relocate out of New England; allocating more defense contracts to communities with high unemployment rates; investigating the discrimination in the costs of New England's trucking, railroad, and ocean freight rates; and providing better housing programs for the middle class. Additionally, Kennedy pointed out that New England would benefit from national policies that cut unnecessary federal spending, restructured international trade policies, effectively enforced antitrust laws, and took steps to safeguard against further inflation or recession. Kennedy summed up his plan: "The theme of the program, if it may be boiled down to a single sentence, would be the importance of the federal government in the preservation of fair competition in an expanding economy."[10]

Kennedy offered his economic agenda with a stern warning that it had implications for U.S. foreign policy. He noted that just months earlier, the local Communist party had distributed leaflets in Lawrence, Massachusetts, attempting to exploit the city's distress. "That attempt was wholly unsuccessful in terms of winning converts in Lawrence; but it serves to illustrate the advantage we are handing to communism, both locally and internationally, when we fail to take action in areas which have suffered several years of serious unemployment and poverty," he said.[11]

During his lengthy presentations on the Senate floor, several senators asked questions and lavished praise on the junior senator for offering a concrete and credible plan. Herbert Lehman from New York praised Kennedy for his "careful analysis of the industrial ills for that great section of our country," adding that it "should be considered seriously by all those interested in the well-being not only of New England, but of the entire Nation." Minnesota's Hubert Humphrey praised Kennedy for "the very splendid study, research and program, which he has presented to the Senate this afternoon." Kennedy, Humphrey said, "has not in any way criticized other areas of the Nation for the fine programs which may have benefitted them." Rather, he had "performed a valuable service, not only for his own people but I think he has set a pattern for the rest of us showing how we can discuss the problems which we face and relate them to the total problem of the United States."[12]

Kennedy followed up his Senate speeches in a number of ways. He wrote major articles for several national publications. "What's the Matter with New England" was published by the *New York Times Magazine* on November 8, 1953. In it, Kennedy insisted that it was not only appropriate but also necessary to spell out New England's challenges. "I believe we must speak frankly about the problems that confront us and I believe that the federal government has to play a role in the alleviation of those problems in its position as catalyst and conservator of the resources of the entire nation." He insisted that he sought no special advantages for Massachusetts or New England but was offering a framework so regional economies could take full advantage of their own resources, initiative, and enterprise to free themselves from the burdens that unfair competition imposed on them.[13]

In his article for the January 1954 edition of the *Atlantic Monthly*, Kennedy focused on the relationship between New England and the South. He argued that unfair competitive practices encouraged many industries to leave New England and relocate in the South. He was not trying to launch a regional economic war but sought policies to affect the "stability and integrity of our entire national economy." Regional competition should take place in the context of a "fair struggle based on natural advantages and natural resources, not exploiting conditions and circumstances that tend to depress rather than elevate the economic welfare of the nation."[14]

Kennedy also had his three Senate speeches, along with some supplementary material, assembled into a 159-page book called *The Economic Problems of New England: A Program for Congressional Action.* He then actively worked to organize the 12 New England senators into a regional bloc that met bimonthly and became a respected force in Congress. Working with the bipartisan New England Council of Senators, Kennedy and his colleagues offered legislation targeted to the region's textile, fishing, and small-business sectors as well as programs for farmers, veterans, and senior citizens.

During his Senate career, Kennedy introduced more than 300 pieces of legislation to implement the agenda he developed in his speeches and writings. Dozens became law. His office closely monitored this legislative effort and issued periodic reports to the citizens of Massachusetts. Writing in December 1957, the year before his reelection campaign, Kennedy discussed initiatives to help the textile, maritime, transportation, and fishing industries, as well as small business, farmers, veterans, and the elderly. "While I have spent a good deal of time and effort on national legislative problems, as a member of the Foreign Relations, Labor and Public Welfare and other committees, I have been ever mindful of my 1952 pledge to 'Do More for Massachusetts,' " he wrote.[15]

III

While Kennedy's detailed and even exhaustive work on the New England economic program was unusual for any lawmaker at that time, it made sense given his emphatic campaign pledge to fight for Massachusetts and New England in the Senate. But Kennedy, though a freshman senator, was already a national figure, although mostly because of his celebrity family and dashing personal style. He was the subject of a swooning cover story in the *Saturday Evening Post*, "The Senate's Gay Bachelor," which clearly had a different meaning in the 1950s. It was one of many articles published around the country celebrating the glamorous young senator.[16]

Kennedy worked out of a suite of three rooms on the third floor of the Senate Office Building. His office was across the hall from a suite occupied by Vice President Nixon, who also served as the president of the Senate. Kennedy's Washington Senate staff included Ted Reardon, Ted Sorensen, Evelyn Lincoln, Mary Barelli Gallagher, Lois Strode, Jean McGonigle Mannix, Lucy Torres, Fred Holborn, and Harris Wofford. He also had a Senate office in Boston, and much of his personal business—and some of his professional work—was done by his father's office in New York.[17]

When his Senate career began, Kennedy was

assigned to two committees. One he actively sought, the Labor and Public Welfare Committee, and one he accepted with some reluctance, the Government Operations Committee. Throughout his Senate career, Kennedy frequently sent letters to Lyndon Johnson, the Senate Democratic leader, requesting membership on more powerful and prestigious committees such as Finance or Foreign Relations. In a sarcastic reference to Kennedy's frustration with his committee assignments, Sorensen sent Kennedy a note in 1955 that said Johnson was finally starting to become helpful. "Lyndon Johnson has finally come through, making up for his failure to appoint you to the Foreign Relations and Finance Committees. He has recommended that you be appointed to the Boston National Historic Sites Commission," Sorensen joked.[18] Kennedy had a wary relationship with the powerful Senate Democratic leader. Florida Democratic senator George Smathers was friends with both Kennedy and Johnson and said they did not enjoy an easy connection. "They abided each other, but they didn't like each other really. Jack Kennedy didn't really like Lyndon. He thought he was a little bit uncouth and somewhat of an oaf. I know Jack Kennedy admired Lyndon's drive. I know he admired Lyndon's cunning. I know he admired Lyndon's dedication. But as a personality, he wasn't a Kennedy type at all."[19]

Evelyn Lincoln, Kennedy's secretary in the

Senate and later in the White House, described her boss as a restless and impatient young senator. "Soon after I went to work for John Fitzgerald Kennedy I learned that if he wanted something done, he wanted it done immediately. He liked to have people around him available at all times. When he called, whether it was ten o'clock in the morning or at twelve o'clock at night, he wanted to be able to reach you." She described a man who was demanding, impatient, and often self-absorbed. "If someone he relied on wanted a few days off, he would say 'I would like a vacation too.'" According to Lincoln, Kennedy didn't sit still, even while dictating. He would pace the room, stroll into his reception room, pick up a golf club, and swing at an imaginary ball. He wrote down numbers and notes on scrap paper and stuffed them into his wallet or pocket and then misplaced them. His handwriting caused Lincoln "endless difficulty and heartache during his first year in office." He often forgot things, leaving clothing and books behind in hotel rooms and on planes. His desk was cluttered. Once, after Lincoln tried to rearrange it and create some order, Kennedy was furious. "Why don't you leave my desk alone?" he snapped. Kennedy's personal office was packed with personal and political items; he had photographs of his wife Jackie and daughter Caroline on his fireplace mantle as well as pictures of former presidents

Harry Truman and Herbert Hoover on his wall. He had a model *PT 109* boat on his mantle and the famous coconut with his scrawled message of distress that helped secure his rescue in the South Pacific encased in plastic and resting on his desk. He called it a "memento of more unpleasant days." The senator also had a large mounted sailfish hanging from one wall; he had caught it near Acapulco while on his honeymoon in the fall of 1953.[20]

When Kennedy was in Washington, he often worked until seven or eight at night despite calls and pleas from his wife to come home earlier. But he was often on the road. His wife said that he rarely spent weekends at home during his time in the Senate, especially in the later years when his political ambitions were on the rise. When about to travel, he frequently worked at his office until 20 minutes before his flight was to depart from National Airport, and Lincoln often had to call the airport to ask the airline to hold his flight. When he was traveling to Hyannis Port, she would often call ahead to tell the household staff when he would arrive and ask them to have a bowl of clam chowder waiting for him. He was disorganized and often late, but he hated to waste time. Kennedy drove his car fast and was known to challenge red lights.[21]

The senator was a man on the move. "Kennedy was a very impatient man. He did not like to be bored," said Harris Wofford, a former Kennedy staffer and later a U.S. senator.[22] He was cool, reserved, and deeply ambitious. Senator Sam Ervin, a Democrat from North Carolina, said his first impression of Kennedy was that he was an introvert but warmed up when he got to know people. "Despite his warm friendships with many of the other senators of both parties, Senator Kennedy was a 'loner' and did not belong to any of the so-called cliques within the Senate," Lincoln recalled.[23]

IV

Shortly after Kennedy began his Senate tenure, the politically charged issue of the St. Lawrence Seaway returned to the congressional agenda. Discussion about U.S. participation with Canada in building a seaway that would link the Great Lakes with the Atlantic Ocean had been swirling around North America for decades. The project under consideration would create a deep-water channel by constructing locks and dams between Ogdensburg, New York, and Montreal, Quebec. There was also discussion of building a hydroelectric power plant at Barnhard Island in the International Rapids, which would provide electricity for northern New York and New England.

After a more than three-decade-long stalemate in the U.S. Congress, seaway legislation was introduced in both chambers on January 23, 1953. Republican senator Alexander Wiley, the chairman of the Senate Foreign Relations Committee, offered a revised version that eliminated the provisions for federal construction of the hydroelectric power plant. Republican congressman George Dondero of New Jersey, chairman of the House Public Works Committee, introduced a similar plan. After two months of hearings, the Senate Foreign Relations Committee approved a clean bill on June 16, 1953, but the Senate took no action on it that year. The House Public Works Committee held hearings in June 1953 on the seaway project and, while there was clear evidence of growing support, the panel did not hold a vote on the matter.[24] The initiative gained new energy when President Eisenhower used his 1954 State of the Union address to advocate for the St. Lawrence Seaway for both economic and national security reasons. "Our relations with Canada, happily always close, involve more and more the unbreakable ties of strategic interdependence. Both nations now need the St. Lawrence Seaway for security as well as economic reasons. I urge the Congress promptly to approve our participation in its construction," he said.[25]

During his three terms in the House, Kennedy,

like his New England congressional colleagues, opposed a seaway. But Kennedy never fully shut the door to supporting the project in the future. In 1952, the senator's staff examined the issue again and wrote a memo analyzing the pros and cons of the project. It was largely critical of it and slanted toward opposition, claiming the St. Lawrence Seaway would harm New England's economy by taking away business from the railroads and the Port of Boston. It expressed skepticism that Canada would build the seaway on its own, as it threatened to do, and questioned whether the project would be self-financing, as its advocates insisted.

The junior senator from Massachusetts received a flood of letters, from both advocates and opponents of the seaway, seeking his current views on the project. One request for his support came from Democratic senator Herbert Lehman of New York. Kennedy replied promptly, saying he could not join him in sponsoring seaway legislation but would like to talk to him personally about the matter. It was clear Kennedy was reconsidering his position.[26] Responding to a letter from John Love, executive vice president of the Revere Sugar Refinery in Charlestown, Massachusetts, Kennedy seemed ambivalent and even confused about his own stance on the seaway. "There appears to be a great deal of conflict with respect to the truth about the effect of the St. Lawrence Seaway on New England," he wrote with evident frustration. "I cannot outline my exact course of action in respect to this measure until I have fully satisfied myself, after reading the hearings and various studies made of the subject, as to the exact effect of the St. Lawrence Seaway upon New England's industries and the Port of Boston; upon the price of consumer goods in the region; upon the economy, defense and welfare of our nation as a whole; and whether or not the Seaway will be constructed in any event by Canada with or without participation by the United States." Kennedy added that he was trying to marry the interests of the nation with the needs of New England.[27]

Kennedy conferred closely with his top aides when the Wiley version of the St. Lawrence Seaway legislation came to a vote in 1954, and he ultimately decided to support the project. A memo from Ted Sorensen suggested his shift of positions could be described as Kennedy's commitment to statesmanship.[28] He could be portrayed as a senator who was determined to look out for the nation's good, rather than be limited by purely regional considerations.

On January 14, 1954, Kennedy announced his new stance on the St. Lawrence Seaway. It was one of the most important speeches of his Senate career. "I am frank to admit that few issues during my service in the House of Representatives or the

Senate have troubled me as much as the pending bill authorizing participation by the United States in the construction and operation of the St. Lawrence Seaway," he began.[29]

He observed that on six different occasions over 20 years, no Massachusetts senator or representative had ever voted in favor of the seaway and that active opposition among some of his state's citizens and industries continued. Though he had undertaken a comprehensive study of the issue, he chose to focus on two narrow questions. First, was the St. Lawrence Seaway going to be built, regardless of the action taken in the U.S. Senate on the pending bill? Second, if so, was it in the national interest that the United States participate in the construction, operation, and administration of the seaway?

Kennedy said that he was "fully satisfied" that the answer to both questions was yes. "The evidence appears to be conclusive that Canada will build the Seaway. Although they frequently overlook this fact, Seaway opponents now appear to take this for granted." Consequently, U.S. lawmakers were confronted only with the second question, which was whether it was in the American interest to participate in the project.

Citing the views of President Eisenhower; the secretaries of defense, commerce, and the army; officials on the National Security Council; and former presidents, Kennedy said that U.S.

ownership and control of this vital strategic international waterway would be lost without passage of the bill. If Canada constructed the seaway on its own, he said, the United States would have to pay for parts of it, but the American government would have no voice over tolls, traffic, admission of foreign ships, defense, and security measures.

Kennedy acknowledged there was political opposition to the St. Lawrence Seaway because some thought it would hurt the Massachusetts economy and there would be no direct benefit to the state. The senator said the evidence as to whether the seaway would hurt New England industries was complex and inconclusive. But the issue was moot because it would be built, so its economic consequences, whether beneficial or not, would be felt regardless of the vote in the U.S. Senate.

Kennedy then tackled the question of whether the seaway would actually help Massachusetts, as some supporters claimed. "There have been a great many claims advanced along the lines that it would be of help to my state; but I have studied them with care and must say in all frankness that I think they are wholly speculative at best. I know of no direct economic benefit to the economy of Massachusetts or any segment thereof from the Seaway. But I am unable to accept such a narrow view of my functions as United States Senator. . . .

Where federal action is necessary and appropriate, it is my firm belief that New England must fight for those national policies." He said that he had asked other senators to support programs to help New England, so it was necessary that he not oppose the seaway just because the direct economic benefits would go largely to other regions, especially the Great Lakes areas of the Midwest.

Kennedy said the arbitrary refusal of many New Englanders to recognize the legitimate needs and aspirations of other areas contributed to the neglect of, and even opposition to, the needs of New England by the rest of the country. "We cannot continue so narrow and destructive a position," he lectured.[30]

The Senate approved the St. Lawrence Seaway authorization legislation on January 20, 1954, on a 51 to 33 vote. The House passed a slightly different bill in early May. The Senate agreed to House amendments soon after, and the bill was sent to President Eisenhower, who signed it on May 13.[31]

The bill Congress approved was less comprehensive than several earlier versions that had called for building channels in the Great Lakes as well as a power project at the International Rapids section of the St. Lawrence River. Nonetheless, the final project remained both consequential and controversial.

Kennedy's vote attracted considerable attention. Newspaper accounts of the Senate debate said Kennedy's vote was critical for psychological as well as practical reasons. "Mr. Kennedy's decision did more than break ranks in Massachusetts. It left a gap in the almost equally solid line-up of Atlantic and Gulf Coast delegations against the Seaway. It seemed likely that others might follow," one account said. "Friends of the Seaway, who earlier had hoped to win by three or four votes, now talked in terms of mustering as many as fifty-six votes for it in the ninety-six member Senate."[32]

Kennedy's vote was discussed back home. The *Boston Post* described it as disastrous for his home state, saying the seaway would help "ruin" Massachusetts.[33] An editorial in the *Everett Leader-Herald* took a gentler stance. "Senator John F. Kennedy recently took a courageous stand against this sectionalism. He announced his support of the St. Lawrence Seaway project, something no other Senator from his state has ever done. It is possible to disagree with the young Senator's point of view as to the benefits that will be derived from the St. Lawrence Seaway. Even his opponents, however, must applaud his courageous refusal to let sectionalism influence him. The welfare of all the states is tied together," the editorial read.[34]

Time magazine's "National Affairs" section took

note of Kennedy's vote but ascribed his support of the project more to pragmatism than to statesmanship. It said that Kennedy realized the seaway was inevitable because Canada was already set to build it, with or without the United States. According to the article, Kennedy saw a chance for some political trading and reasoned that if he supported the bill, the states that stood to benefit from the seaway might be more willing to help New England on other matters.[35]

After the Senate vote, Stephen Benedict, a special assistant to Eisenhower, sent a private letter to Kennedy, saying he admired the senator's action. "It seems to me that it was statesmanship in the most genuine sense, a clear and responsible judgment of the facts, with the long-term interests of the country as a whole uppermost in mind. How rare that so obvious quality so often seems."[36]

Kennedy's vote on the St. Lawrence Seaway was consequential. It positioned him as a senator with a national perspective, willing to break from purely parochial considerations. Political observers assumed Kennedy's vote was an indication of larger ambitions. "I knew Jack was serious about running for president back in 1954, when he mentioned that he intended to vote for the St. Lawrence Seaway," wrote Tip O'Neill. "The whole Northeast delegation was opposed to that bill, because once you opened the seaway you killed the port of Boston, which was the closest port to Europe. The Boston papers were against it, and so were the merchant marines and the longshoremen. But Jack wanted to show he wasn't parochial, and that he had a truly national perspective. Although he acknowledged that the seaway would hurt Boston, he supported it because the project would benefit the country as a whole."[37]

V

John Kennedy was involved in labor issues throughout his congressional career, from his earliest days in the House through his years in the Senate. When he entered the House in 1947, he was immediately assigned to the House Education and Labor Committee, as was another freshman congressman, Republican Richard Nixon of California. "He and I shared the dubious distinction of sitting at the opposite ends of the committee table like a pair of unmatched bookends," Nixon later wrote.[38] Congressmen Kennedy and Nixon received an immersion course in labor history and policy.

The power of labor unions and their influence on the American economy was a serious and contentious issue in Congress at the end of World War II. The year 1946 became the most contentious in the history of labor-management relations in the United States. There were nearly 5,000 work stoppages by 4.6 million workers, or about one of every 14 Americans in the labor force. In that year alone, the number of worker days lost was 116 million, three times the previous high in 1945.[39]

The Taft-Hartley act that Kennedy opposed in the House continued to dominate the debate on labor policy. Since it limited union rights, required members to sign non-Communist affidavits, and curbed labor's political influence, it was quite unpopular among progressive Democrats. Truman vetoed the bill in 1947 but was overridden when conservative Democrats joined with Republicans. Kennedy's mixed position to it—opposition to the law but firm conviction that labor reforms were needed—continued in the Senate. His first year there, Congress spent months debating legislation that sought changes to Taft-Hartley. The Senate Labor Committee held hearings on the law as well as on broader labor issues that spring. The panel heard from dozens of representatives from business and labor. At the same time, the House held parallel hearings. Attempts by Republicans in both chambers to craft a bill revising Taft-Hartley faltered, and Labor Secretary Martin Durkin resigned in frustration, blaming the White House for not being sufficiently committed to labor reform. Durkin learned that congressional Republicans and even Republicans in the

Eisenhower administration were divided, with some seeking an even tougher Taft-Hartley law, while others sought to ease its harshest provisions.

In addition to trying to overhaul Taft-Hartley, the Congress of the 1950s became deeply concerned with increasing evidence of corruption within organized labor. In 1957 the Senate created the Select Committee on Improper Activities in the Labor or Management Field, known as the McClellan Committee. It brought together lawmakers from both the Senate Labor Committee and the Permanent Investigations Subcommittee of the Government Operations Committee. The eight-member bipartisan panel included Democrats John McClellan of Arkansas, who chaired the panel, Sam Ervin of North Carolina, Pat McNamara of Michigan, and Kennedy, and Republicans Joseph McCarthy of Wisconsin, Karl Mundt of South Dakota, Irving Ives of New York, and Barry Goldwater of Arizona. When McCarthy died on May 2, 1957, Carl Curtiss of Nebraska replaced him. Robert Kennedy served as the select committee's chief counsel.[40]

The McClellan Committee's high-profile hearings initially focused on labor racketeering and management malpractices, but the scope expanded to include union violence, corruption, and secondary boycotts. The hearings frequently generated front-page headlines across the nation.

The 1957 hearings led to the expulsion of the Teamsters from the AFL-CIO. The 1958 hearings on labor racketeering featured riveting appearances by former Teamster president David Beck and current president Jimmy Hoffa.

While the McClellan Committee hearings were capturing national attention and President Eisenhower called for new labor legislation, Kennedy was assigned to write new legislation by the chairman of the Labor Committee. As chairman of a key subcommittee, Kennedy worked with a blue-ribbon panel of labor experts, including Archibald Cox and Arthur Goldberg, who served as advisers on his staff. Kennedy drafted several bills in 1958. The first attempted to improve the federal-state unemployment insurance program and set national payment standards that would allow workers to receive benefits for 39 weeks. The next bill Kennedy proposed required administrators of employee welfare and pension plans to provide participants with annual financial reports upon request and to file copies with the secretary of labor.

The third bill was a broader effort to implement the findings of the McClellan Committee. Working with Senator Ives, Kennedy held 15 days of hearings before crafting a bill that sought to address many of the issues the McClellan Committee raised. It required reporting and disclosure of union financial data; required the election of national and local union officials by secret ballot; prohibited organizational picketing for the purpose of extortion; and partially closed a jurisdictional gap between state govern-ments and the federal government in the handling of certain labor disputes.[41]

The Senate took up the Kennedy-Ives bill on June 12, 1958, and a wide-ranging and contentious debate on labor policy ensued. The Senate considered more than 50 amendments, most of which were Republican efforts to rewrite the bill. However, a dozen Republicans joined with a majority of Senate Democrats to reject those amendments that were opposed by key labor leaders. The Senate passed the Kennedy-Ives bill 88 to 1 on June 17.

The measure was then sent to the House, where House Speaker Sam Rayburn, a tough and terse Democrat from Texas, delayed consideration of the bill because Democrats were divided on labor issues. Additionally, the business community felt the Kennedy-Ives bill represented too little reform; labor groups insisted it was too harsh. An effort by some House members on August 18, one of the final days of the session, to force a vote on the Kennedy-Ives bill was rejected.[42]

Kennedy was furious that House leaders did not take up his bill. He argued it was "sabotaged" by Secretary of Labor James P. Mitchell, Durkin's successor. His Republican Senate partner, Irving

Ives, said it was killed by a lobbying alliance of the National Association of Manufacturers, the Chamber of Commerce, the American Retail Federation, the United Mine Workers, and the Teamsters. More neutral observers noted that the bill's failure was due largely to the division among House Democrats.

An angry Kennedy took to the Senate floor on August 22 and lamented Congress's failure to pass labor reform. "Those who voted against this bill and those who lobbied for its defeat must bear a heavy responsibility during the coming months when racketeering and gangsterism in the labor movement continue unchecked. That this bill displeases extremists is not surprising, for these same extremists have been the ones who have prevented the enactment of any progressive labor legislation since 1947."[43]

He said the Kennedy-Ives bill represented a real opportunity for effective labor reform, and the failure of Congress to pass it meant that Hoffa and the handful of irresponsible and arrogant leaders who plagued an otherwise clean labor movement would continue to operate with impunity. "Of one thing we may be sure: Next year, there will be more scandals, more racketeering, more abuses by the hoodlums who have infiltrated a tiny fringe of the labor movement. But we shall lack an effective remedy to stop them."[44]

The defeat was particularly painful given that it negated two years of work by the McClellan Committee and months of congressional hearings and debate. Kennedy's own subcommittee had devoted countless hours to labor reform legislation. Kennedy blamed Republicans and business groups for scuttling sensible labor reform. "Neither Senator Ives nor I have ever sought to make this labor reform measure a partisan political issue. We know that there is too much at stake. . . . Until this week it was never a party measure. The bill had bipartisan origin and sponsorship and included the recommendations of the President as well as those of the bipartisan McClellan Committee."[45]

Kennedy said partisanship had killed the legislation. He went after Labor Secretary Mitchell for working to derail the bill, accusing him of talking long and piously about the need for labor reform and blaming Democratic leaders for inaction. "But the facts of the matter are that the chief stumbling block to labor reform legislation in this Congress has been Secretary Mitchell," Kennedy said. "The reason is plain, Mr. Mitchell did not want a labor reform bill." The labor secretary sought to placate Republicans who wanted a more restrictive bill and to "maintain a synthetic political issue," Kennedy insisted.[46]

Clearly disappointed and frustrated about the stalemate, Kennedy decided to try again to pass legislation the following year. In 1959, he proceeded methodically, trying to build a solid case based on expert testimony. Now working with Democratic senator Sam Ervin, who assumed a key role following the retirement of Ives, Kennedy's bill was basically the same package but with new provisions added to secure the strong support of labor.

The Senate passed Kennedy's bill on April 25 on a 90 to 1 vote after a long and vigorous debate. In the process, the bill adopted several amendments that many labor leaders opposed, including the American Federation of Labor, which dropped its support of the legislation.

President Eisenhower wanted a bill that eased some parts of Taft-Hartley but also limited union rights by restricting picketing and secondary boycotts. As a response to the Kennedy-Ervin bill, the House passed a tough anti-labor bill that August. A House-Senate conference was convened and presided over by Kennedy to draft a final compromise that resolved differences between the two versions. The conference ran nearly two weeks, and the final version of the bill more closely resembled the House version than the Senate bill that Kennedy had initiated. The Senate approved the final package on a 95 to 2 vote on September 3. The House passed the same bill on a 352 to 52 vote on September 4, which Eisenhower signed on September 14, 1959.[47]

Kennedy had envisioned a new law to attack the labor racketeering and labor-management collusion that was exposed by the McClellan Committee. But the final bill was far more sweeping and, from Kennedy's perspective, more pernicious than he wanted. It included the first major changes to Taft-Hartley since 1947. However, rather than easing the law's toughest provisions, it strengthened several of them. In other words, it moved in the opposite direction from what Kennedy had intended. On the day the Senate considered the final package, Kennedy spoke on the Senate floor to express his ambivalence about the final version. "This bill is a compromise. I must frankly state that it goes a good deal further in some areas than I think is either desirable or necessary—this is especially true on the Taft-Hartley amendments." He said the final package was the only bill that was possible to pass under the circumstances. The House version had serious flaws and would have restricted normal, legitimate trade union activity. Though he had been able to soften some of the changes the House sought, he acknowledged the final bill was not perfect but was acceptable. "I have no apologies for the bill we are now bringing before the Senate," he said defensively. "I believe that any Senator, regardless of his views on these matters, can vote for the conference report. I do not claim that it is a perfect bill or that it is a model of fairness. But taking it as a whole, it is the best bill we can pass."[48]

Kennedy later said that his agenda had been fundamentally different than that of many Republicans. "We were trying to curb racketeers and crime—that was clear. Their bill was trying to curb honest unions at the bargaining table—that also was clear. The Administration's bill in the form in which it passed the House threatened to set back the trade union movement to the dark ages before the Wagner Act. The right to picket, even the right to strike, and thus the right to bargain collectively and effectively, would have been drastically restricted," he said. "I do not say that the bill is now satisfactory. I do not say that all arbitrary or burdensome restrictions on honest members and leaders have been lifted. . . . The Labor-Management Reform Bill of 1959 is a strong bill. It is a responsible bill. No Democrat ever need to be ashamed of his vote for it—and no Republican campaign orator can ever again accuse our party of being the tool of the corrupt labor bosses."[49]

Kennedy vowed he would continue the battle for labor law reform. "There will be more labor legislation in future sessions of Congress. Those who loudly proclaimed their devotion to the worker's interest while voting to restrict his traditional right will be given more opportunity to demonstrate their concern."[50]

Kennedy's attempt to pass labor policy reforms was probably the most sustained legislative effort in his Senate career. Kennedy impressed his colleagues with his diligence and grasp of the subtlety of labor issues. Senator Paul Douglas said Kennedy plunged into the intricacies of labor matters, mastered a highly arcane area of law, and established himself "as a man with a truly first rate intellect." He said Kennedy's labor speeches were a "combination of politician and PhD. I think it was an amazing performance," adding that Kennedy "came to the correct conclusions down to 100th of an inch. It was like seeing a skilled surgeon operate."[51]

Working with Kennedy on the bill, Ervin said Kennedy developed an impressive command of the issue and worked diligently and fairly. Senator Hubert Humphrey also praised Kennedy's work, saying that he delved into the misuse of health and welfare funds by some of the unions and was able to probe union wrongs without losing their confidence.[52] Ted Sorensen said Kennedy immersed himself in labor legislation with an intensity and purpose that was greater than that which he displayed toward any other issue during his Senate career.[53]

Kennedy's foray into labor legislation also demonstrated his ability to master the art of political theater. During his participation in the McClellan Committee and his questioning of business and labor leaders and Secretary of Labor Mitchell in his subcommittee, Kennedy showed himself to be quick on his feet and in possession of a penetrating and agile intelligence. Kennedy's exchanges with his colleagues on labor issues on the Senate floor showcased his intelligence, wit, and ability to engage in robust give and take.

Kennedy's experiences with labor legislation confirmed that his legislative skills were solid, but not overwhelming. By all accounts the final bill to emerge in 1959 was a far cry from what he wanted, and he later distanced himself from it, going so far as to remove his name from the final version. Whether a more experienced legislator, such as Lyndon Johnson, could have negotiated more effectively is a matter of conjecture. Some of Kennedy's struggles were due to factors over which he had no control. Democrats were deeply divided over labor legislation, with southern Democrats willing, and often eager, to break from their northern counterparts and work with Republicans, thus crippling Kennedy's negotiating position. For their part, Republicans wanted to prevail in the labor fight because they believed in the substance of their cause, they wanted to help their allies in the business community, and they were determined to deliver a tough blow to organized labor. The stakes were high, and they were willing to use all the tools at their disposal to prevail.

As Kennedy worked doggedly on labor legislation in 1958 and 1959, he was a rising Democratic political star with clear presidential aspirations. His opponents in both parties saw him as a potential challenger; many couldn't resist taking shots at him as he toiled over labor legislation. After the bruising legislative battle ended in 1959, Kennedy appeared eager to set aside this kind of politically risky lawmaking and concentrate on his presidential campaign.

Kennedy's work on domestic issues during his Senate career revealed important components of his political personality. His initial effort to develop a New England revitalization plan showed a politically savvy young senator who understood that he needed to act visibly on his central campaign pledge to help fix his state's and region's economy. Failing to do so could make him a one-term senator. Kennedy's decision to support the construction of the St. Lawrence Seaway was riskier. But he calculated that he was politically strong enough at home that he could afford to cast a vote that signaled that he had a national perspective and aspired to be a statesman. His foray into labor legislation was mostly a responsibility that he inherited as a subcommittee chairman of the Labor Committee. He showed his ability to master a complex set of issues, but the experience likely confirmed that intense involvement in the legislative trenches would complicate his political ambitions. Kennedy's decision to act cautiously on civil rights legislation and on the condemnation of Joseph McCarthy revealed a calculating aspect of his political personality that frustrated some but persuaded others that he was a senator carefully cultivating higher ambitions.

Six
The High Realm of Foreign Affairs

I

In 1951, during a year of intense preparations for his coming Senate campaign against Henry Cabot Lodge and at a time of almost nonstop travel throughout Massachusetts, Congressman John F. Kennedy took two extensive overseas trips. While he was not a member of the House's appropriations, foreign affairs, or defense committees, Kennedy still wanted to see two critical regions of the world, meet international leaders, and bolster his foreign policy credentials. The trips were not elaborately staged photo opportunities, but lengthy and grueling fact-finding missions by a man who wanted to understand the world and be respected as a foreign policy expert.

Undaunted by the fact that Congress was still in session, Kennedy spent five weeks that January and February traveling through western Europe, visiting the United Kingdom, France, Italy, Spain, and Yugoslavia. The congressman met with important figures at every stop: French and German generals, several prime ministers, cabinet ministers, ambassadors, Marshal Josip Tito, and Pope Pius XII.

When he returned to the United States, Kennedy gave a speech that was carried by 540 radio stations of the Mutual Broadcasting Company. He discussed his impressions of Europe in the face of the continuing and seemingly escalating menace of the Soviet Union. He reflected on the necessity of a strong western European defense capability that was able to resist the Soviet threat. "Upon the correct solution of that problem hangs the fate of millions of American lives—indeed the very survival of the Nation may hinge upon it," Kennedy declared.[1]

He summarized the challenges facing each nation that he visited and observed that the continent was still traumatized from World War II and fearful of a future war. In England he was struck by "a deep spiritual and physical weariness over the thought of war." France, he said, would have to contribute the lion's share of troops to any western European army. But he was not sure she would be up to the task: "France gives me a sense of division and confusion, of hesitation and doubt." West Germany was on the mend but was struggling for a clear role after the devastation the Nazi government had inflicted on Europe and the world. Kennedy observed that West Germany's neighbors both lectured her on the evils of militarism and implored her to rearm to counter the Soviet threat. He saw Italy as a fragile, chaotic nation, and Yugoslavia as a "sparse and grim country." Spain's military was a mess and lacked "almost everything needed for a modern war."[2]

Taking a broader view, Kennedy said Europeans needed to sacrifice in order to survive the Soviet threat, but "the plain and brutal fact today is that Europe is not making these sacrifices."[3] Several weeks later, Congressman Kennedy testified to a joint hearing before the Senate Foreign Relations and Senate Armed Services committees about his impressions of Europe's challenges, and he emphasized the need for European nations to spend far more on defense programs.

In the fall of that year, Kennedy took a nearly two-month Asian trip with a small group that included his brother Robert and his sister Jean. "It was a long journey," he later recalled. "Some 25,000 miles of flying, some seven weeks of being constantly on the move. It was eastward, always eastward—to Israel, to Iran, to Pakistan, to the teeming millions of India. And then to Singapore, to Thailand, to embattled Indochina, north to the rough, fighting country of Korea, to Tokyo and finally home across the blue Pacific."[4]

As with his European trip, Kennedy met with a remarkable assortment of people, including American generals Dwight Eisenhower, Lawton Collins, and Matthew Ridgway; Jean de Lattre, the commander in chief of the French troops in Indochina; and prime ministers David Ben Gurion of Israel, Jawaharlal Nehru of India, and Liquant Ali of Pakistan. He later offered vivid impressions of the countries he saw. India was "anti-Western and anti-American, but not with the passion of the Arab, rather with a sullen lack of concern for the way of life we have to offer. Russia and America are nations of whose quarrels India wishes no part." He saw a region in turmoil and lamented that the United States had not made any new friends since World War II and had actually lost some old ones.[5]

Upon returning from Asia, Kennedy challenged American lawmakers to study the world and participate in the foreign policy debate. "Seven weeks is a short time to try and grasp these many problems. But any Congressman, any Senator today, to be worthy of his salt must lift his vision from the immediate problems of his constituency to reach for an understanding of the role that America should play in this world," he said.[6] Kennedy argued that foreign policy was the dominant issue confronting America, and policymakers and the public needed to pay attention to it. "Just as Clemenceau once said, 'War is much too important to be left to the generals,' I would remark that 'Foreign policy is too important for all of us to leave to the experts and the diplomats.' "[7]

During his eight years in the Senate, Kennedy

made a constructive and often impressive contribution to foreign policy. He secured a seat on the powerful and prestigious Senate Foreign Relations Committee in 1957, but even before that, he jumped into debates, gave important speeches, offered bills and amendments, challenged Senate elders, and scrutinized everything the Eisenhower administration said and did. "Foreign policy, the world, was the one thing he was very, very interested in. It was what excited him," said Harris Wofford, a former staffer for Senator Kennedy and later a senator in his own right.[8]

President Dwight Eisenhower and his combative secretary of state John Foster Dulles confronted crises in Asia, Europe, the Middle East, and Latin America during a difficult period in the Cold War. Driving almost all of the administration's actions was the ongoing struggle with the world's other superpower, the Soviet Union, and its sometimes ally, China. At various times as tensions escalated, the Eisenhower administration contemplated or threatened the use of nuclear weapons, such as in response to crises in the Taiwan Straits, French Indochina, and the Korean peninsula. Shrewd and tough, Eisenhower sometimes posed as a detached observer in Washington but was in fact the driving force behind his administration's policies. Dulles was preachy, confrontational, and sometimes bellicose. He was, according to Winston Churchill, "the only bull who carried his own China closet with him."[9]

Kennedy sometimes supported the administration but more frequently served as a tough critic. At various times, he scorched the administration for vacillation in the Middle East, timidity in Eastern Europe, neglect of Latin America, NATO's deterioration, lack of imagination toward India, indifference to the rise of China, alienation of the underdeveloped world, and stumbling into crises in Berlin and the Formosa Straits. The junior senator from Massachusetts showed his colleagues, constituents, and the foreign policy community in the United States and around the world that he was a man of substance. Well informed, confident, and sometimes controversial, he placed issues in their historical context and sharpened his arguments with historical analogies. Possessing a broad view, he also could dive into details. His detractors would say that he was willing to grandstand and offer criticisms that were hyperbolic and even dangerous, such as his provocative warnings about a missile gap that the United States allegedly faced with the Soviet Union. He seemed determined to position himself to the right of the administration in many areas, accusing it of passivity, out-of-date thinking, and failing to adequately fund defense programs. Senator Kennedy found a way to force himself into the American foreign policy debate.

II

Of all the places that Congressman Kennedy visited in 1951, none affected him more deeply than Indochina. While in Saigon, he met with diplomats, military officers, and journalists, receiving wide-ranging, if not encouraging, briefings. At the time of Kennedy's visit, the French were struggling to regain their colonial empire in Indochina. President Franklin Roosevelt believed France should be forced to relinquish Indochina after the war, but he died in 1945; his successor, Harry Truman, did not resist France's return to Indochina. In 1950, the Truman administration decided to actively support the French war effort in Indochina. That year, France established Vietnam, Laos, and Cambodia as semi-autonomous states within the French Union in Indochina, but there was a strong nationalist movement in all three that wanted the French to leave.

Kennedy arrived at Saigon's Tan Son Nhut airport in October 1951 and almost immediately heard small-arms fire, an indication of turmoil just outside the city. The next day he went to the apartment of Seymour Topping, the Associated Press's Saigon bureau chief. They spoke for two hours, and Topping told the senator that France was losing the war in Indochina and was unlikely to reverse its fortunes. Ho Chi Minh had captured the leadership of the nationalist movement, and his forces controlled the mountain passes to China, whose leader, Mao Zedong, was supplying the Vietminh with weapons and training. Topping said the United States was resented by many Vietnamese who viewed the Americans as supporters of France's war effort and as representing another wave of Western colonialism.

Kennedy also had a meeting with Edmund Gullion, a counselor at the American legation, a diplomatic outpost in Saigon, who also offered a discouraging assessment of France's political and military prospects. Kennedy's meetings grew more contentious when he pressed a senior American diplomat, Donald Heath, and France's high commissioner and military commander, General Jean de Lattre, to describe a scenario in which France prevailed. Both were annoyed by Kennedy's tough and skeptical line of questioning, and he was underwhelmed by their answers. Writing in his trip journal, Kennedy echoed the pessimistic views he had heard in Saigon. "We are more and more becoming colonialists in the minds of the people," he wrote.[10]

When Kennedy returned to the United States, he expressed deep doubt that the French effort to regain control of Indochina was succeeding and questioned if America's assistance to France was appropriate. In a radio address, he said,

In Indochina, we have allied ourselves to the desperate effort of a French regime to hang on to the remnants of empire. There is no broad, general support of the native Viet Nam Government among the people of that area and there will be none until the French give clear indications that, despite their gallantry, they are fighting not merely for themselves but for the sake of strengthening a non-Communist native government so that it can move safely toward independence. . . . To check the southern drive of Communism makes sense but not only through reliance on the force of arms. The task is rather to build strong native non-Communist sentiment within these areas and rely on that as a spearhead of defense rather than the legions of General de Lattre, brilliant though he may be. And to do this apart from and in defiance of innately nationalistic aims spells foredoomed failure. To the rising drive of nationalism, we have unfortunately become a friend of its enemy and as such its enemy and not its friend.[11]

Several months after entering the Senate in 1953, Kennedy plunged into a debate about the future of Indochina, specifically how the United States should try to prevent a Communist takeover. By the end of 1953, the United States had spent nearly $1 billion in assistance to the French war effort, with American officials arguing that the war between the Vietminh and France was a struggle to halt Communism, not a colonial war. During a Senate debate in the summer of 1953 on a foreign aid bill, which included about $400 million for the French war in Indochina, Kennedy took center stage. He offered a wide-ranging history of the French effort in Indochina, discussed the current struggle, and made a vigorous case for refocusing American aid so that it encouraged France to grant freedom and independence to the three states of Indochina: Vietnam, Laos, and Cambodia.

Kennedy reminded his colleagues that the French took control of Indochina in 1860 and maintained it until 1945, when Japan seized Indochina near the end of World War II. A guerilla movement in Vietnam against Japan was led by Ho Chi Minh, who had a long history of support of Communism but an even longer history as a forceful critic of French colonialism in Southeast Asia. As France was seeking to regain control of Indochina, French leader Charles de Gaulle envisioned an Indochinese federation with Vietnam, Cambodia, and Laos presided over by a governor general representing France. Subsequent talks between France and Ho Chi Minh led to provisional agreements, but they unraveled because France never offered Ho Chi Minh and his followers the one thing they insisted upon: independence for Vietnam.[12]

In his historical review, Kennedy said the war between France and Ho Chi Minh began in December 1946 and was continuing with building fury. The United States, the senator said, needed to understand the nature of this war before it deepened its involvement there.

Kennedy argued that if France withdrew its troops from Indochina, Communists would overrun not only French Indochina but also much of Southeast Asia. "But it is because we want the war to be brought to a successful conclusion that we should insist on genuine independence. The war has been going on since 1946. There is evidence that the position of the French is not improving. Meanwhile the assistance the United States is giving is steadily increasing." Kennedy said the Western effort to defeat the Communists would fail "unless large numbers of the people of Vietnam are won over from their sullen neutrality and open hostility to it and fully support its successful conclusion. This can never be done unless they are assured beyond doubt that complete independence will be theirs at the conclusion of the war."[13]

Kennedy said the French were fighting because they were convinced that if they retreated, all of Southeast Asia would fall to the Communists, their position in North Africa would become endangered, and even the security of metropolitan France would be threatened. Kennedy apparently believed that France would still have a motive to fight in Indochina even if it relinquished its control over the region. He argued that it was important that at a time when the United States was committing itself to the war in Indochina, the nation's influence and prestige with the French be used to promote the independence of the three states. If the United States did this, the prospects of victory would be increased, and the position of the United States and France and the Western Alliance in Asia would be advanced.

Kennedy's remarks during the Senate's funding debate concluded with a sense of gloom. "The conditions are not now present in French Indochina that would permit a victory for the French forces. Indeed, indications are against such a victory, regardless of the steady increase in U.S. assistance since 1950. Continuation of an obviously fruitless campaign will certainly be more likely to result in the French withdrawing."[14]

Kennedy offered an amendment in the Senate urging France to give more independence to Vietnam, Laos, and Cambodia. His amendment was opposed by the administration and rejected by the Senate because opponents said it put too must pressure on France during a difficult, even delicate, time for that nation.

The senator continued to follow events closely

in Indochina and remained active in the congressional debate regarding American policy in the region. The spring of 1954 was a tumultuous time in Indochina. The French military position weakened dramatically, and an important part of its army in Indochina was surrounded by Communist forces at Dien Bien Phu. French leaders appealed to Eisenhower for help. The president feared the consequences of a French defeat in Indochina, believing the loss of Indochina just five years after the West "lost" China would be politically devastating. He also believed that a Communist victory in Vietnam would imperil the rest of Southeast Asia with its important sea routes, natural resources, and markets. Eisenhower seriously contemplated U.S. air and naval intervention in Indochina and even thought about the use of nuclear weapons. But congressional leaders balked at a greater American commitment to Indochina unless Great Britain joined the effort and France pledged independence for the three states. Weeks of intense diplomacy in March and April by Dulles failed to secure the desired commitments from Great Britain and France. At the same time, an international conference was about to begin in Geneva to consider the fate of Indochina.[15]

On the eve of the final Communist assault at Dien Bien Phu and the start of the Geneva Conference, Kennedy offered a sweeping assessment of events in Indochina on the floor of the Senate. "Mr. President, the time has come for the American people to be told the blunt truth about Indochina," he began, noting critical talks were about to begin in Geneva that could substantially deepen American involvement in Indochina. The American people needed to take notice because the United States was on the cusp of a possible war in Indochina, a war that would "threaten the survival of civilization." Kennedy said two alternatives were likely to emerge from Geneva. First, the talks might produce a negotiated peace, based either on the partition of Vietnam, possibly along the 16th parallel, or on a coalition government in which Ho Chi Minh was represented. The other alternative was that the United States would persuade the French to continue their war in Indochina by offering more American support, including troops. But he said it would be misguided for the United States to "pour money, materiel, and men into the jungles of Indochina without at least a remote prospect of victory." This, he said, "would be dangerously futile and self-destructive."[16]

Kennedy then took the Eisenhower administration to task for years of overly optimistic assessments of political and military developments in Indochina. In a devastating recitation, Kennedy listed examples of years of official expressions of confidence by Dulles, Defense Secretary Charles

Wilson, the chairman of the Joint Chiefs of Staff Admiral Arthur Radford, and even President Eisenhower. "Despite this series of optimistic reports about eventual victory, every member of the Senate knows that such a victory today appears to be desperately remote . . . despite tremendous amounts of economic and material aid from the United States and despite a deplorable loss of French Union manpower."[17]

He said many officials in France were reluctant to continue the war in Indochina without greater help from America and that the United States must proceed with caution. "I am frankly of the belief that no amount of American military assistance in Indochina can conquer an enemy which is everywhere and at the same time nowhere, an 'enemy of the people' which has the sympathy and covert support of the people." He said that without offering political independence to the people of Indochina, other Asian nations had made it clear that they regarded this as a war of colonialism.[18]

The overriding American interest, Kennedy declared, was the defense of Southeast Asia from Communist aggression, not to maintain the French colonial empire. He hoped the administration would see the futility of sending American men and machines into that "hopeless internecine struggle." This was the time for American policymakers to think clearly and plan carefully, "for upon our decisions now may well rest the peace and security of the world and, indeed, the continued existence of mankind."[19]

Kennedy's speech sparked a lengthy debate on the Senate floor, with some of the Senate's senior leaders applauding Kennedy for his wise and provocative assessment of the American dilemma in Indochina. Senate Majority Leader William Knowland, a California Republican, said there was "much, and probably the predominance of what the Senator from Massachusetts has said with which I would fully agree." He praised Kennedy for a "very well thought out and provocative speech which I think both the Senate and the country should read with interest." Henry Jackson, a Democrat from Washington, congratulated Kennedy for his "brilliant analysis of the problem we face in Indochina." Mike Mansfield, a Montana Democrat and an expert on Asian affairs, praised Kennedy's "scholarly and statesmanlike address." Stuart Symington, a Missouri Democrat, said he was impressed with Kennedy's presentation. John Stennis, a Democrat from Mississippi, said Kennedy had delivered the "finest statement I have ever heard on this subject. It is a statement which certainly needed to be made."[20]

Everett Dirksen, a Republican from Illinois, agreed with many of Kennedy's points but disagreed that the situation in Indochina required immediate presidential attention. Kennedy responded that if the French were not willing to make sufficient concessions to win the support of the native people, then the cause was hopeless. He said the negotiations between the French and Vietnamese had broken down, and two treaties were urgently needed: first, a grant of complete independence to the three states of Vietnam, Laos, and Cambodia; and second, a treaty binding the states to the French Union on the basis of equality. "I am certain that the long period of French colonialism has ended. But unless the French are willing to change . . . it seems to me that our hopes in that area, regardless of how extensive our intervention may be, are doomed to failure," Kennedy concluded.[21]

Kennedy's assessment of France's predicament was astute, as was his understanding about the clamor for independence from the people of Vietnam. But it doesn't appear that he had fully thought through France's dilemma in the region. Why would France continue to fight a dangerous, bloody war that would end in the withdrawal of French interests in Asia? Put differently, if France were going to lose its control over Indochina, why wouldn't it just pull out its troops and head home rather than stay and fight with the Americans to combat the spread of Communism?

Seeking to broaden the debate even further, Kennedy traveled to Chicago in late May 1954 and spoke to the Executives' Club. He gave a sober briefing on the challenges the United States faced in Indochina. Kennedy said that American policy toward Indochina had been hampered by a number of miscalculations and contradictions: the mistaken view that France's military plan for Indochina was working; the inability to recognize the nature and significance of the independence movement in Indochina; the inability to recognize that the Communists were viewed by many in the region as a force for independence; and the Eisenhower administration's decision to shift to a military strategy that relied heavily on nuclear weapons and provided insufficient resources to fight "brushfire wars" such as the one occurring in Indochina. He warned that before the United States became more ensnared in the region, it needed to carefully assess the military situation in Indochina. "The terrain in Indochina is more complex than Korea and we would not have the support of a friendly population. We would be forced to throw our widely dispersed ground troops into the jungle war where conditions favor the Communists," he said.[22]

Events in Indochina were troubling, and he hoped the situation would allow American leaders to learn hard lessons about the importance of allies, the need to reverse recent defense spending cuts for fiscal austerity reasons, and the fact that the United States was strongest when it adhered to its core values, such as helping oppressed peoples even if that required the United States to pressure friends who had colonial empires.[23] These remarks encapsulated his central critique of the administration's policy toward Indochina.

As Kennedy spoke about Indochina in 1953 and 1954, events on the ground in the region were rapidly undermining France's position. The French military was routed at the battle of Dien Bien Phu on May 7, 1954, effectively ending France's willingness to fight any more in Indochina. The Geneva Agreement of 1954 decided on a temporary division of Vietnam near the 17th parallel, with reunification set to occur in July 1956 after a national election. Until then, the North was to be led by Ho Chi Minh, the long-time freedom fighter and leader of the Communists, and the South by Bao Dai, who was later replaced by Ngo Dinh Diem, an aristocratic Catholic. The French began withdrawing their forces from Saigon in May 1955; by April 1956 the final French troops had left Vietnam. Eisenhower didn't want to send U.S. ground troops to Vietnam but also feared that South Vietnam would fall to the Communists. He and many other American leaders became convinced that supporting Diem would provide a bulwark against Communism in the region.

While initially troubled about the partition of Vietnam agreed to in Geneva, and fearful that Communists would take over the entire country,

Kennedy thought Diem was an effective leader and that South Vietnam was a promising, if fragile, young democracy. He began to speak of a "Diem miracle" in South Vietnam and urged American backing for his regime. He accepted, as did other American leaders, Diem's decision not to go forward with national elections in 1956 as had been promised in Geneva.[24]

By the spring of 1956 Kennedy was an informal member of a group called the American Friends of Vietnam, a pro-Diem, pro-Vietnam lobby in the United States. He was joined by other senators, including Hubert Humphrey, Mike Mansfield, William Knowland, and Karl Mundt, as well as other opinion leaders and intellectuals. Kennedy gave the keynote address when the group met at the Willard Hotel in Washington on June 1, 1956, to discuss "America's Stake in Vietnam."[25] He exulted over the "amazing success of President Diem in meeting firmly and with determination the major political and economic crises which had heretofore continually plagued Vietnam." American support, he declared, was critical to the fledgling democracy of South Vietnam. This support, he said, "can't buy the friendship of the Vietnamese. Nor can we win their hearts by making them dependent upon our handouts. What we must offer them is a revolution—a political, economic and social revolution far superior to anything the Communists can offer—far more peaceful, far more democratic and far more locally controlled."[26]

Kennedy said the United States could help replenish capital drained by centuries of colonial exploitation, provide technicians to train those hampered by deliberate policies of illiteracy, offer guidance to assist a nation taking its first steps toward a republican form of government, and extend military assistance to rebuild the new Vietnamese Army, which every day faced the peril of Vietminh armies across the border. "This is the revolution we can, we should, we must offer to the Vietnamese people—not as charity, not as a business proposition, not as a political maneuver, nor simply as soldiers against Communism or as chattels of American foreign policy—but a revolution of their own making, for their own welfare, and for the security of freedom everywhere. The Communists offer them another kind of revolution, glittering and seductive in its superficial appeal. The choice between the two can be made only by the Vietnamese people themselves."[27]

Then in a sweeping formulation about the importance of Vietnam, Kennedy declared, "Vietnam represents the cornerstone of the Free World in Southeast Asia, the keystone in the arch, the finger in the dike." The success of South Vietnam was a test of American respons-ibility and determination. "This is our offspring. We cannot abandon it," he stated.[28]

Kennedy's transformation from a shrewd critic of France's missteps in Indochina to a full supporter of American involvement in Vietnam continues to fascinate and perplex historians. The Kennedy who as a young congressman in 1951 had visited Indochina and asked searching questions about the ability of the West to have its way in that part of the world seemed to lose his skepticism when it came to how his own country would fare in Indochina.[29]

Doubts about Diem began to intensify among some American military and political leaders even before Kennedy spoke approvingly about him in 1956. Diem showed himself to be an autocratic and repressive leader whose government was never able to consolidate its hold on the South. Ho Chi Minh's government had firm control over the North and even promoted insurrections in the South.

But even as late in his Senate career as 1960, Kennedy appeared to believe that backing Diem was a reasonable strategy for the United States. In his campaign book, *The Strategy of Peace*, published in 1960, Kennedy said that Indochina presented a case study about the power of the anticolonial revolution sweeping Asia and Africa. It showed, he said, that national independence could lead to genuine resistance to Communism. "It is a long, sad story with a hopeful chapter, but the end is not in sight," he wrote. His fear that

Ho Chi Minh and his Communists would ultimately come to dominate all Indochina had not come to pass, at least not yet. Despite the misgiving of many, the Vietnamese were uniting behind Diem to channel the power of nationalism to create an independent, anti-Communist Vietnam. That "brave little state is working in friendly and free association with the United States, whose economic and military aid has, in conditions of independence, proved to be effective."[30]

III

John Kennedy joined the Senate Foreign Relations Committee in 1957, which gave him entrée into the American foreign policy establishment. But he shocked that establishment when he went to the Senate floor in the summer of 1957 to speak again about France. This time he discussed France's increasingly bloody war in Algeria, a struggle he framed in sweeping terms. "The most powerful single force in the world today is neither Communism nor capitalism, neither the H bomb nor the guided missile—it is man's eternal desire to be free and independent. The great enemy of that tremendous force of freedom is called, for want of a more precise term, 'imperialism,' " he began. Kennedy said there were many examples of the clash between independence and imperialism in the West, but the situation in Algeria was the most significant. "The war in Algeria," Kennedy warned, "confronts the United States with its most critical diplomatic impasse since the crisis in Indochina—and yet we have not only failed to meet the problem forthrightly and effectively, we have refused even to recognize that is our problem at all."[31]

The war in Algeria in which the indigenous people sought their freedom from French control began in 1954 and was a signal event in the history of decolonization in Africa. The war mobilized the Algerian people and sharply divided the French. For the most part, France contained the insurgency on the battlefield but lost the political struggle. The war in Algeria was the first sustained armed uprising against colonial rule in Africa and shaped other national liberation movements. Under pressure, in 1956, France decided to grant full independence to Morocco and Tunisia, but it was determined to retain French Algeria.

Kennedy was reluctant to criticize France, given its long history of friendship with the United States, but the stakes in Algeria were too large for that country, the Western Alliance, and North Africa for him to remain silent. The war in Algeria, he said, had engaged 400,000 French soldiers, thus stripping the continental forces of

NATO to the bone. The turmoil the war caused had damaged efforts to create a European Common Market and strengthen NATO. The war "steadily drained the manpower, the resources, and the spirit of one of our oldest and most important allies—a nation whose strength is vital to the Free World. No, Algeria is no longer a problem for the French alone—nor will it ever be again," Kennedy declared. It was necessary to have a frank discussion with France about Algeria, even if it caused discomfort. "Did we not learn in Indochina, where we delayed action as the result of similar warnings, that we might have served both the French and our own causes infinitely better, had we taken a more firm stand much earlier than we did? Did that tragic episode not teach us that, whether France likes it or not, admits it or not, or has our support or not, their overseas territories are sooner or later, one by one, inevitably going to break free and look with suspicion on the Western nations who impeded their steps to independence?"[32]

The senator argued it was not important to preserve the myth of French empire, but it was critical to save the French nation as well as respect independence movements throughout Africa. If the French wanted to retain their influence in North Africa, they should grant independence to Algeria as they had to Morocco and Tunisia. If concrete steps were taken to do this there still could be a French North Africa with strong economic and cultural ties persisting between France and Africa. The lessons of Tunisia and Morocco, like the lesson of Indochina, underscored the futility of France's current course in Algeria. Prompt settlement was an urgent necessity—for North Africa, France, the United States, NATO, and the Western world, Kennedy declared. He brushed aside France's proposed arrangement with Algeria as a largely cosmetic gesture, one not sufficient to satisfy the demands of Algerians. American leaders should grasp that this was not just a French problem and that piecemeal adjustments or plans to incorporate Algeria into France would not work. As the leader of the free world, the United States should help forge the transition to political independence in Algeria.[33]

As a step in that direction, Kennedy urged the Senate to adopt a resolution committing the United States to work with others to achieve "the independent personality of Algeria" and secure a settlement with France. The United States should endorse a framework of political independence for Algeria that allowed for close economic interdependence with France. Such American leadership would win over those wary of the United States' "negative and vacillating record on colonial issues." The senator introduced a resolution calling for an "international effort to derive for Algeria the basis for an orderly achievement of independence" as a way to ignite a debate within the United States and across the world.[34]

The senator's speech and resolution triggered a powerful reaction in Algeria, France, and the American foreign policy establishment. He drew sharp rebukes from Secretary of State Dulles and two-time Democratic presidential nominee Adlai Stevenson. "Algeria is a French problem," Stevenson snapped. A newspaper in New Hampshire chastised the senator, saying it wished Kennedy were as tough on America's enemies as he was on her friends. It was unusual, and some thought inappropriate, for a junior senator to publicly attack one of the United States' most important allies—especially from the floor of the U.S. Senate.[35]

Kennedy addressed the Senate about a week later to acknowledge the sharp reactions his earlier remarks had provoked both at home and abroad. Those reactions only bolstered his conviction that the situation in Algeria was "drifting dangerously," with the French authorities reluctant to take a fresh approach and American leaders not able to grasp the serious international implications of this impasse. The current tumult, he said, should not obscure the central fact that the Algerians would some day be free. Whether Algerians turned to the West or Russia or China depended on who helped bring about their independence. "We dare not overlook, in our concern over legal and diplomatic niceties, the powerful force of man's eternal desire to be free and independent. The world-wide struggle against imperialism, the sweep of nationalism, is the most potent factor in foreign affairs today. We can resist it or ignore it, but only for a little while; we can see it exploited by the Soviets, with grave consequences; or we in this country can give it hope and leadership and thus improve immeasurably our standing and our security," he said.[36]

With angry reactions continuing in the United States and France to his two speeches on the Senate floor, Kennedy offered a comprehensive statement about his views to answer his critics. In October 1957, Kennedy wrote an essay about Algeria in *America*, a respected publication. The imperatives of Western unity and the need to sustain Western influence in the uncommitted areas of the world made the Algerian question one of the pivotal issues in world politics, he wrote. Algeria was "pulsating from cross pressures and influences" from France, within NATO, across Africa, and especially within the neighboring states of Tunisia and Morocco. A durable settlement in Algeria could only be achieved by adopting a course that would, within a reasonable period of time, lead to Algerian independence, preferably within a federative or interdependent framework. Kennedy also posited that direct negotiations between France and the opposition groups in Algeria were preferable to mediation by the United Nations.[37]

In the essay, Kennedy acknowledged his critics' argument that it was inappropriate for an American lawmaker to openly discuss Algeria because it was an internal matter for France. Kennedy countered that the crisis had serious implications around the world. He went on to counter criticism that Americans should focus on their own uneven record on civil rights as it pertained to blacks, Native Americans, and the people of Puerto Rico. Kennedy responded by saying that while America's record was imperfect, steps were being taken to correct these problems, and the United States' flaws were not relevant to French control of Algeria.[38]

Kennedy wrote that some critics argued that events in Algeria should run their natural course and the United States should step aside and let France and Algeria resolve the crisis. Kennedy said this was too passive an approach, and the United States and others should press France to find a solution. The criticism Kennedy gave the most credence was that loosening French control in Algeria would provide an opening for either Communists or extremist Arabs to transform North Africa into an arena of terrorism or anarchy. "I must say that I share the fear of these critics;

I differ with them, however, in the view that the continuance of present policy better insulates Algeria from these dangers," Kennedy wrote.[39]

Kennedy said the Algerian impasse made it difficult for the West to mobilize opinion in the uncommitted world against the greater imperialist outrages of the Soviet Union in Eastern Europe. He acknowledged there were some indications that French leaders were contemplating a new statute for Algeria but said the proposals in circulation were not a significant improvement over the current situation. A French offer to provide a little more decentralization wouldn't solve the core problem in Algeria. However, a new law that offered far more autonomy for Algeria would be a positive step. France must begin moving toward political independence for Algeria, and the United States should then respond favorably.[40]

Kennedy argued that the implications of the Algerian crisis touched the core interests of the free world: NATO, emerging proposals for a common market for Europe, and the precarious growth of the new states of Africa. "All of these great enterprises and visions will, I fear, come to nothing if we cannot close the Algerian wound," Kennedy wrote. He concluded that the real interest of the Franco-American friendship would be promoted by a resolution of the Algerian crisis. Neither France nor the Western Alliance could afford another Indochina debacle. "It is not a sentimental and dogmatic anti-colonialism, but the harsh realities of the world we live in, which call on all nations to help in the search for an Algerian solution," he concluded.[41]

In letters to private citizens who commented on his speeches and writings regarding Algeria, Kennedy wrote that the United States should face up to the situation in Algeria before it was too late. The American position in the world would be compromised if "we denounce Soviet imperialism in Hungary and accept the French position in Algeria." He admired the French, sympathized with their problems, and hoped U.S. policy was never anti-French. "But, as in the case of Indochina, there are occasions when we would serve the interests of our friends better by speaking out frankly on the facts they refuse to face," he wrote. As fighting continued to rock North Africa, Kennedy remained engaged on Algeria. There were several possible solutions, Kennedy said. First, France could abandon Algeria as it did Indochina. This was not the preferred course, but it was the most likely given the flow of events. Second, the French could attempt to reconquer all of North Africa, but this would, at best, provide only a temporary victory, for Algerian nationalism was stronger than France realized. Third, there could be partition along national lines in Algeria. But in Kennedy's view, time had run out for such a solution. Finally, there could be a Mediterranean pact with a North African federation in which Algeria was offered a realistic timetable for self-determination. This would give the best chance for peace in North Africa, Kennedy said. "There is still a chance to make the Mediterranean not a moat but a bridge between Europe and North Africa."[42]

Senator Kennedy's warnings to France about Algeria proved prescient. Charles de Gaulle ended up offering Algeria options in 1959 that were along the lines that Kennedy suggested in 1957. By 1962, Algeria had secured its independence after a bloody war in which 10,000 French troops died, more than a million Muslim Algerians were killed, and as many European settlers were driven into exile. The eight-year Algerian war caused the fall of six French governments, led to a constitutional crisis and the collapse of the Fourth Republic, and caused profound civil unrest in France.[43] Far better than most American political leaders, Kennedy grasped the perils of Algeria for France and the West, though his urgent warnings went largely unheeded.

IV

Senator Kennedy traveled to Poland in 1955. He came away impressed by the spirit and tenacity of the Polish people and frustrated the West was not doing more to reach out to Poland and other nations of Eastern Europe. Kennedy was angered by the disconnect between the administration's soaring "liberation" rhetoric, which encouraged the people of Eastern Europe to resist Soviet control, and its seeming indifference to providing tangible assistance to ease the daily struggles of those living behind the Iron Curtain. In March 1957, he wrote to Secretary Dulles that there was strong support in Congress to extend economic assistance to the people of Poland. The Polish people were trying to secure some independence from the Soviet Union. "If there is even a slight chance that this demonstration of friendship on our part will help the Polish people to loosen further the bonds of Soviet domination then the obvious gains to this nation and the free world will have been well worth the effort," he wrote. "To deny them help because they have not yet been able to shake free of total Communist control would be a brutal and dangerous policy, either increasing their dependence on Russia or driving them into the slaughter of a fruitless premature revolt." The United States, Kennedy argued, should offer aid that would directly benefit the Polish people, such as surplus foodstuffs and the sale of farm machinery.[44]

Dulles was unmoved by Kennedy's appeal, and his ideas were initially brushed aside by the administration and strongly opposed by the

Republican leader in the Senate, William Knowland, who argued that aid to Poland would bail out a Soviet satellite country in Eastern Europe, which he didn't want to see happen. Kennedy was convinced that a new U.S. approach to Poland and other nations of Eastern Europe was needed, especially in the aftermath of the Soviet Union's brutal crushing of the Hungarian rebellion in 1956.

On August 21, 1957, Kennedy took to the Senate floor and connected the West's challenges in Algeria to those in Poland, arguing that just as the specter of Western imperialism was confronting the United States in Algeria and North Africa, Soviet imperialism challenged American foreign policy in Eastern Europe, especially in Poland. American policies toward Eastern Europe and Poland were not adequate, Kennedy said, adding that it was easy to decry the treachery of the Yalta agreement and implore the captive peoples of Eastern Europe to resist Soviet brutality. But it would be far more productive for the United States to offer tangible assistance to those nations that wanted to loosen the tight grip of Communism.[45]

Kennedy said Poland was the country of both America's greatest failures and its greatest hope— and the country most urgently requiring a reexamination of current U.S. policies. Poland was unique, with its fragile accommodation between the Catholic Church and the government, which was an anti-Stalinist regime led by President Wladyslaw Gomulka. "It is not my intention today to dwell on Soviet brutality or Polish bravery—for I am sure this body is well aware of both," Kennedy declared. He said the United States' loan agreement of the previous summer to Poland was both meager and tardy and extended only after protracted haggling. The administration pulled back from a more generous assistance package because it was uncertain how the Soviets would react, and also because outdated American foreign aid statutes contemplated only two categories of governments: friends or foes. Kennedy argued that more flexible foreign assistance programs were needed so the United States could offer aid to governments such as Poland that weren't yet allies but wanted to distance themselves from the Soviet Union. "Other satellites, we may be sure, are watching—and if we fail to help the Poles, who else will dare stand up to the Russians and look westward?" Kennedy asked. The senator then proposed a plan to help Poland that might drive a wedge between the Polish government and the Kremlin. Kennedy's package called for more educational and people-to-people exchange programs, expanded trade, greater technical assistance to the Polish government, and humanitarian relief to repatriates finally returning to Poland from Russia in the belated aftermath of World War II. Additionally, the United States needed to be ready to move quickly to offer assistance to Poland or other nations of Eastern Europe if they found opportunities to ease the control of the Soviet Union. Kennedy acknowledged there was no easy solution by which Poland could gain its freedom, but he urged the United States to replace hollow rhetoric with specific plans.[46]

To create more flexible foreign assistance programs, Kennedy worked closely with Republican senator George Aiken of Vermont to amend the Battle Act so it would permit the president to extend assistance to nations behind the Iron Curtain if such assistance would help detach them from Communist control. If the United States were to offer practical assistance to the subjected peoples of Eastern Europe, it needed a flexible set of economic tools to do so. "At the present time the cumbersome Battle Act, passed in other circumstances and under other conditions, inhibits such efforts and does not give the President sufficient authority to act in a situation such as briefly existed in Eastern Europe in the fall of 1956. It is time that we attempt to build our policy to Eastern Europe on more than rhetoric," he said.[47]

Kennedy and Aiken tried to pass their package in the Senate in 1958 but failed by a single vote.

The administration said it supported congressional efforts to provide more flexibility to give aid to satellite nations resisting Soviet domination, but it had procedural concerns with the approach of Kennedy and Aiken. Kennedy vowed to press ahead: "We have found from sad experience that our own arsenal of weapons for use behind the Iron Curtain is very nearly empty. The pleasant slogans of liberation have had a hollow echo."[48]

Kennedy argued the United States couldn't expect freedom for Eastern Europe by means of dramatic or violent revolution. The best hope was to encourage nations to follow the examples of Poland, Yugoslavia, and Finland and move gradually, if cautiously, away from total Soviet political domination and also seek greater economic independence. "We are not going to help them revolt or send them arms. We made that clear in 1956. Neither are we helping by woodenly lumping all Eastern European nations together under one label regardless of the differences in their aspirations or operation. We can help by offering the best possible concrete alternatives— by being ready to take advantage of the first opening—by having ready alternative forms of economic aid to lessen their dependence upon the USSR or China. Unfortunately we cannot do more, certainly we dare not do less."[49]

Kennedy and Aiken continued to work with the administration and in 1959 pushed a revised version of their bill through the Senate. It amended the Battle Act, and several other laws, to permit loans or grants to Poland or other Communist satellites seeking to resist Soviet and Chinese domination. His effort showed Kennedy's ability to find tangible ways to break free from rigid Cold War thinking.

V

John Kennedy used the Senate as a platform to challenge the Eisenhower administration's foreign and national security policy and to outline his own vision of America's role in the world. As his stature grew, he became one of the Democratic Party's most visible spokesmen on national security issues. He was frequently asked to, or insisted that he, offer assessments of the administration's international policies.

He did not wait long in his Senate career to embrace the role of a vocal critic of the administration's foreign policy. About a year after taking office, Eisenhower, having reviewed the status of America's standoff with the Soviet Union and China, as well as the challenges it faced around the world, announced a new national security policy. Eisenhower and Secretary of State Dulles unveiled the so-called "New Look," a strategy that emphasized the importance of air power, nuclear weapons, and a smaller conventional force.

Just weeks after the plan was announced, Kennedy addressed the Cathedral Club in Brooklyn, New York, and forcefully challenged the administration's new approach. Kennedy argued that a robust military is a critical component of national strength and questioned the administration's decision to make military budget cuts and contemplate the use of nuclear weapons. This was one of Kennedy's first—but hardly his last—efforts to criticize Eisenhower's proposed defense cuts.

Several years later, Kennedy wrote a much-noticed essay, "A Democrat Looks at Foreign Policy," in the prestigious *Foreign Affairs* journal. Published in October 1957, Kennedy argued that two central weaknesses were crippling American foreign policy. First was the failure to appreciate how the forces of nationalism were changing the geopolitical map of the world, especially in North Africa, southeastern Europe, and the Middle East. Second was a lack of decisiveness from the administration on foreign policy. It tended too often, Kennedy charged, "to substitute slogans for solutions." After reviewing the history of the U.S.'s containment strategy, which began in 1947, Kennedy said the Eisenhower administration's new approach raised far-reaching issues. The administration appeared to be calling for a "unilateral worldwide Monroe Doctrine for the atomic age," which Kennedy argued would unsettle both allies and adversaries. He questioned how this strategy would apply to current situations, such as the war in Indochina. How would the Eisenhower-Dulles doctrine of nuclear retaliation actually work in a guerilla war in the jungles of Indochina? How would the threat of nuclear retaliation work in circumstances in which Communists advanced by local insurrection and political unrest rather than by overt military invasion? He questioned how this new doctrine would alter the constitutional role of Congress in declaring war. "In an era of supersonic attack and atomic retaliation, extended public debate and education are of no avail," he said. Kennedy concluded by challenging the administration to think more deeply and articulate its policy more clearly, for upon its implementation might rest "the very continued existence of mankind."[50]

The next year, 1958, Kennedy continued his critique of the administration in ways that were both consequential and symbolic. As an example of the latter, Kennedy charged the administration with squandering a wonderful opportunity to showcase American life at the World's Fair in Brussels. He believed the fair was an opportunity to promote the United States and highlight the creativity and vigor of American life. The Eisenhower administration took it far less seriously and saw it as simply a global festival. In a speech on the Senate floor, Kennedy said it was apparent the United States was going to be "outspent, outmanned and outshone in this competition for international prestige and good will" by the Soviet Union. He contrasted the $60 million the Soviet Union was spending on its exhibition in Brussels with the U.S. investment of less than $15 million. But he had a suggestion: Congress should approve the administration's funding request, but also authorize and fund a small project by the Department of Health, Education and Welfare that would highlight American successes in rehabilitating disabled workers. In Kennedy's view, this proposed exhibit would underscore "what American science and research have accomplished, not in missiles and weapons but in vaccines and sanitation." It would demonstrate what the United States could do "not in the way of snuffing out lives, but saving them, not in maiming the bodies of men, but reclaiming them." He urged others in Congress to join with him in this effort to "demonstrate to a wondering world that our chief concern is not with wars or material things but the helping of all mankind." Kennedy's idea never generated much support in Congress but demonstrated his creative thinking and outside-the-box diplomacy.[51]

On a more consequential note, Kennedy gave a major Senate speech on August 14, 1958, arguing the United States was falling behind the Soviet Union in important military areas. The United States, he said, faced a missile gap in which American offensive and defensive missile capabilities were about to lag so far behind those of the Soviets as to place the nation in a position of substantial peril. In Kennedy's view, the most critical phase in the missile gap would be between 1960 and 1964; during this time, the Soviet Union might have available a "new shortcut to world domination." He warned that the United States could not expect the Soviet Union to sit back and not take advantage of its relative strength. "In the years of the gap, the Soviets may be expected to use their superior striking ability to achieve their objectives in ways which may not require launching an actual attack. Their missile power will be the shield from behind which they will slowly, but surely, advance—through Sputnik diplomacy, limited brush fire wars, indirect non-overt aggression, intimidation and subversion, internal revolution, increased prestige or influence, and the vicious blackmail of our allies. The periphery of the Free World will slowly be nibbled away."[52]

Kennedy said the United States needed to reassess its national security posture, devote whatever resources necessary to meet those challenges, and not place fiscal security ahead of national security. Undue focus on budgetary concerns, he charged, helped cause the sluggish American response to the Soviet threat. Citing nineteenth-century British historian Edward Gibbon's contention that the Romans maintained the peace by constantly preparing for war, Kennedy said the United States should use all elements of national power—economic, military, and diplomatic—to prepare for "the most serious test in our nation's history, which will be impending in the next five years."[53] Kennedy's dire warnings were partly based on the findings of the Gaither Report, a study by a blue-ribbon task force that concluded the United States was facing the gravest danger in its history as the Soviet Union raced ahead of it in many aspects of national power. Many believed the report was hyperbolic, but Kennedy seized on its findings to attack the administration.

The following year, Kennedy continued his critiques of Eisenhower's national security policies. In a speech to the Wisconsin Democratic Party in Milwaukee on November 13, 1959, Kennedy argued that since January 1953, the month of Eisenhower's first inauguration, the United States had wasted time and squandered many of its advantages. "When we should have sailed hard into the wind, we, too, drifted. When we should have planned anew, sacrificed, and marched ahead, we, too, stood still, sought the easy way, and looked to the past." But the Soviet

Union used these years to catch up and then surpass the United States, stripping away American prestige, influence, and even power in the world.[54]

In Kennedy's view, the United States of 1952 was the unchallenged leader in every sphere, but by 1959 the Soviets had caught up in the space race and were challenging American interests in Indochina, Hungary, Latin America, and the Middle East. As Kennedy saw the balance sheet, the Soviets had made major advances militarily as the United States fell behind the Soviet Union in the development and production of ballistic missiles, rocket engines, jet engines, new types of fuel, and modern submarines. The United States was also lagging in education, science, and research, and its economy had fallen into a slump, fluctuating between inflation and recession with high unemployment. He also saw the Soviet Union surging past the United States in agriculture, trade, and foreign assistance. Kennedy's assessment of the Eisenhower years was withering. "Eight gray years—'years that the locusts have eaten.' Years of drift, years of falling behind, of postponing decisions and crises. And as a result, the burdens that will face the next administration will be tremendous." But he said the United States could still close the gaps and pull ahead with determined national effort.[55]

In the summer of 1960, just as Kennedy was

poised to formally become the Democratic nominee for president, he once again took to the Senate floor to hammer the Eisenhower administration on national security and describe a way forward for the United States. Articulating themes that were central to his presidential campaign, Kennedy said the collapse of the Eisenhower-Khrushchev summit in May 1960 should give American leaders and the public a renewed awareness of the perils the nation faced, the sacrifices it had to make, and the urgent need for leadership. Kennedy said the real issue behind the implosion of the Paris summit, which many had hoped would ease the tensions of the Cold War, was the lack of a coherent national strategy backed by strength.[56]

The next American president, Kennedy said, must summon the country's vast resources against the "most dangerous threat it has ever faced." He would inherit "far flung commitments without the strength to back them up" due to the limits set by "budgeteers without regard to world conditions or America's needs." The next president needed fresh ideas to break stalemates in Berlin and in arms control negotiations. "We have as our grand strategy only the arms race and the cold war," he lamented. Instead, the United States needed a comprehensive set of carefully prepared, long-term policies designed to increase the strength of the non-Communist world. "And unless this task is accomplished, as we move into the most critical period in our nation's history, since the bleak winter at Valley Forge, our national security, our survival itself, will be in peril. The hour is late, but the agenda is long."[57]

Kennedy then outlined his agenda for American foreign policy—an agenda that he had refined on the campaign trail as he pursued the Democratic presidential nomination and that he would use to challenge his Republican opponent, Vice President Richard Nixon, in the fall. The nation needed an invulnerable nuclear retaliatory power; it had to produce missiles to close the gap and ensure that the United States couldn't be wiped out by a surprise attack. It needed to regain its ability to intervene effectively "in any limited war anywhere in the world." The nation needed to rebuild NATO into a viable and consolidated military force able to deter any kind of attack. It needed to work with western Europe and Japan to send capital to underdeveloped parts of Asia, Africa, the Middle East, and Latin America. It needed an entirely revamped foreign aid program.

The United States needed to rebuild relations with Latin American democracies, forge a new approach to the Middle East, and extend a hand of friendship to newly emerging nations in Africa. It needed plans premised on the inevitable triumph of nationalism in Africa. The nation needed a long-range solution to Berlin and more flexible and realistic tools in Eastern Europe. The liberation rhetoric of the Eisenhower administration had proved to be a "snare and a delusion." Failed uprisings in East Germany, Hungary, and Poland proved the United States had neither the intention nor the capacity to liberate Eastern Europe—and the false hopes raised by U.S. promises were cruelly crushed.

The United States needed to offer Poland fresh new initiatives on aid, trade, tourism, and student and teacher exchanges. It needed a new China policy, as the current one had failed to weaken Communist rule in the mainland. It needed new workable programs for peace and the control of arms, with an arms-control research institute. And finally, the United States needed to rebuild its science, research, and space programs. Despite his lengthy "to do" list, Kennedy ended hopefully, proclaiming that "the coming years will bring new problems, undreamt of challenges, unanticipated opportunities."[58]

Kennedy used his time in the Senate to become schooled in international affairs and developed into a forceful, if partisan, foreign policy player. He gave a number of provocative, even prescient, speeches on Indochina, Algeria, and Soviet control over Eastern Europe. As a member of the Senate Foreign Relations Committee, he became skilled at direct, even blunt, questioning of administration officials. He crafted his own foreign policy agenda that blended lofty idealism and hardball politics. His frequent critiques of the Eisenhower administration gave him considerable visibility but also ensured the administration would not turn to him for solutions. He was willing to live with that bargain.

Senator John Kennedy questioning Dave Beck, a controversial leader of the Teamsters Union. This hearing took place in the Senate Caucus Room, which was renamed the Kennedy Caucus Room in 2009 in memory of John, Robert, and Edward Kennedy, all of whom served in the U.S. Senate. *Photo courtesy of U.S. Senate Historical Office.*

Senator John Kennedy shares a light moment with his brother Robert who managed John's 1952 campaign in which he defeated incumbent senator Henry Cabot Lodge. Robert Kennedy later served on the staff of several Senate committees before heading up his brother's 1960 presidential campaign. *Photo courtesy of U.S. Senate Historical Office.*

Senator Kennedy poses with his staff, and the birthday cake they gave him, in his office in what is now called the Senate Russell Office Building. Kennedy was a polite but demanding boss who expected his staff to be available whenever he wanted to reach them. *Photo courtesy of the JFK Presidential Library.*

John and Robert Kennedy leave the U.S. Capitol and head toward their offices. Behind them is the East Front of the Capitol where John Kennedy later delivered one of the most memorable Inauguration Addresses of the twentieth century on January 20, 1961. *Photo courtesy of the JFK Presidential Library.*

Senator Kennedy grilling a witness during a Senate hearing. Often charming and charismatic, Kennedy could be a tough, even curt, questioner. *Photo courtesy of the JFK Presidential Library.*

During his four-year quest for the presidency, Senator Kennedy often left Washington to campaign around the country. Here his wife, Jackie, sees him off at Washington's National Airport as he heads toward a plane. *Photo courtesy of the JFK Presidential Library.*

Senator Kennedy devoted more time to labor reform than any other domestic issue during his Senate career. Here Kennedy meets informally with a group of labor leaders in his office. Copies of his book, *Profiles in Courage*, are stacked on his desk. *Photo courtesy of the JFK Presidential Library.*

John F. Kennedy was not a natural politician, and during the early part of his congressional career, he was often a halting and unimpressive speaker, but he grew into an effective campaigner. Here he speaks at an outdoor rally in central Massachusetts. *Photo courtesy of U.S. Senate Historical Office.*

Senator Kennedy files a campaign document as his wife looks on. During his Senate career, he often traveled on weekends to political events, and Jackie usually stayed behind in Washington. *Photo courtesy of U.S. Senate Historical Office.*

Senator John F. Kennedy's official photograph. He served in the Senate from January 1953 to December 1960, resigning a month before his Inauguration as the thirty-fifth president of the United States. *Photo courtesy of U.S. Senate Historical Office.*

Senator Kennedy poses with Senate Majority Leader Lyndon Johnson. The two men were wary rivals during much of the 1950s and battled for the 1960 Democratic nomination for president. Kennedy prevailed, and Johnson became Kennedy's vice presidential running mate. *Photo courtesy of U.S. Senate Historical Office.*

Senator Kennedy poses with two Senate colleagues from Pennsylvania: Hugh Scott, a Republican, and Joseph Clark, a Democrat. *Photo courtesy of U.S. Senate Historical Office.*

John Kennedy with other lawmakers involved in the labor reform debate. Republican senator Barry Goldwater is on the far left. *UPI photo provided by U.S. Senate Historical Office.*

John F. Kennedy is reviewing a bill with Jacob Javits, a liberal Republican from New York. Javits served with Kennedy in both the House and Senate. *Photo courtesy of U.S. Senate Historical Office.*

Senator John Kennedy "playing" baseball with two other Democratic senators in a Georgetown park: Mike Mansfield and Henry "Scoop" Jackson. Kennedy is the catcher, Mansfield the umpire, and Jackson the batter. The photo was staged. Kennedy arrived late to the gathering in his convertible, joined his Senate colleagues who had been waiting impatiently for him, posed for the picture, and then raced off. *Photo courtesy of U.S. Senate Historical Office.*

Senator John Kennedy in the Senate Reception Room in March 1959 during the official unveiling of the portraits of the five best senators in American history. Kennedy was the chair of the special committee that made the selection, and during the ceremony he was joined on the dais by Senate Majority Leader Lyndon Johnson and Vice President Richard Nixon. Here he listens to the Senate Republican leader, Everett Dirksen. *Photo courtesy of The Dirksen Congressional Center.*

Seven
The Scholarly Senator

I

John Kennedy was a solid and usually constructive senator on domestic issues and a consequential and often creative one as it pertained to foreign policy. However, what distinguished Kennedy from his Senate colleagues was his ability to write and speak with literary flair and striking historical perspective.

Kennedy's writing career began when he was at Harvard. An indifferent student during his first several years in college, he became deeply interested in current events, politics, and government during his final two years. He received permission from the university to spend a semester in Europe to work on an honor's thesis in the winter of 1939. Kennedy crossed the Atlantic Ocean on the eve of World War II, just before the German army moved into Czechoslovakia. During his time in Europe, Kennedy worked for his father in the American embassy in London and traveled throughout the United Kingdom, France, Poland, Latvia, Russia, Turkey,

Palestine, and the Balkans. Since his father was the U.S. ambassador to Great Britain, Kennedy took advantage of his father's diplomatic contacts to arrange travel to places not easily accessible with war on the horizon. George Kennan, then a relatively junior diplomat based in Prague, grumbled that Ambassador Kennedy "has chosen this time to send one of his young sons on a fact-finding tour around Europe and it was up to us to find means of getting him across the border and through the German lines so that he could include in his itinerary a visit to Prague." The culmination of Kennedy's European trip was being in the House of Commons when Prime Minister Neville Chamberlain declared war on Germany on behalf of his country on September 3, 1939. Kennedy also saw Winston Churchill address the House of Commons that same day and pledge, as the First Lord of the Admirality, a relentless effort to defeat the Nazis.[1]

Kennedy returned to Harvard at the end of that year, immersed himself in a rigorous academic schedule, and plunged into his honor's thesis on England's foreign policy since 1931. For the first time in his life he became consumed by a topic and worked passionately to master it. With continuing assistance from the staff of the American embassy in London, which sent him cartons of important documents, and with considerable secretarial help in Cambridge, Kennedy submitted his thesis,

Appeasement at Munich: The Inevitable Result of the Slowness of Conversion of the British Democracy to Change from a Disarmament Policy to a Rearmament Policy.

The 148-page paper was a carefully researched study of British politics that most of his examiners found generally impressive, though marred by spelling and grammatical errors and tangled syntax. One professor said the thesis was a "laborious, interesting and intelligent discussion of a difficult question." Another was more critical, saying the fundamental premise of the thesis was never analyzed, and the paper was "much too long, wordy, repetitious." Nonetheless, Kennedy received Harvard's second highest honors for the thesis, magna cum laude.[2]

Arthur Krock, a family friend and *New York Times* columnist, read the thesis during a visit with the Kennedys in Florida and concluded it was an interesting and timely study. He suggested that Kennedy publish it as a book. Krock helped Kennedy secure an agent who in turn found a publisher, Wilfred Funk. With editing assistance from Krock, Kennedy's book, *Why England Slept*, was published in the summer of 1940 as war raged in Europe.

In the book, Kennedy analyzed why England so poorly prepared in the 1930s for the rising threat of Nazi Germany. He argued that it was unfair to dismiss England's failures as merely the miscalculations of a handful of leaders such as Neville Chamberlain and Stanley Baldwin. Rather, British society as a whole had failed, Kennedy argued, assigning responsibility to business, labor, the press, political leaders, and the British public, which was determined to stay out of another European war. From 1931, when Prime Minister Ramsay MacDonald was chosen to head the new National Unity Government, until the end of the decade, Britain slowly awoke to the dangers posed by Nazi Germany and began to rearm. But the agonizingly slow process only intensified after the Munich crisis in September 1938 and then shifted into high gear in September 1939 after Germany invaded Poland and Great Britain and France declared war on Germany.[3]

Kennedy believed Chamberlain's accommodation with Hitler at Munich was largely an effort to buy time until Great Britain was better prepared to resist. If Chamberlain had taken Britain into war in 1938, he would have been playing into Hitler's hands because Germany was then far stronger militarily than the U.K. and was ready for war. As Hitler invaded Holland and steamrolled through France in the spring of 1940, Churchill became prime minister, assumed vast domestic war powers that rivaled Hitler's, and drove Britain's massive rearmament. "With this new spirit alive in England my story ends," Kennedy wrote. "England was now awake; it had taken a great shock to bring home a realization of the enormity of the task it was facing. . . . This is a supreme test of democracy's ability to survive in this changing world."[4]

Why England Slept then moved from the specifics of Britain's failures to a broader assessment of the relative strengths and weaknesses of democratic-capitalist systems, such as those in the United States and U.K., compared with a totalitarian regime such as Nazi Germany. Kennedy concluded that in the long run, democratic-capitalist systems are superior, but totalitarian systems are built for war and democracies are not. "For democracy and capitalism are institutions which are geared for a world at peace. It is our problem to find a method of protecting them in a world at war," he wrote. Kennedy argued that many of the weaknesses displayed by Britain in the 1930s were apparent in the United States, and Americans must understand the weaknesses of their system and be prepared to make sacrifices to preserve their way of life in the future. "Any person will awaken when the house is burning down. What we need is an armed guard that will wake up when the fire first starts or, better yet, one that will not permit a fire to start at all."[5]

The book quickly became a best seller, in both the United States and Great Britain. Praise came from many quarters. Henry Luce, the publisher of *Time*, penned the book's foreword and called it "the most dispassionate and factual account yet written of the development of British policy in the light of democratic British public opinion in the last decade." Luce described the book as a striking accomplishment for such a young man, adding he could not recall anyone of his college generation who could have written such a mature book on such an important subject during his senior year. "This book has the rare and immensely appealing quality of combining factuality and breadth of understanding with the truest instincts of patriotism," Luce wrote.[6]

Why England Slept received mixed reviews. S. T. Williamson in the *New York Times* called it a book of "such painstaking scholarship, such mature understanding and fair-mindedness and of such penetrating and timely conclusions that is a notable textbook for our time." Williamson said he had read no other discussion of prewar Britain that offered better insights than did Kennedy's book. "He has taken the hard way and the thorough way to show how and why Britain slept while Germany whetted her sword."[7] Another review by R. J. Cruikshank said the book revealed Kennedy's "quick-silver intelligence," adding that "one sees in this book how a warm absorption of the sympathies by men and events can be combined with a cool, objective appraisement of historic forces."[8] Some critics were cooler. Ole H. Lexau, writing in the *Atlanta Constitution*, said the book was a solid effort but didn't probe deeply enough into the reasons England failed to rearm in the face of the Nazi threat. "There isn't any why," he concluded of the book. "To say that England slept because England slept is sound enough, as far as it goes, but doesn't go anywhere."[9]

In the U.K. the book generated disagreement on its merits. Harold Laski, a leading economist and intellectual, wrote Ambassador Kennedy and offered a withering review of his son's book. "For while it is the book of a lad with brains, it is very immature, it has no structure and dwells almost wholly on the surface of things. In a good university, half a hundred seniors do books like this as part of their normal work in the final year. But they don't publish them for the good reason that their importance lies solely in what they get out of doing them and not of what they have to say." But B. H. Liddell Hart, the famous British military historian, found considerable value in the book and sent a warm note to John Kennedy. "I would like to express my admiration for the outstanding way it combines insight with balanced judgment, in a way that nothing that has yet been written here approaches. It is all the more impressive by comparison with other recent books which I have read, by both English and American writers who were apt to get led astray by superficial appearances."[10] On balance, the book was an impressive and timely study of an issue in which much of the world was interested. Even so, the book would likely have attracted only modest attention had the author not come from a prominent family whose father who was the controversial American ambassador to the U.K.

The book sold 80,000 copies and earned Kennedy about $40,000 in royalties. Kennedy took considerable pride in the book, giving copies to friends and acquaintances for years, quipping that it was his favorite book by his favorite author.

While he was working on the book, his father sent him an encouraging note saying that writing a respected book would be a boost for his career. "So whether you make a cent out of it or not, it will do you an amazing amount of good, particularly if it is well received. You would be surprised how a book that really makes the grade with high class people stands you in good stead for years to come."[11]

II

After graduating from Harvard, Kennedy considered careers in journalism, writing, academia, and politics. These long-term career reflections were interrupted by his World War II service. His heroic actions to save members of his crew after their PT boat was sliced in half in the South

Pacific became legendary—even if the full facts behind the sinking and rescue remain unclear. After the war, Kennedy worked briefly as a newspaper correspondent. His journalism consisted of articles that ranged from 300 to 400 words and blended analysis and opinion. They were simple, clear, and occasionally perceptive essays with flashes of wit and irony. The format of the articles did not allow for inspired writing or deep analysis. But they showed a young man with a facility for language and a fascination with international affairs. His tone was realistic and even skeptical.

When Kennedy entered the political arena in 1946 and ran for the House, his campaign focused on the domestic needs of his constituents and the challenges of the impending Cold War. His speech announcing his candidacy was a simple and straightforward statement about the need for housing, education, price controls, and jobs legislation and the imperative of a strong military for the United States to prevail in the messy world following the war. His agenda was expressed in terse prose; there was no poetry or literary lift to his statement. During his six-year career in the House, his writing remained the same. His speeches were straightforward and constrained. He had not yet found his distinctive voice. Kennedy's 1952 campaign speeches and writings were equally parochial and pedestrian.

Ted Sorensen was one of the first assistants Kennedy brought into his Senate office in 1953. They developed an intense and effective partnership. Sorensen became a policy adviser, speechwriter, and sounding board for the senator. Kennedy called Sorensen "my intellectual blood bank." He later told Tip O'Neill, "I never had anyone who could write for me before Ted came along." With Sorensen at his side, Kennedy's writings and speeches took on a new flavor. There was a noticeable increase in their range, eloquence, rhetorical power, and concision. Both Kennedy and Sorensen were fans of *The Elements of Style*, the book on writing by William Strunk Jr. that emphasized brevity and precision.[12]

Kennedy and Sorensen developed a collaborative process in which Kennedy sketched out his ideas for an article or a speech. Sorensen then wrote a draft that Kennedy would edit. Kennedy would often dictate a new draft and then work again with Sorensen to refine it. "Kennedy was as compulsive about his important speeches as he was about his food, clothes and sex life," said Thurston Clarke, an expert on Kennedy's writings and speeches. "He fussed over every word, dictating, re-dictating and editing an address until moments before it was delivered, then making further changes as he spoke." John Kenneth Galbraith, then an informal adviser to Kennedy, said the senator took great pride in his writings. Kennedy, he said, "did not suffer fools gladly nor did he suffer bad prose."[13]

Kennedy scribbled random thoughts and substantive ideas on any piece of paper that was handy. The senator jotted notes on the backs of letters, envelopes, airline tickets, or telegrams. But he did most of his writing through dictation, which was "ideally suited to a restless man, uncomfortable with solitude, who liked doing everything at top speed," said Clarke.[14] Kennedy had kept a loose-leaf notebook since his war years with his favorite quotations. He also frequently consulted *Bartlett's Familiar Quotations* for additional adages. Fascinated with the art of rhetoric, Kennedy loved listening to recordings of Churchill's speeches and reading those of Lincoln. He both read and recommended a book given to him by Sorensen, *A Treasury of the World's Great Speeches*. During his House and early Senate career, Kennedy was a mediocre speaker with a hurried delivery and a high-pitched voice. His speeches were fact-filled and detailed and often seemed to drain sentiment out of situations. But Kennedy was aware of his shortcomings and was determined to get better— both in spoken and written expression. "I can't afford to sound just like any other senator," he told Sorenson.[15]

In the way that the Sorensen partnership was

critical to Kennedy's intellectual and rhetorical maturation, the senator's lifelong devotion to reading history and biography was critical to infusing his ideas with heft and context. "He would read walking, he'd read at the table, at meals, he'd read after dinner, he'd read in the bathtub," recalled his wife, Jackie. "He'd open some book I'd be reading, you know, and just devour it. He really read all the times you don't think you have time to read." She said that he read almost exclusively history and biography and rarely touched a novel. "He wasn't just reading for diversion. He didn't want to waste a single second," she said, recalling that every Sunday he would study the *New York Times Book Review* and circle the books he wanted her to pick up for him.[16] When he met with academics, he would often ask them to send him a suggested reading list—and he would actually read the books. During his time in the Senate, his office was a seemingly endless borrower from the Library of Congress. His long-time friend Lem Billings said Kennedy was always a voracious reader. "There has never been a moment when he didn't have something to read and usually he has been working on at least two books at the same time."[17]

Kennedy was particularly fond of American and British history and biography. His favorite books were *Pilgrim's Way* by John Buchan, *The Young*

Melbourne by David Cecil, *The Seven Pillars of Wisdom* by T. E. Lawrence, *John Quincy Adams and the Union* by Samuel Flagg Bemis, and *The Emergence of Lincoln* by Allan Nevins. He read all of Churchill's books and listened to tapes of his wartime speeches. He read *War and Peace* while serving in the navy in the South Pacific during World War II. When asked by a reporter in 1957 what he had been reading recently, he cited *Oliver Cromwell* by John Buchan, *Crisis of the Old Order* by Arthur Schlesinger Jr., and *Road to the White House* by Arthur Link. Kennedy told another interviewer the books he would take with him to the proverbial desert island were the Bible, *Pilgrim's Way*, *The Oxford Book of American Verse*, and *The Oxford Anthology of American Literature.*[18]

Historian Arthur Schlesinger said Kennedy had a historical cast of mind and was particularly intrigued by large figures who dominated their times. "History was full of heroes for him and he reveled in stately cadences of historical prose. His memory of what he read was photographic. Situations, scenes and quotations stuck in his mind for the rest of his life," Schlesinger wrote. "Kennedy read seldom for distraction. He did not want to waste a single second. He read partly for information, partly for comparison, partly for insight, partly for the sheer joy of felicitous statement."[19] Sorensen described him as an analytical historian, saying he was "not only a scholar of history but a severe judge of historical and biographical work."[20] He was intensely interested in the past. Aides said he could not pass a historical marker without stopping to read it. He also understood how policymakers used history. He enjoyed Romain Rolland's observation that "history furnishes to politics all the arguments it needs for the chosen course."[21]

Kennedy liked to talk about and debate history and was willing to change his mind about past events and controversies. He devoured Civil War histories and because of them fundamentally changed his view on the Reconstruction period, coming to believe that northern Republicans were far more fair-minded than southerners often contended.[22] After Kennedy delivered a speech at Harvard, Schlesinger sent the senator a note of congratulations but also challenged him on a statement he made about the 1856 presidential campaign. Kennedy asked Congress's Legislative Reference Service to research the disagreement and report back to him. (Kennedy was presumably disappointed to learn that Schlesinger was right and he had been wrong.) He also frequently sought historical background from this research service. Before giving a speech on Thomas Jefferson and Andrew Jackson, he asked for a memo from the Legislative Reference Service on the correspondence between the two. Kennedy's description of Jackson shows his love of vivid personalities in history. Jackson, Kennedy said, had

> both the judicial qualities of a Tennessee Superior Court Judge and the mud of America's rivers and swamps. He was both a picture of dignity and the master of profanity. His body bore the scars left by savage Indians—the bullets of Tennessee duelists—the shattered ribs suffered in battle for his country. He took with him a warm heart and a cool head—a folksy cob pipe and a sharp, bitter tongue. He was both simple and shrewd, both beloved by the many and suspected by the few. He had, in Sandburg's phrase, "lived on acorns and slept in the rain"; and now he was to be the President of the United States.[23]

Nearly all observers of Kennedy as historian return to his fascination with individuals who shaped their times. "His view of history, it is very clear, is very largely in personal terms—great men and their influence," said historian and biographer David Donald.[24]

III

Early in his Senate career, Kennedy came across a reference in one of his favorite books, *The Price of Union* by Herbert Agar, about John Quincy Adams's decision as a senator to support a trade embargo on Great Britain imposed by President Thomas Jefferson. The embargo was strongly opposed by the economic interests of his state, Massachusetts, because it was expected to severely damage the shipping industry. Moreover, Jefferson had been a fierce rival of Adams's father, John Adams, and had defeated him in the 1800 presidential race. But John Quincy Adams was convinced the embargo was in the national interest and deserved his support, even if this support damaged him politically. Kennedy was intrigued by this example of senatorial bravery and instructed Sorensen to track down background information so they could write a broader article about senatorial courage. A survey during the 1954 Army-McCarthy hearings about senators who had taken courageous positions may also have piqued his interest in the subject.[25]

While convalescing in Palm Beach after major back surgery in late 1954, Kennedy decided to expand his article, "Patterns of Political Courage," into a full book. He signed a contract in May 1955 with Harper & Brothers and received a $500 advance. Sorensen began sending Kennedy cartons of books, memos, and research materials on the topic. Kennedy assembled an informal research team for the project, including Sorensen; James Landis, a Kennedy family attorney; and historians Arthur Holcombe, James MacGregor Burns, and Jules Davids. Kennedy oversaw the project, but Sorensen coordinated the research, gathered background material, and sent Kennedy memos and draft chapters. Kennedy edited them and dictated new drafts and concentrated on the first and final chapters, which described the broad challenges of political courage.[26]

Profiles in Courage was published in January 1956 and focused on eight senators who took courageous stands in defiance of the apparent will of their constituents: John Quincy Adams, Daniel Webster, Thomas Hart Benton, Sam Houston, Edmund Ross, Lucius Lamar, George Norris, and Robert Taft. In each profile, Kennedy described how the senator took career-threatening risks to do what he thought was right. Adams supported the Louisiana Purchase and Jefferson's Embargo Act; Webster backed the 1850 Compromise to save the Union; Benton battled to keep Missouri from joining the Confederacy; Houston supported the Kansas-Nebraska Act of 1854; Ross opposed the impeachment of Andrew Johnson; Lamar sought national unity by offering a powerful eulogy for abolitionist Charles Sumner; George Norris fought the armed ship bill on the eve of

World War I; and Taft criticized the Nuremberg trials of Nazi war criminals on the grounds that the American Constitution prohibits ex post facto laws.

The book also served as Kennedy's meditation on political courage and the Senate. The eight senators he chronicled were willing to endure personal and professional risk to support the national interest. For each, self-respect was more important than popularity, and integrity took precedence over the desire to stay in office. Kennedy said the American public doesn't always understand the pressures that discourage acts of political courage and "which drive a Senator to abandon or subdue his conscience." One pressure was the simple desire to be liked and respected by colleagues. "We are anxious to get along with our fellow legislators, our fellow members of the club, to abide by the clubhouse rules and patterns, not to pursue a unique and independent course which would embarrass or irritate the other members. We realize, moreover, that our influence in the club—and the extent to which our objectives and those of our constituents—are dependent in some measure on the esteem with which we are regarded by other senators," he wrote. "Going along means more than just good fellowship—it includes the use of compromise, the sense of things possible. We should not be too hasty in condemning all compromise as bad morals. For politics and legislation are not matters for inflexible principles or unattainable ideals."[27]

Kennedy confided to his readers something they probably already suspected: that most senators want to get reelected and have an instinctive reluctance to go down in defeat in support of a single principle or cause, in part, because they will not be around to fight for that or any other cause in the future. "Few senators 'retire to Pocatello' by choice," he wrote. "The virus of Potomac Fever, which rages everywhere in Washington, breaks nowhere in more virulent form than on the Senate floor." Most senators are reluctant to lose their membership to the most exclusive club in the world because it would require them to give up interesting work, elegant trappings, and the comfortable prerogatives of congressional office. The desire to get reelected exercises a strong deterrent to independent courage.[28]

There are also relentless and seemingly endless pressures coming from constituents, interest groups, and voters. "But to decide at which point and on which issue he will risk his career is a difficult and soul-searching decision," Kennedy wrote. "We must on occasion lead, inform, correct and sometimes even ignore constituent opinion." Kennedy acknowledged that it's often difficult for a senator to sift through letters and review comments from interest groups to determine his state's views on an issue. "Yet, in truth I rarely know how the great majority of the voters feel, or even how much they know of the issues that seem so burning in Washington."[29]

Kennedy lamented that American political life was "becoming so expensive, so mechanized and so dominated by professional politicians and public relations men, that the idealist who dreams of independent statesmanship is rudely awakened by the necessities of election and accomplishment." He said the case studies he presented showed that courage requires no exceptional qualifications, magic formulas, or special blend of time, place, and circumstance. "It is an opportunity that sooner or later is presented to all of us. Politics merely furnishes one arena which imposes special tests of courage." Examples from the past could instruct, offer hope, and provide inspiration and guidance. "But they cannot supply courage itself. For this each man must look into his own soul."[30]

Shortly before the publication of *Profiles in Courage* in January 1956, excerpts were printed in a number of popular magazines, such as *Harper's*, *Reader's Digest*, and *Collier's*. An essay in the *New York Times Magazine*, "The Challenge of Political Courage," came out on December 18, 1955. It was largely a portion of the book's first chapter and explained the pressures that confront conscientious lawmakers. "Perhaps if the American public more fully comprehended the terrible pressures which discourage acts of political courage, which drive a Senator to abandon or subdue his conscience, then they might be less critical of those who take the easier road—and more appreciative of those still able to follow the path of courage."[31]

Profiles in Courage seized the public's attention, garnering mostly excellent reviews and generating robust sales. In a major review in the Sunday *New York Times*, Cabell Phillips lavished praise on the book, saying it was "refreshing and enlightening to have a first rate politician write a thoughtful and persuasive book about political integrity." In each of Kennedy's case studies, the senators "at some moment of crisis staked his principles against the massed furies of bigotry, sectionalism and conformity." Phillips continued, "These are stirring tales, packed with drama, suspense, high purpose, reward and retribution. Each character took a stand—some fearlessly, others in frank trepidation—on some critical issue of his day that was unpopular with his constituents or his party but which his conscience would not let him evade." Kennedy wrote from the "dual eminence of a perceptive and reflective mind and of practical, first-hand political experience." Like some other younger members of Congress, Kennedy had thought about the role of the legislature and the legislator, as well as their potential weaknesses, and wondered whether the days of the giants were over. *Profiles in Courage*, Phillips concluded, "would restore respect for a venerable and much abused profession."[32]

A more critical review ran in the *New York Times*'s "Books of the Times" section. Charles Poore wrote that while Kennedy's book was "splendidly readable" and offered an impressively varied cast of characters, it also had weaknesses. One troubling aspect was the men in the book "showed their most conspicuous courage in defying the very forces that had chosen them for leadership." It did not take "sufficient account of the enduring good sense of the American people as a whole who, as in the past, always will preserve constitutional government, no matter what the demagogue advocates in any passing time." He also challenged Kennedy's assertion that it did not matter whether one of his subjects, George Norris, was right or wrong on a particular issue, only that Norris was courageous and true to himself. "It almost urges us to admire courage as courage, no matter where it appears. And this has its repugnant aspects. . . . Our view of true courage, somehow, is inextricably woven into the fabric of the cause for which it is displayed," Poore wrote.[33]

Kennedy gave each of his Senate colleagues a copy of *Profiles in Courage*. Evelyn Lincoln, his Senate secretary, recalled sitting by his desk, handing him books to sign. After he autographed about two dozen copies, he would take a break while she made sure they were hand-delivered to his colleagues. Kennedy also dictated a list of personal friends and prominent people to whom he wanted to send an autographed copy. He worked for hours at a time signing books, checking lists, and adding more names. One grateful recipient was a former colleague, Vice President Richard Nixon, who wrote Kennedy a warm note thanking him for his copy. Kennedy later told Nixon that book writing was good for a political career, saying, "There's something about being an author which really builds the reputation of a politician."[34]

Profiles in Courage was on the U.S. best-seller list for more than a year, eventually selling more than 2 million copies. It played a key role in establishing Kennedy as the Senate's preeminent historian and also as an advocate for public integrity. The book, and its author, reached an even higher level of prominence with remarkable news in the spring of 1957. On May 7, John Kennedy learned that *Profiles in Courage* was the recipient of the Pulitzer Prize for biography. It came as a surprise to him and to almost everyone who followed the award closely. The two judges for biography were historians Julian Boyd and Bernard Mayo. They submitted to the Advisory Board on Pulitzer Prizes a list of recommendations that did not include *Profiles in Courage*. They recommended five books: *Harlan Fiske Stone* by Alpheus Mason; *Roosevelt: The Lion and the Fox* by James MacGregor Burns; *James Madison: The President, 1808–12* by Irving Brant; *John Quincy Adams and the Union* by Samuel Bemis; and *Old Bullion Benton* by William Chambers. Boyd and Mayo suggested several other books worth consideration; this additional list also did not include *Profiles in Courage*. But the Advisory Board ignored their recommendations and gave the award to Kennedy. According to one analyst, they decided to "override the weightier works recommended by the historians" and selected a book that appealed to a popular audience. Journalist and Kennedy family friend Arthur Krock lobbied hard for Kennedy's book to the Advisory Board. Kennedy's father may also have weighed in with calls to board members.[35]

Winning the prestigious prize is a signal event for any author, but for a sitting U.S. senator with political ambitions and literary aspirations this award was a remarkable and much-welcomed achievement. As news spread that Kennedy won the Pulitzer, the senator received congratulations from friends, colleagues, rivals, and even strangers.

Connecticut governor Abe Ribicoff, New York governor Averell Harriman, and Massachusetts governor Foster Furcolo, a bitter Kennedy rival, all sent their congratulations. "Massachusetts hails its great Democratic senator as the first member of Congress ever to win a Pulitzer Prize," Furcolo wired, perhaps through clenched teeth. "It brings great credit to our commonwealth."[36]

Congresswoman Edna Kelly, a Democrat from New York, sent effusive words of praise to the senator. "I am so proud, not only knowing you, but also having served in the House of Representatives with you," she gushed. "Incidentally, you neglected to autograph my copy, an oversight which I will attempt to have corrected in the very near future." Representative Isidore Dollinger, also a Democrat from New York, was delighted for the senator, observing that he had achieved considerable fame for such a young man. "To be able to write a Pulitzer Prize winning book while at the same time carrying out the arduous duties of a Senator in a brilliant and outstanding manner is indeed a great achievement."[37]

Senator Richard Neuberger, a Democrat from Oregon, went to the Senate floor to praise Kennedy for his accomplishments in the House, Senate, and now the literary world. He inserted a *New York Times* article about Kennedy into the *Congressional Record* that described his political, and now literary, accomplishments. Kennedy, the article noted, was elected to the House at age 29, the Senate at 36, and won the Pulitzer Prize at 39.

It described him as having "poise, polish, education and money." Senator Mike Monroney, a Democrat from Oklahoma, congratulated Kennedy personally on the floor of the Senate and then sent him a warm note. "The Pulitzer Committee, in recognizing the great value of your book, not only has brought honor to you, but to the subject which you treated. I feel that you have distinguished yourself and the Senate in which we both serve. I am proud and happy with you."[38]

Words of praise also arrived from the diplomatic corps. Agha Shahi, a diplomat from Pakistan's embassy in Washington, sent a note to Kennedy praising *Profiles in Courage*. He was confident it would be "permanently accorded a high place in the field of American biography." Ahmed Hussein, Egypt's ambassador to America, sent a wire extending his "hearty congratulations" to Kennedy for winning the coveted award.[39]

Members of the press sent the senator congratulatory notes that edged to the line of professional detachment and propriety. Warren Duffee, a reporter for United Press International, told Kennedy the award was "quite an honor and I know you're justly proud of it." "Dear Jack," wrote Cabell Phillips of the *New York Times*. "It couldn't have happened to a nicer guy and a better book. It's also comforting, of course, to have my judgment as a book critic confirmed by so august a body of double-domes as the Pulitzer board." Phillips was referring to the laudatory review of the book he wrote for his paper when *Profiles in Courage* was published in 1956.

Accolades also came from unlikely sources. Fred Seaton, President Eisenhower's secretary of the interior, sent Kennedy a note saying he was eager to "join the many who will be extending congratulations to you." He added that Kennedy's book had "long since become a permanent addition to my personal library. Enjoyed it tremendously." Sister Mary Frumentia of Swartz Creek, Michigan, sent the senator a Holy Card as an expression of congratulations. Bernard Gimbel, chairman of the board of the famous Gimbel Brothers department store in New York City, told Kennedy that the award confirmed he was on the road to great success. "In the relatively few years that you've been around, you have shown great versatility and are rendering your fellow citizens splendid service." The staff of the Hotel Vendome in Boston wired words of congratulation to the senator, as did the presidents of Notre Dame University, Loras College, and the registrar of Ana Maria College in Paxton, Massachusetts, who also invited the senator to stop by the campus that coming weekend to look at a new building.[40]

Bernard Weitzer, the national legislative director of the Jewish War Veterans, told Kennedy the award confirmed his literary prowess, and he attempted to put it into an appropriate historical perspective. "No one can now question the fact that you are a great author. I hope that you may have the opportunity soon for a repeat performance. Being an author does not happen too often for a Senator. The only one I can recall offhand is the late Senator Albert Beveridge of Indiana. He wrote an excellent biography of John Marshall and also a good little book called *Tales from the Bible* or *Heroes from the Bible*."[41]

Kennedy also received a letter he must have valued greatly from one of the nation's most venerable historians, Henry Steele Commager at Amherst College. "Just a word to congratulate you on winning the Pulitzer—and on the Pulitzer for awarding the prize to you. I trust you are deep in another book now, even with all of your Senatorial and other public duties."[42]

Kennedy responded with thank you notes to those who had sent him their congratulations, which blended pride with self-deprecation. "Needless to say I was most gratified by the announcement; and the pleasure of it all was heightened by the generous messages I received from you and other friends. Thanks for thinking of me—but don't count on a repeat performance!"[43]

About a week after the award was announced, Gilbert Seldes, a columnist for the *Village Voice*, wrote an article that claimed Kennedy had a "collaborator" for *Profiles in Courage*. He also dismissed the book as being below Pulitzer quality. "It shows no research. It hasn't a point of view beyond the one indicated in the title: courage is a Good Thing. It is the most innocuous book published in a generation."[44] Several months later, Kennedy received a letter from Emma Sheehy, a professor at Columbia University, who said she had heard a rumor that Kennedy's book was "entirely ghost written by somebody else." She asked Kennedy to assure her this was not true.[45] He immediately wrote back and told Sheehy the rumor was "completely and utterly untrue," adding the "apparent source of this rumor" was Seldes's column that may have been misunderstood. "I suppose the natural growth of a false rumor made the step from 'had a collaborator' to 'completely ghost written' inevitable," Kennedy wrote. With more than a little defensiveness, Kennedy said, "The false rumors concerning my book did not start until it had been awarded a Pulitzer Prize."[46]

However, the controversy did not end with this correspondence and in fact dramatically escalated on December 7, 1957, when journalist Drew Pearson charged on Mike Wallace's ABC television show that *Profiles in Courage* was ghostwritten. Kennedy was furious at Pearson's charge and clearly fearful for his reputation. His father hired Washington attorney Clark Clifford to secure a public retraction from Pearson and

ABC. As part of this process, Sorensen agreed to the Kennedy family's request that he submit an affidavit declaring he was not the author of *Profiles in Courage* and that Kennedy "originally conceived its theme, selected its characters, determined its contents and wrote and rewrote each of its chapters."[47] During the controversy, Kennedy called Sorensen at home and said a vigorous rebuttal was needed to Pearson's charge. "We might as well quit if we let this stand," Kennedy told Sorensen.[48] The controversy over the Pulitzer Prize threatened to demolish all that Kennedy and his staff had been laboring to promote about the senator's talents and credibility.[49] Kennedy's aggressive rebuttal won the day and the matter faded, but the primary authorship of *Profiles in Courage* remains a controversy more than half a century later.

Sorensen remained careful, even evasive, about his contribution to the book for the rest of his life. "As I said under oath, the book's concept was his, and the selection of stories was his. He immersed himself in the book's research, provided its philosophy, wrote or rewrote each of its chapters, chose its title, and provided constant directions and corrections to those of us supplying him raw material," Sorensen wrote in his 2008 memoir.[50]

IV

Despite the continuing debate about Kennedy's authorship of the book, it was a huge boon to his Senate career and later to his presidential candidacy. After the publication of *Profiles in Courage*, Kennedy was frequently invited to write articles for publications of all kinds. Articles under Kennedy's byline appeared in popular magazines and in smaller journals, including *Vogue*, *Life*, *Look*, *New York Times Magazine*, *Kiwanis Magazine*, *General Electric Defense Quarterly*, the *Bulletin of Atomic Scientists*, and the *National Parent-Teacher*. Many of the articles revolved around the theme of courage, such as an article Kennedy wrote for *McCall's* about "three American women of courage"—Anne Hutchinson, Jeannette Rankin, and Prudence Crandell. Kennedy also wrote several prominent book reviews, including one of a new book on the Senate, *Citadel*, by *New York Times* reporter William White, and another on a biography of Al Smith by historian Oscar Handlin.

Kennedy also spoke frequently about the need to bridge the worlds of power and ideas. He gave the keynote speech at the National Book Award banquet in New York in February 1956. Combining humor and self-deprecation with a serious message, Kennedy called for a truce in the battle between writers and politicians. Speaking as a politician, he said that writers were "the one army whose weapons we most fear." He observed wryly that he had traveled to New York from Washington to "appeal for peace and understanding" between the two communities. "I have not come through the enemy's lines today to accentuate our differences, but to plead for recognition of our similarities." Writers and political leaders shared a common ancestry since the nation's first great politicians were also its leading writers. He cited Thomas Jefferson, James Madison, Benjamin Franklin, Thomas Paine, Alexander Hamilton, and John Adams as prime examples. "Books were their tools, not their enemies," Kennedy said, adding that for more than a century this link between the American literary and political worlds was unbroken. But this link was now shattered to the detriment of the country. "Where are the scholar-statesmen of yesteryear?" he asked.[51]

Speaking at Harvard's commencement in June 1956, Kennedy told the graduates and their families that politicians had much to learn from the academy, declaring, "The political profession needs to have its temperature lowered in the cooling waters of the scholastic pool. We need both the technical judgment and the disinterested viewpoint of the scholar, to prevent us from becoming imprisoned by our own slogans." But academics and intellectuals should conduct their research aware of the importance of practical advice and mindful of the messy and often unsatisfying realities of political life. It was regrettable, he said, that the gap between the intellectual and the politician seemed to be widening. "Instead of synthesis, clash and discord now characterize the relations between the two groups much of the time. Authors, scholars and intellectuals can praise every aspect of American society but the political." He said his desk was stacked with books, articles, and pamphlets criticizing Congress, but rarely, if ever, had he seen any intellectuals praise the political profession or any political body for its accomplishments, its ability, or its integrity— much less for its intelligence. "It seems to me the time has come for intellectuals and politicians alike to put aside those horrible weapons of modern internecine warfare, the barbed thrust, the acid pen and, most cynical of all, the rhetorical blast. Let us not emphasize all on which we differ but all we have in common," he implored. Kennedy said there was a need for greater cooperation and understanding between politicians and intellectuals. "What we need are men who can ride easily over broad fields of knowledge and recognize the mutual dependence of our two worlds," he said, presumably thinking of himself. "If more politicians knew poetry and more poets knew politics, I am convinced the world would be a little better place in which to live on this commencement day of 1956."[52] Lyndon Johnson enjoyed Kennedy's speech so much he put it into the *Congressional Record*, calling it "the most eloquent defense of politics and politicians that has ever been my pleasure to read."[53]

In a similar vein, Kennedy reflected on what he called "The Education of an American Politician," in a 1957 speech to a group of school administrators. "It is disheartening to me, and I think alarming for our Republic, to realize how poorly the political profession is regarded in America. Mothers may still want their favorite son to grow up to be President but, according to a famous Gallup poll of some years ago, they do not want them to become politicians in the process." There was a need for leaders with a "broad range of talents" to enter the political arena. He cited an obituary for Senator Thomas Hart Benton with evident admiration. He saw Benton as a kind of rustic Renaissance man and greatly admired his range of interests and talents: "With a readiness that was often surprising, he could quote from Roman law or a Greek philosopher, from Virgil's *Georgics*, *The Arabian Nights*, Herodotus, or Sancho Panza, from Sacred Carpets, the German reforms or Adam Smith; from Fenolon or Hudubras, from the financial reports of Necca or the doings of the Council of Trent, from the debates on the adoption of the Constitution or intrigues of the kitchen cabinet or from some forgotten speech of a deceased member of Congress."[54]

Kennedy said there was need for scholarship that was "fitted for practical action." When teaching political science, it was important to avoid the confusion of political idealism with political fantasy or rigidity—otherwise any compromise was viewed as immoral. The academic world needed support from politicians, and political leaders needed the ideas and perspective offered by the academy. "I ask for your thoughtful attention to the task of uniting our two worlds still further," he told the group.[55]

With the 1960 campaign looming, Kennedy asked law professor Harris Wofford and historian Allan Nevins to assemble a book composed largely of his major Senate speeches on foreign policy with several additional essays. It was designed to show liberals that Kennedy was one of them and to show the world that he was a man of ideas and intellectual firepower. The book, *The Strategy of Peace*, was most striking in displaying the range of Kennedy's interests, his willingness to offer detailed and carefully articulated programs, and the depth of his grasp of history. Speech after speech was packed with historical analogies and references. With apparent ease, he quoted Arnold Toynbee, Edward Gibbon,

Abraham Lincoln, and Herodotus, and he discussed the War of 1812, life on the Oregon Trail, and the medieval Crusades.

In one speech describing how the United States needed to confront the growing missile threat from the Soviet Union, Kennedy discussed Great Britain's challenge after the loss of Calais in the sixteenth century. The British were devastated by the loss of their last foothold in Europe, which was surrendered to the French in 1558. "Once they had recovered from their initial panic, the British set about adjusting their thinking and their policies to the loss they had suffered," Kennedy said. "With their gateway to the Continent gone, they sought new power and influence in the seas. A navy built, new trade routes promoted, a new maritime emphasis established; and when the Spanish Armada was defeated in 1588, the panic and pessimism that had followed the loss of Calais were forgotten as Britannia ruled the waves. The old power, the foundation for old policies, was gone—but new policies had brought a new power and new security."[56]

Kennedy argued that the English loss of Calais altered the course of British diplomatic and military policy. Acceptance of the loss and the adjustment of policy were not easily or quickly accomplished, but they occurred eventually and allowed Britain to reestablish its preeminence on a different foundation. "There is every indication that by 1960 the United States will have lost its Calais—its superiority in nuclear striking power," he said, adding, "There is no reason why we, too, cannot successfully emerge from this period of peril more secure than ever." Kennedy concluded that the United States should use all the elements of its national power—economic, military, and diplomatic—to prepare for the most serious test in the nation's history. Summoning a tone of urgency, Kennedy quoted Churchill: "Let us go forward together in all of the [land]. There is not a week, nor a day, nor an hour to be lost."[57]

Kennedy's office sent out 250 copies of *The Strategy of Peace* to intellectuals and opinion leaders across the country. One note of appreciation he received was from a young Harvard professor named Henry Kissinger. "A copy of your book has just come into my office. And I am writing to thank you for having it sent and to tell you that I am looking forward with great interest to reading it."[58]

V

As a senator, Kennedy could have sought many possible roles: Democratic Party leader, spokesman for New England, advocate for a particular interest group, lobbyist for a cause, or policy specialist. While seeking to establish a reputation as a foreign policy expert, Kennedy's temperament, talent, opportunity, and cast of mind persuaded him to embrace the role of the Senate's intellectual, a statesman-scholar who could bridge the worlds of action and ideas. This gave him a niche and a role that became an integral part of his political persona.

Kennedy positioned himself to run for president in 1960 as a modern, practical politician who was also steeped in history and comfortable in the realm of ideas. This image was ripe for caricature. "Senator Kennedy's role in the Senate is like that of the visiting literary professor," quipped a writer for *The Progressive* magazine. "The glamorous young man who wows the students, makes a hit with the faculty wives and stays aloof from the dull grind of the campus. This exasperates some of Kennedy's colleagues. They see him running about the country making headlines and reaping political hay while they attend to the chores."[59]

Lyndon Johnson, the Democratic leader of the Senate during Kennedy's Senate career and a political rival, admired Kennedy for his academic and literary accomplishments but also derided him as a man of talk rather than action. "He never said a word of importance in the Senate and he never did a thing," Johnson once said of Kennedy. "But somehow with his books and his Pulitzer Prizes he managed to create the image of himself as a shining intellectual, a youthful leader who would change the face of the country."[60] Johnson's assessment of Kennedy was too harsh but did touch on an important part of the young senator's appeal. Winning the Pulitzer Prize was a pivotal moment in Kennedy's political career given his ambition to be a man of action and letters. Like his hero Winston Churchill, Kennedy sought to inhabit and excel in both of these worlds. He aspired to be a man of action and intellect and a historian-scholar-statesman. The Pulitzer and many of his other writings and speeches helped him establish this identity.

Eight
The Kennedy Committee

I

On August 2, 1955, as Congress was approaching the end of its legislative year, the acting Senate majority leader, Earle Clements, and the minority leader, William Knowland, went to the Senate floor to offer a resolution to create a special Senate committee to determine five outstanding senators in U.S. history. After a brief discussion, it was approved on a voice vote. Senate majority leader Lyndon Johnson, who was recovering in Bethesda Naval Hospital from a heart attack he suffered the previous month, had conceived of the idea. Speaking on Johnson's behalf, Clements and Knowland said those selected would have their portraits displayed in the ornate reception room adjacent to the Senate chamber in the spaces left vacant when Italian artist Constantino Brumidi designed the room nearly a century earlier.[1]

Johnson had a deep interest in the Senate as an institution and thought such an inquiry into excellence within it would direct the attention of the country toward Congress's upper chamber. Johnson said on several occasions that the project was designed to identify the five *greatest* senators in American history, but the resolution the Senate passed on that August day was less clear, saying only that the committee would choose five *outstanding* senators. Others said the panel would identify the *most illustrious* senators in American history. Johnson believed the committee would capture the nation's attention, with opinion leaders debating the merits of various senators and schools across the country holding contests in which students would research and write about their state's great senators. Johnson also hoped the project would help educate the large influx of recently elected senators about the Senate's history and encourage them to embrace role models from American history. This project was unique, reflecting Johnson's respect for the Senate and his belief that the upper chamber should be better appreciated in America and around the world. It also reflected the Senate's institutional self-confidence and its conviction that such a project would be compelling to the public and would be seen as an appropriate way of validating the strength of the U.S. political system.

Vice President Richard Nixon, the president of the Senate, formally appointed five members to the committee in September 1955, and to no one's surprise, Johnson was selected as the committee's chairman. Nixon also named Democrats Richard Russell of Georgia and Mike Mansfield of

Montana and Republicans Styles Bridges of New Hampshire and Eugene Millikin of Colorado to the panel. The men chosen to form the special committee were noteworthy because each was a formidable lawmaker and one of the handful of members who drove the Senate's agenda and accomplished much of the chamber's essential work, often behind the scenes.

Johnson was delighted to chair the committee that would pick the Senate's so-called Hall of Fame or Famous Five.[2] Johnson directed his aide, William Kittrell, to work with historian Walter Webb, a professor at the University of Texas, on an operational plan for the Johnson Committee. Kittrell envisioned a massive survey of all current senators, some former senators, former presidents and first ladies, historians, and commentators to determine the five outstanding senators in American history.[3]

But the Johnson Committee never got going. As Johnson spent the summer and fall of 1955 convalescing at his Texas ranch, he lost interest in the special committee and became more focused on developing a legislative agenda to propose when the Senate convened in January 1956. He was also preparing for a major debate on President Eisenhower's interstate highway proposal and a looming battle over civil rights legislation. Johnson was ready to get back to the serious business of lawmaking.

II

Given his best-selling *Profiles in Courage* and his growing reputation as the Senate's historian, Kennedy was an obvious successor to Johnson. On April 11, 1956, Vice President Nixon named him to replace Johnson as the new chairman of the Senate's special committee.[4] Kennedy jumped into the assignment with alacrity. His first task was to create a credible selection process so his committee could choose the five outstanding senators. He sought the advice of Allan Nevins, one of the nation's most popular and respected historians, with whom Kennedy had worked on other projects. Kennedy asked Nevins to chair an advisory board of nine prominent historians and political scientists, balanced by region and political affiliation, to establish criteria for selecting the winning senators. That advisory board then suggested 150 scholars to be surveyed to narrow the list of senators to be considered for the Hall of Fame. Kennedy told Nevins that he wanted to select the most deserving senators and not get bogged down by political considerations. He recalled that Arthur Schlesinger Sr. had polled historians several years earlier to determine the best presidents in American history. Kennedy wondered if his panel could devise a similar survey to identify the five best senators. While he was determined to get the best advice from the academic world, Kennedy made it clear that the senators on his committee would make the final decisions.

On June 1, Kennedy sent a memo to the four other members of what became known as the Kennedy Committee to bring them up to date on the project since he had assumed the chairmanship six weeks earlier. He said he was continuing to think about how they should conduct their work and had consulted with the executive directors of the American Historical Association, the American Political Science Association, and the archivist of the United States, along with other scholars. Kennedy wanted to make the process as merit oriented as possible. "It seems important to insure that careful consideration be given to the selection of the outstanding Senators so that those most deserving the honor will be chosen; at the same time it is important to separate the selection process from political or log-rolling considera-tions," he wrote to his colleagues.[5]

The Kennedy Committee met a week later in the senator's office and agreed on Kennedy's basic approach to the project. They also agreed to modify the Senate resolution so that all five of the senators would be selected by May 1, 1957, rather than have a single individual named each year as called for in the original 1955 resolution. Johnson and Knowland, the two Senate leaders, approved of the Kennedy Committee's modified plan.

Nevins was joined on the advisory panel by Wilfred Binkley of Ohio Northern University, Fletcher Green of the University of North Carolina, Ernest Griffith from the Library of Congress, John Hicks of the University of California–Berkeley, Arthur Holcombe of Harvard University, Merritt Pound of the University of Georgia, Walter Webb of the University of Texas, and Leonard White of the University of Chicago. The advisory board agreed on criteria for the five outstanding senators. They should be chosen without regard to their service in other offices, they should be distinguished for acts of statesmanship transcending state and party lines, and the statesmanship should include leadership in national thought and constitutional interpretation as well as legislation.

Kennedy sent the survey to 150 scholars in February and March 1957 and included this request: "Although the final decision must rest with the Senate Committee, the counsel of the panel will play an important role in our determination. The choice must of course be made with care and with attention to the claims of different groups, parties and sections," he wrote. "The Committee will be extremely grateful if, after careful thought, you will furnish us the names of the five Senators whom you regard as most worthy of this distinction, indicating the reasons for your choice."[6]

Nearly all the surveys were returned in the late winter and early spring of 1957. Samuel Flagg Bemis of Yale, James MacGregor Burns of Williams, Henry Steele Commager of Amherst, Edward Corwin of Princeton, Dumas Malone of Columbia, Arthur Schlesinger Jr. and Sr. of Harvard, C. Vann Woodward of Johns Hopkins, Richard Current of the University of North Carolina, and Kenneth Stampp of the University of California–Berkeley were among the scholars who sent responses. Some wrote elegant, carefully reasoned essays, while others submitted cryptic notes that simply listed their top five senators.[7]

"Of the hundreds of illustrious men who have served in the Senate, most spent their time on the legislative stage and disappeared in the wings of oblivion," proclaimed George Galloway from the Library of Congress's Legislative Research Service. "But a few mighty men of old writ large their names on the scroll of time and achieved lasting fame," he said, and then offered his suggestions of Henry Clay of Kentucky, Daniel Webster of Massachusetts, John Sherman of Ohio, George Norris of Nebraska, and Robert Wagner of New York. Earl Latham, a professor at Amherst College, was less convinced that his ideas would be taken seriously in the decision making of the Kennedy Committee. "Dear Sir," he wrote, "I am sure that your advisory committee is capable of picking five senators without my advice. For whatever it is worth, my choice would be as follows," he said, suggesting Webster, Calhoun, Norris, Arthur Vandenberg of Michigan, and Oliver Ellsworth of Connecticut. Kenneth Stampp of Berkeley said the task of selecting the five senators "doubtless seems simpler to me than it will to your committee." There was, he declared, a powerful case for naming Calhoun, Webster, Clay, Robert LaFollete Sr. of Wisconsin, and Norris, not feeling the need to elaborate on his selections. "The role of each of these men is so familiar to you that further comment from me is pointless," Stampp wrote. Lynwood Holland at Emory University offered his choices quickly: Clay, Calhoun, Webster, Norris, and LaFollette. He then lavished praise on Kennedy's new book and moved on to what appeared to be the central point of his letter. He invited Kennedy to speak at Emory "if and when you are ever in Atlanta." Arthur Schlesinger Jr. outlined five choices he said would make a "fairly balanced ticket." They were Clay, Calhoun, Webster, Norris, and Wagner. However, his father, Arthur Schlesinger Sr., seemed to find the exercise less than enthralling. "Dear Jack," he wrote, "I am not as 'happy' as you assumed I would be to be on the panel to help choose the five senatorial immortals since I do not believe your committee is in a position to act purely on the basis of merit." But he grudgingly offered his picks. They were the same as his son's except that he chose Justin Smith Morrill of Vermont rather than Wagner.

Clinton Rossiter of Yale, a friend of Kennedy's, said he was "delighted that you turned to an old colleague" for advice. Rossiter named Webster as "the orator," Calhoun as "the constitutionalist," Clay as the "genius of compromise," Norris as the "model progressive," and Robert Taft of Ohio as the "model conservative." Henry Steele Commager of Amherst was certain who the first selection should be. "Daniel Webster is so obvious a choice that it would be superfluous to attempt a justification. Indeed if a single name were to be selected, that name would be, almost by common consent, Webster." Samuel Bemis of Yale suggested Sam Houston of Texas, John Quincy Adams of Massachusetts, Webster, Clay, and Vandenberg. He ended his note with a lofty flourish. "Let us hope, my dear Senator, that your reaction toward some chapter of events in an unknown future may lead a panel of historians a century hence to choose your name and portrait for such high distinction."

When the scholarly submissions were calculated by the Kennedy Committee, the top vote getter was Norris, followed by Clay, Webster, Calhoun, and LaFollette.[8]

The panel also asked for recommendations from current senators, prominent former senators, and other public figures, including the two living former presidents, Herbert Hoover and Harry Truman. "Dear Senator," Truman wrote to Kennedy from Independence, Missouri, "At long last, and after much study and research, I have assembled the names of those Senators who are considered great, if only in my own estimation. There are so many to be considered that I do not see how you will ever be able to arrive at the five greatest." Truman then attached a long memo, outlining 42 senators he found impressive and offering intriguing nuggets on many of them. Albert Beveridge of Indiana was worth considering, Truman said, but added he was "noted more for his literary ability than his political career. His life of John Marshall is considered an authority." Truman described Hiram Johnson of California as a "great progressive" while Alva Adams of Colorado was a "great conservative in times when the Democratic Party needed a safety break." John Ingalls of Kansas was also a senator with a literary flair, Truman said, but added that he probably "plagiarized his great poem, *Opportunity*." The former president praised Clay as a "truly great legislator" who "was never treated fairly by the New England historians." He was less convinced of Webster's merits. "Mr. Webster's public ethics were practically nonexistent. He was in the pay of Biddle's United States Bank." James Blaine of Maine was a "great politician," Truman said, adding, "My old rebel Democratic grandfather always said he was the smartest Republican of his time." Truman told Kennedy he was coming to Washington in about a month and would enjoy meeting with the senator and his panel to discuss his recommendations. Truman liked the project so much that he said he was going to suggest that House Speaker Sam Rayburn organize a similar one for the lower chamber.[9]

President Hoover was less enamored with the exercise. Writing from his suite at the Waldorf Astoria in Manhattan, he had little to say. "My dear Senator," he began. "I simply do not have enough knowledge to pick out the five greatest Senators. I suppose Clay and Webster would be eligible for consideration. Also, the Sherman Anti-Trust Law was one of the greatest preservatives of the American way of life. With kind regards, Yours Faithfully, Herbert Hoover." It's unclear how Kennedy regarded this perplexing letter from the former president that identified two senators and a law as his recommendations for the Senate's Hall of Fame.[10]

Intriguing letters drifted in from Kennedy's colleagues in the Senate. Ranging from the perfunctory to the profound, they were variously addressed to "John," "Jack," "Senator Kennedy," and "Senator" depending on the sender's relationship to Kennedy. Russell Long of Louisiana and Al Gore Sr. of Tennessee wrote back to Kennedy to say they didn't have any nominations—at least yet. Barry Goldwater of Arizona, a recently elected senator, said it would be "presumptuous" for "one as young as I am to attempt to pick any one of that number." But then he added, "If you want me to" offer some names, he would. And he did: Henry Ashhurst from Arizona and Robert Taft.[11]

Paul Douglas of Illinois wrote a short, elegant note, naming Clay, Thomas Hart Benton of Missouri, LaFollette, and Norris, "the noblest of them all." He stopped at four nominations. "I think I will stand on these," he wrote. "I should like to protest the possible inclusion of Daniel Webster because while able and influential, he was undoubtedly venal."

Frank Barrett of Utah wrote a long, rambling, touching essay about one of his predecessors, Francis Warren, who was the last Union soldier to serve in Congress. He had been a farmer, soldier, war hero, pioneer rancher, politician, and statesman who, according to Barrett, held firm to his principles and was able to reach compromises without sacrificing his values. Several weeks before the committee's final decisions were announced, Senator John Marshall Butler of Maryland sent Kennedy a peculiar note in which he not only nominated the five senators who would eventually be selected but also offered the services of a Maryland painter to create the portraits of the eventual honorees. The painter,

Butler informed Kennedy, "has been working on the project for many months and has already completed what I believe to be excellent portraits of Senators Taft, Clay, Calhoun and Webster. The artist's research for portraits of Senators LaFollette and George W. Norris is now underway." Butler either had good sources within the Kennedy Committee or was a confident predictor to have commissioned the paintings that were then in his office awaiting Kennedy's review. Butler did hedge his bets by also requesting a sixth painting of Norris, who was not selected. There is no record of whether Kennedy ever strolled down the hall of the Senate Office Building to examine the unsolicited artwork in Butler's office.

Many current senators only nominated former senators from their own state. Strom Thurmond suggested South Carolinians Burnett Rhett Maybank, Charles Pinckney, Wade Hampton, and Benjamin Tillman, as well as John Calhoun. Sam Ervin of North Carolina nominated two almost comically obscure senators from his state: Willie Person Mangum and Zebulon Vance. William Fulbright of Arkansas nominated Joseph Robinson. Stuart Symington of Missouri took the state-centric course, but first buttered up Kennedy. "Dear Jack," he wrote, "I most certainly would recommend Missouri's first Senator, about whom you have written so splendidly, Thomas Hart Benton." Senator Edward Martin of Pennsylvania wrote, "Dear Jack, I am limiting my suggestions to Pennsylvanians because I presume that other Senators will nominate the great Senators from their respective states." But the other Pennsylvania senator, Joe Clark, was more modest. "I am afraid my knowledge of Senate history does not qualify me to make much of a contribution to the work of your special committee." But then he added, "For what it is worth, and largely off the top of my head, the following names occur to me: Clay, Webster, Benton, William Borah, LaFollette and Norris." Clark concluded, "I deeply regret the absence of any Pennsylvanian on my list; but I am afraid it would be difficult for any former senator from our Commonwealth to meet the competition of the above names."[12]

Senator A. Willis Robertson of Virginia sent Kennedy an edgy, cantankerous letter. He had studied the opinions of the 150 historians and political scientists Kennedy had polled and was not impressed. "Their conclusions about who has been great in the Senate really astound me," he snapped. He derided Kennedy's "so-called historians" for rating Wagner and Norris highly. "Then your so-called experts give 42 votes to LaFollette," he wrote before accusing LaFollette of being corrupt. Senator Carl Curtiss of Nebraska declined to submit the name of any senator but offered a suggestion that seemed a thinly veiled threat. Curtiss suggested that before Kennedy's

Committee issued its report, a state's current senators must concur with the inclusion of any past senator from their state. "I am sure you understand the spirit in which I make this suggestion," he wrote.[13]

III

For their final deliberations, the Kennedy Committee members drew on detailed biographies prepared by the Library of Congress and their own independent research. They received more than 600 letters from the public and reviewed newspaper editorials opining on the Senate's Hall of Fame. The committee's survey of more than 150 academics yielded 65 nominations. They had much to discuss.

Kennedy presided over a committee that was composed largely of Senate elders. Since it was initially formed, John Bricker, a Republican from Ohio, replaced Eugene Millikin, the Colorado Republican, who did not run for reelection in 1956 and thus left the Senate in January 1957. And Kennedy, of course, replaced Johnson as a member and as the chairman of the committee.

The elder statesman on the Kennedy Committee was Richard Russell, arguably the most respected man in the Senate. A native of Georgia, Russell was elected to the Georgia General Assembly at the age of 23 and served in that chamber for a decade. He became Speaker of the Assembly during his last two terms. Russell was elected governor of Georgia in 1930 but did not serve long. The death of Georgia senator William Harris in 1932 opened up a U.S. Senate seat for which Russell ran and won. He was sworn in in January 1933 and served in the Senate until his death in 1971. Russell rose to senior positions on the powerful Senate Appropriations and Armed Services committees and could have been elected Senate Democratic leader on a number of occasions if he had wanted the job. But he didn't, preferring to focus on legislation. Russell was an expert on agriculture, budget, and national security issues. The author of the school lunch program, he was also an early champion of food stamps for the poor. By the 1950s, Russell had emerged as one of the most powerful senators in Washington. He was a member of the Democratic Policy Committee and the Democratic Steering Committee, two panels with influence on committee assignments and the legislative agenda.[14]

Russell spoke sparingly on the Senate floor, preferring to work behind the scenes to exert influence. He was frequently praised for his integrity, fairness, wisdom, and ability to forge compromises. Respect for him within the Senate grew in 1951 when he cochaired hearings in the aftermath of the firing of General Douglas MacArthur by President Truman. Russell insisted the hearings be held behind closed doors to quiet the public uproar that had erupted across the nation. He also expanded the hearings so they focused on broader national security issues rather than the personality clash between Truman and MacArthur. And in a shrewd move, he opted not to issue a final report, which would only underscore partisan differences on the matter.

Russell was also a passionate segregationist and a ferocious opponent of civil rights legislation. As chairman of the Southern Caucus, he resisted reforms from the 1940s through the end of his career. He played a major role in drafting the Southern Manifesto that was published in March 1956 in the aftermath of the sweeping *Brown v. Board of Education* Supreme Court ruling. The manifesto, signed by 19 senators and 77 House members, urged southern states to resist integration, as mandated by the Supreme Court, by any lawful means. According to one biographer, his prolonged battle against civil rights legislation "took an unbelievable amount of Russell's time and energy" and diminished his ultimate legacy.[15] But even with this major flaw, Russell was a revered and respected figure in the Senate.

Russell liked and respected Kennedy and described him as a "very capable young man."

They shared a love of history and discussed the topic frequently. Edward Kennedy recalled one Christmas Eve when he was discussing Civil War history with his brother Jack, who could not recall the details of a specific 1863 battle in which the Confederate forces halted a Union advance into Georgia. Jack called Russell at his Senate office and got a detailed account of the three-day Battle of Chickamauga.[16]

The other Democrat serving on the Kennedy Committee was Mike Mansfield. Born in New York City, Mansfield lost both of his parents as a young boy and was adopted by relatives living in Montana. While still in his teens, he ran away from home to enlist in the navy. He later served in the army and marines. After World War I, Mansfield worked as a miner in Butte, attended the Montana School of Mines, and graduated from Montana State University with a degree in history. He had been a history professor at Montana State University for nearly a decade when he decided to run for Congress. Elected to the House in 1942, he served for decade. He was a member of the House Foreign Affairs Committee, became an expert on Asia, and in 1944 he served as a special envoy to China for President Franklin Roosevelt.[17]

Mansfield was elected to the Senate in 1952, the same year as Kennedy, and quickly became a star of the class. He was immediately selected to sit on the Senate Foreign Relations Committee by Democratic leader Lyndon Johnson, as was another young senator, Hubert Humphrey. Johnson quipped that he wanted Mansfield on the prestigious panel to outthink Republican Robert Taft, while Humphrey's role would be to outtalk Taft.[18] A loyal Democrat, Mansfield was also willing to cooperate with the Eisenhower administration on some issues, especially regarding foreign policy. He took several trips to Indochina, was consulted by the White House, and generally supported the Eisenhower administration's stance toward the region.

Mansfield traveled extensively in the 1950s, solidifying his reputation as a foreign policy expert. He took 18 trips abroad in his first 14 years in the House and Senate and typically wrote detailed reports and delivered major speeches about his travels. In 1956, Mansfield delivered ten major foreign policy speeches to the Senate, and the following year he gave a 49-page address, "The Next Stage in Foreign Policy." His speeches were scholarly and restrained. When he criticized the administration's foreign policy, he usually offered alternatives.[19]

Honest, direct, and soft-spoken, Mansfield became the Democratic whip in 1957, making him the second-ranking Democrat in the Senate behind Lyndon Johnson. When he first arrived in the Senate, Mansfield sat next to Kennedy in the back row. Although they came from very different social and political worlds, the two men shared a deep interest in foreign policy and history and got along well. Mansfield said early in Kennedy's Senate career that he believed his colleague from Massachusetts could win the presidency.

Styles Bridges of New Hampshire was the senior Republican on the Kennedy Committee. He began his professional career working on agricultural issues, serving as the executive secretary of the New Hampshire Farm Bureau Federation. Bridges became a protégé of former Governor Robert Bass; in 1930, he was appointed to the New Hampshire Public Service Commission. In 1934, he secured the Republican nomination for governor of New Hampshire and won the election that year, becoming the nation's youngest governor. Two years later he was elected to the Senate despite FDR's landslide. When he entered the Senate in 1937, Bridges was one of only 16 Republicans in the upper chamber.[20]

Bridges was a fierce critic of most of FDR's domestic agenda, especially his plans to enlarge the Supreme Court and reorganize the executive branch. He voted against most New Deal domestic legislation but generally supported Roosevelt's internationalist foreign policy even before World War II. Shrewd and effective in face-to-face dealings, Bridges quietly grew into a Senate power. He was able to mediate between the GOP's internationalist and isolationist factions and also strike deals with Democrats such as Johnson and Russell. He served on the Senate Appropriations and Armed Services panels throughout his career and twice chaired the Appropriations Committee. Bridges served as the Senate Republican leader in 1952, the Senate president pro tempore from 1953 to 1954, and chairman of the Senate Republican policy committee from 1955 to 1960. Although he wrote no major legislation, for decades Bridges was widely considered the Senate's prime Republican power broker. He earned a reputation as a man who knew the Senate and who could work with politicians on both sides of the aisle. A tough partisan, he was also pragmatic. "He was a subtle, sophisticated political leader," conservative columnist Robert Novak wrote of Bridges. "A master of negotia-tions in his hideaway office just off the Senate floor, Bridges flourished during the heyday of the bipartisan Senate oligarchy. Other oligarchs declined in influence with the advent of Lyndon B. Johnson as Majority Leader in the early 50s, but Bridges maintained his leverage as the Republican leader closest to LBJ."[21] Richard Russell called his colleague a "Senate man," adding that Bridges protected the prerogatives of the Senate and "appreciated the fact that this was a body unique in all the parliamentary history of the world."[22]

John Bricker of Ohio, a hard-charging Republican conservative, rounded out the Kennedy

Committee. Bricker was elected attorney general of Ohio in 1932 and reelected in 1934. His run for governor in 1936 ended in defeat. But he ran again in 1938, was elected, and was reelected twice. Bricker sought the Republican presidential nomination in 1944 and was defeated by New York governor Thomas Dewey, who then chose him as his vice presidential running mate. Roosevelt and his running mate, Harry Truman, trounced the Dewey-Bricker ticket. Bricker rebounded by winning election to the Senate in 1946 and was reelected in 1952. He resided squarely in the conservative wing of the GOP. He tried to cut federal spending, opposed government regulation, resisted most foreign aid, and defended Joseph McCarthy. "Joe," he famously said to McCarthy, "You're a son of a bitch, but there are times when you've got to have a son of a bitch around, and this is one of them."[23]

Bricker was a significant foreign policy figure in the Senate of the mid-1950s as the sponsor of a constitutional amendment that sought to limit the impact of treaties on domestic law and prevent the use of executive agreements as a substitute for treaties. The Senate was consumed by debates and votes on variations of the Bricker amendment for several years. Eisenhower strongly opposed most of them, arguing they would limit presidential flexibility to conduct foreign policy. "I am so sick of the Bricker Amendment I could scream. The whole damn thing is senseless and plain damaging to the prestige of the United States," Eisenhower once snapped.[24]

Stately and even regal-looking, with a mane of white hair, Bricker looked like a senator from central casting. But many disputed that he comported himself as one. In his book *Inside USA*, journalist John Gunther offered a withering assessment of Bricker that resonated in the political world. "Little record exists that Bricker has ever said anything worth more than 30 seconds of consideration by anybody. Intellectually, he is like interstellar space—a vast vacuum occasionally crossed by homeless, wandering clichés." Even Taft, the senior Republican senator from Ohio, was not impressed with Bricker. On the eve of Bricker's 1944 presidential campaign, Taft said, "He hasn't got the ability to speak and say anything and is almost certain to make a lot of mistakes."[25]

The five-member Kennedy Committee consisted of several of the Senate's heavy hitters. It had the Senate's leading statesman in Russell, two rising stars from the Democratic Party in Kennedy and Mansfield, the Senate's shrewdest operator in Bridges, and one of the Republican Party's most stalwart and forceful firebrands in Bricker. As the committee intensified its deliberations in the spring of 1957, the members easily agreed on their first three choices: the "Great Triumvirate" of Senators Daniel Webster, Henry Clay, and John

Calhoun. These three dominated American politics and government before the Civil War and were widely touted as the gold standard of effective and forceful senators.

Kennedy generally agreed with these selections but was also aware that each had serious detractors with specific objections. He wrote to historians Arthur Schlesinger Jr., Arthur Holcombe, and Allan Nevins, asking if criticism of Webster, Clay, and Calhoun was sufficiently serious to disqualify any of them from the final list. Kennedy knew that some historians contended that while Webster was a powerful orator, his skills as a legislator were less apparent. Others wondered if Webster's financial dealings with Nicholas Biddle and the Bank of the United States should take him out of the running. Some historians observed that while Calhoun offered a clear political philosophy and was a leading regional spokesman, he had also advocated disunion and slavery. Kennedy wondered if these stances should disqualify Calhoun from the final five. Kennedy questioned if Clay, while clearly a legendary Speaker of the House, had accomplished enough in the Senate to deserve recognition as one of its greats.

The three historians confirmed that Webster, Clay, and Calhoun were senators of the first rank and deserved to remain on the Kennedy Committee's final list. "I take it that your committee is selecting, not the most irreproachable or blameless senators, but the greatest ones," wrote Schlesinger Jr. "Great men often have bad habits, unpopular opinions and enemies; they are very often ambitious, tough and ruthless. But the committee, I take it, is not selecting a Sunday school superintendent, nor even a model for contemporary behavior. It is not awarding good conduct medals. It is trying to name the men whose presence in the Senate have most affected our history."[26]

Once the Kennedy Committee settled on Webster, Clay, and Calhoun, they debated their final two selections. After discussion, they decided to choose a leading conservative and a leading progressive from the twentieth century. The panel selected Robert Taft over John Sherman as the conservative and Robert LaFollette Sr. over George Norris as the progressive. According to Kennedy aide Ted Sorensen, Bridges rejected Norris "either because he had tangled with Norris many years earlier, as he admitted, or because he was acting for Nebraska's conservative senator Carl Curtiss, whose earlier request that each state's current senators be permitted to block the selection of any previous senator from their state had been politely rejected by Kennedy." Though Kennedy himself would have preferred Norris over LaFollette, he agreed to drop his personal choice in the interest of achieving a unanimous vote within his committee.[27]

IV

As his committee was nearing final agreement on its selections, Kennedy wrote an essay in the *New York Times* to build interest in the panel. On April 14, 1957, just two weeks before the committee's May 1 deadline, Kennedy's essay, "Search for the Five Greatest Senators," emphasized the difficulty of their task. Kennedy wrote, "The value of a Senator is not so easily determined as the value of a car or a hog, or even that of a public utility bond or a ballplayer. There are no standard tests to apply to a Senator, no Dunn & Bradstreet rating, no scouting reports. His talents may vary with his time; his contribution may be limited by his politics. To judge his true greatness, particularly in comparison with his fellow Senators long after they are all dead, is nearly an impossible task."[28]

Kennedy insisted the Senate, in its effort to identify the best senators, was not "idly engaged in some sort of historical quiz contest or game." The value of the deliberations went well beyond the mere selection of portraits. "For in these days when political and legislative service is too often ridiculed or disdained, it is particularly desirable that we focus the nation's attention upon the Senate and its distinguished traditions, stimulating interest in our political problems and motivations and understanding of the Senate's role in our government," he wrote.[29]

In order to illustrate how difficult it was to choose the five best senators, Kennedy identified some of the most obvious criteria and explained how they yielded more ambiguity than certainty. For example, some urged the panel to focus on senators associated with landmark legislation. But Kennedy noted that courageous opposition to flawed legislation is often as important as championing fresh ideas and writing new laws. And associating a senator with a particular bill can be misleading. There were a number of historical examples, Kennedy archly observed, where senators were credited with legislation they actually had little to do with and possibly didn't even understand.[30]

Some suggested the Kennedy Committee represent each major period of American history in its selection of the five senators. But Kennedy said some periods, such as from 1820 to 1868, conjured exceptional statesmanship from Congress, while other periods did not summon comparable greatness. "For the times and issues required greatness —to meet recurring crises between North and South, to meet the challenges of Western expansionism, to meet the tangled and tense problems of slavery, tariffs and national fiscal policies."[31]

Others called on his committee to give special consideration to senators with long records of service in the upper chamber. But Kennedy responded that some with relatively few years in the Senate made a large impact, such as Edmund

Ross of Kansas, John Henderson of Missouri, and Albert Beveridge of Indiana. Kennedy also challenged the idea that national leadership was essential, noting that John Calhoun "lived, and died, for Southern principles" but was still widely viewed as a Senate giant. Kennedy also felt that criteria such as public popularity during a senator's career and the respect of his contemporaries had to be evaluated carefully and should not be seen as definitive proof of greatness.[32]

Kennedy released his report on April 30, 1957, and the next day made the formal announcement on the Senate floor of his committee's selection of Henry Clay, Daniel Webster, John Calhoun, Robert LaFollette Sr., and Robert Taft as the five outstanding senators in American history. He personally invited the current senators from the states represented by the Famous Five to come to the Senate floor and hear his presentation and respond if they wished. Kennedy acknowledged that objections could be raised to all five choices, but it was important to celebrate "their overall statesmanship, their service to the Nation, and their impact on the Senate, the country, and our history." They were not necessarily the five greatest senators, nor the most blameless or irreproachable, nor models of contemporary behavior. Allowances needed to be made, Kennedy said, for the times, the morals, and the practices of the period in which they served.[33]

Kennedy said his panel was aware of the hazards of attempting to pass judgment on other members of the Senate. None of them were totally detached from the senators in question, nor were they professional historians themselves. The compelling nature of so many nominations made their assignment a nearly impossible task, he said, adding that he personally had the most difficulty excluding George Norris, Thomas Hart Benton, and Oliver Ellsworth from the final list.

Kennedy acknowledged that other senators might disagree with the committee's selections and said they should voice their objections or suggest their own preferences to the Senate. If a majority were opposed to the recommendations contained in the report, the Senate could reject his committee's work. Although individual senators had been asked to submit nominations, no attempt was made to seek approval of the committee's choices by the senators from the home states of the honorees as some had proposed. The committee was glad to defend its choices and methods against whatever objections might be raised. Kennedy also noted that of his committee's $10,000 budget, they spent only $532.32, and of that sum, $500 went to the Library of Congress for research.[34]

Describing the project's accomplishments, Kennedy said there was "considerable merit in stimulating interest among the general public and the Senate itself in the high traditions of the Senate, in the political problems faced by even our most distinguished statesmen and in the high standards of the past which might be inspiring or emulated today." He added that he hoped the project would be of value "at a time when the democratic way of life is under pressure from without and the problems and conflicting pressures involved in the political profession are frequently misunderstood within our country." He concluded, "The committee has attempted in a small way to focus the Nation's attention upon the Senate and its distinguished traditions, upon the high quality of men who have served in the Senate, and upon the significant role that the Senate has played in the history of our Nation."[35]

The committee also provided an honorable mention to some of the senators who were nominated by members of the Senate, the panel of scholars, and the public. These were Alben Barkley of Kentucky, Thomas Hart Benton of Missouri, William Borah of Idaho, Stephen Douglas of Illinois, Oliver Ellsworth of Connecticut, Carter Glass of Virginia, Justin Smith Morrill of Vermont, George Norris of Nebraska, John Sherman of Ohio, Charles Sumner of Massachusetts, Lyman Trumball of Illinois, Oscar Underwood of Alabama, Arthur Vandenberg of Michigan, Robert Wagner of New York, and Thomas Walsh of Montana.

V

The Kennedy Committee's final report was widely covered in the United States, both as a news story and as a topic of discussion in the nation's editorial pages. "Five 'Outstanding Senators of the Past' Named," read a *New York Times* article, which included extensive profiles of the five senators selected and described the work of the Kennedy Committee. The *Washington Post* noted the work of the Senate's "Hall of Fame" committee and said the final five senators were selected "after long deliberation and research." The Associated Press story proclaimed, "Five Named to Senate's Hall of Fame." The nation's major news magazines, *Time* and *Newsweek*, ran articles about the findings of the Kennedy Committee. *Life* published an extensive feature in its May 6 edition with a luminous Sophia Loren on its cover. It included color photographs of the Famous Five and an essay entitled, "The Immortals for the United States Senate."[36]

Several dozen articles ran in American newspapers discussing the work of the Kennedy Committee, largely in positive terms. The *New York Herald Tribune* said the panel's decision was a "balanced one and represents a fair judgment by this generation of Americans of their own history. It was a choice worth making, too, for the past always needs to be assessed if the present is to be intelligently interpreted. It speaks well of the Senators that they undertook to make the choice themselves."[37]

The *Evening Journal* of Wilmington, Delaware, said the Kennedy Committee had done the "all but impossible task" of selecting five outstanding senators in American history. "History, we believe, will confirm the committee's verdict. But perhaps it would be wiser, as the committee itself suggests, to expand the pantheon to include such other men as Thomas Hart Benton of Missouri, William Borah of Idaho, Carter Glass of Virginia, Charles Sumner of Massachusetts, Arthur Vandenberg of Michigan and Robert Wagner of New York. For all of them, and others too, left marks on the Senate and on history for good or ill which men will long remember."[38]

The *Standard-Times* of New Bedford, Massachusetts, said Kennedy had been selected to chair the committee because "he is recognized by his colleagues as an authority on Senate history, because his sound judgment commands the highest respect, and because he is a man of integrity who does not hesitate to give credit where credit is due irrespective of political party."

The editorial went on to state that it was a tribute to Kennedy's fairness and courage that, though a Democrat, he acknowledged the greatness of Robert Taft, a conservative Republican.[39]

However the *Globe Times* of Bethlehem, Pennsylvania, described the committee's entire purpose as "Worse Than a Baby Contest."[40] And even before the report was released, the *Washington Post*'s editorial page derided the Kennedy Committee's work as a "silly game," adding that if the Senate was determined to do the project, it should have left the selections with historians.[41] Kennedy sent an immediate response to the *Post* in which he said that historians played an important role in the committee's deliberations and defended the selection process as rigorous and nonpolitical.[42]

An essay in the *Christian Century* magazine ridiculed the decisions of the Kennedy Committee. "The three 19th century senators are remembered principally for their part in the debates that failed to prevent a civil war that may have settled the issues of secession but left the race question unsettled. Senator Taft, undoubtedly a technician of high ability among lawmakers, was the last hope of futile isolationism. Robert LaFollette, champion of lost causes, left the 'most progressive' American state spiritually unprepared for depression, disillusionment and McCarthy." The essay went on to challenge the concept of political greatness, citing the Kennedy Committee's selections. "Outstanding senators? Yes. Important men? Yes. Famous men? Yes. But to what ends did their oratory lead? Is there for any one of them a monument of lasting achievement that compares with the schools of Horace Mann, the electrical inventions of Thomas Edison, the steel mills of Andrew Carnegie, the world missions of John R. Mott, the conquest of disease of Walter Reed? Of all the kinds of success, political success is perhaps the most ephemeral. Of all the causes, the causes of political partisanship are among the least certain."[43]

The Senate's interest in, and support for, the selections of the Kennedy Committee's findings continued after the announcement. The Senate voted in August of that year to officially accept the decision of the Kennedy Committee and to create another commission to procure paintings of the five outstanding senators. This new commission was composed of the architect of the Capitol, George Stewart; the director of the National Gallery of Art, John Walker; and the chairman of the Commission of Fine Arts, David Finley. After considerable discussion and debate they selected five artists to paint the portraits: Allyn Cox of New York City to paint Henry Clay; Adrian Lamb of New York City to paint Daniel Webster; Arthur Conrad of Baldwin, Maryland, to paint John Calhoun; Chester LaFollette of New York City to paint his cousin Robert LaFollette Sr.; and Dean Keller of Hamden, Connecticut, to paint Robert Taft.

As the portraits were being painted, journalist Holmes Alexander published a book called *The Famous Five*, a tribute to the senators selected. Kennedy wrote the book's foreword, saying the profiles captured the essential greatness of the five senators. "The life of each of these senators is a drama in itself. Each made a distinct historic impression during the period of his public service, and each has become a part of America's broad constitutional heritage. Clay, Webster, Calhoun, LaFollette, Taft were all men who knew the value and limits of constructive partnership, yet each also made solitary pilgrimages at times when they differed with the prevailing mood of opinion in Congress and in the country." Alexander's book, Kennedy said, showed that "statesmanship is not a cliché but a quality within the reach of politicians with the vision and courage of the five Senators included in this fine volume."[44]

The paintings of the Famous Five were completed in late 1958, approved by the special procurement commission and the Senate Rules Committee, and quietly installed in the Senate Reception Room in the final days that year. Each painting was about two feet high and 20 inches wide and placed in a massive and ornate gold frame. Clay's portrait was hung on the south wall of the Senate Reception Room, the paintings of Taft and Calhoun on the east wall, and the paintings of Webster and LaFollette on the west wall. The Senate Rules Committee ordered that the five paintings remain covered until "appropriate unveiling ceremonies" could be scheduled early in 1959.

Kennedy spent three years working with the committee, from 1956 to 1959. It was arguably the one project that he was in charge of during his Senate career. The committee's deliberations showed Kennedy's ability to negotiate with senior senators, forge a bipartisan agreement, and present it to the public. He created a disciplined and rigorous selection process, took the project seriously, consulted with the nation's leading congressional experts, and produced a final report that was praised at the time and has withstood the test of history.

Kennedy's biographers agree that he relished his experience as the chairman of the special committee. It allowed him to delve into a topic that fascinated him—political greatness—and engage with the nation's leading historians and political scientists. It cemented his reputation as the Senate's historian and kept him in the news during a critical time in his political career. Kennedy spoke proudly of his committee and its selections. The work of the Kennedy Committee is still considered Kennedy's greatest contribution to the institution of the Senate.

In the spring of 1958 Kennedy addressed a conference of historians and reflected on their profession, calling himself "at best a provisional member" of the guild. He discussed in a partly tongue-and-cheek way the deliberations of the Kennedy Committee. During his Senate career, he said, he had faced hard issues in which he had to confront political division and sectional conflicts such as civil rights, agriculture, foreign aid, and the St. Lawrence Seaway. "All of these I would willingly face again, for the slings and arrows they brought are part of the fortunes of politics. But one Senatorial duty I cannot recall without shuddering, without a sigh of relief that it will not confront me again—and that was my assignment, as Chairman of a Special Committee on Portraits for the Senate Reception Room, to pick the five outstanding senators of all time."[45]

No doubt exaggerating the committee's political difficulties and controversies for effect to the historians, Kennedy said the choices his panel faced were daunting. "If we omitted Calhoun, would there be a filibuster? If we neglected Sam Houston, would the Majority Leader cut off our appropriation? There were suggestions of a congressional investigation of Daniel Webster's fees and Henry Clay's morality. We were under pressure to pick a second team, or award honorable mention, or vote on another five every year."[46]

Shifting to a broader perspective, Kennedy told the historians that their insights were critical for policymakers as they attempt to understand the past and make decisions for the present and the future. He saluted the historian as the "interpreter of our times" who is best suited to bridge the gap between the intellectual and political worlds. He urged historians to study large structural forces driving world events, but also to fully appreciate the importance of individuals who shape the world. He chided them by recalling Oscar Wilde's quip: "It is much more difficult to write about a thing than to do it. Anybody can make history. Only a great man can write it."[47]

"I do not underestimate the number of great men in this audience. But neither would I under-estimate the importance of great men whose actions have shaped our history," Kennedy said. The senator said he agreed with Abraham Lincoln's admission that he did not control events but was controlled by them. "But while admitting the large amount of truth in this, it is a foolhardy man, indeed, who would maintain that the crucial years between 1860 and 1865 would have been quite the same if Stephen Douglas or William Seward had occupied the White House."[48]

He cited a number of specific cases of political bravery and noted how individuals had altered history. "What if Columbus were cowardly, John Wilkes Booth sane or Paul Revere a poor rider?" he asked rhetorically.[49]

He urged historians to better appreciate the

work of politicians who seek practical solutions that often involve compromises. "I do not wish to overstate my case. I would not pretend that history is all biography—and I know that all biography these days is not history. But I would ask the historian to appreciate a bit more fully the role of the politician—of his frequent stand against these groups and masses and trends that might otherwise be shaping our history."

As Kennedy extolled the critical role played by brave individuals in American history, he may have been thinking about those eight senators he wrote about in *Profiles in Courage* or those five outstanding senators identified by the Kennedy Committee. Or he may have dreamed of what might be said of him one day, either as a senator or as the holder of an even higher office.

Nine
The Total Politician

I

John F. Kennedy's political career skyrocketed in 1956. Through a mixture of careful planning, hard work, tough-minded organization, and remarkably good fortune, Kennedy catapulted from promising politician to potential star. There was a clear cascading effect: each opportunity and success engendered future opportunities and successes. He was on a seemingly continuous upward cycle. By the summer of 1956, with the November presidential election approaching, Kennedy's name began to appear on lists as a possible vice presidential nominee on a ticket that Adlai Stevenson, the former Illinois governor and the 1952 Democratic nominee, was expected to head. Stevenson had run a spirited and competitive race against Dwight Eisenhower in 1952 and was widely seen as the Democratic Party's best hope against the incumbent president. A *Newsweek* article that summer mentioned Kennedy as one of the leading contenders for the vice presidential nomination, along with Senator Hubert Humphrey of Minnesota, Senator Estes Kefauver of Tennessee, and Governor Robert Meyner of New Jersey.[1]

As Kennedy was discussed as a possible vice presidential nominee, his staff quietly, but forcefully, advanced his candidacy for the number two spot. Ted Sorensen researched and wrote a memo that argued that Kennedy's Catholicism could be an asset rather than a liability for the Democratic ticket that fall. The Sorensen memo was given to John Bailey, chairman of the Democratic Party in Connecticut, who circulated it under his own name. The Bailey memorandum, titled "The Catholic Vote in 1952 and 1956," argued that there were 14 electorally critical states with large adult Catholic populations, ranging from 20 percent in Ohio to 60 percent in Rhode Island. Democrats needed to win those 14 pivotal states to regain the presidency. The Bailey memo argued that a Catholic vice presidential candidate could help accomplish the objective.[2]

With his political stock rising, Kennedy, then 39, was asked by Democratic officials to narrate a film about the Democratic Party that would kick off their August convention. Kennedy traveled to Los Angeles in July for the recording. "All of us who were in contact with him immediately fell in love with him because he was so quick and so charming and so cooperative, and obviously so bright and skilled," the film's producer recalled.[3]

The Pursuit of Happiness opened the Democratic convention in Chicago on August 13 and began with the words: "Ladies and Gentlemen: I am Senator John F. Kennedy. To some, the Democratic Party represents a philosophy, a way of life and a point of view. Others think in terms of personalities; the great Democratic leaders of past and present. To some, the Party is an old friend of the family; to others a crusading cause; to still others a treasury of fundamental truths." Kennedy went on to praise the Democratic Party as the oldest political party in the world and as a continuing beacon of hope. Recalling Democratic leaders from Thomas Jefferson, James Monroe, and Andrew Jackson to William Jennings Bryan, Woodrow Wilson, Franklin Roosevelt, and Harry Truman, Kennedy said his party provided inspired leadership when it was most needed. "The unchanging destinations of the Democratic Party remain as always," he said in conclusion. "Free enterprise . . . prosperity, not for the few but the many . . . freedom of thought and conscience . . . freedom from fear . . . social progress . . . security . . . peace . . . and the pursuit of happiness."[4]

After the film and Tennessee governor Frank Clement's fiery keynote speech, the Massachusetts delegation staged a brief parade on the convention floor for their senator, waving "Kennedy for President" placards. It was the nation's first real introduction to the junior senator from Massachusetts. Kennedy became an instant celebrity at the convention and across the country. "Kennedy," a *New York Times* story declared, "came before the convention tonight as a movie star."[5]

Based largely on the positive reaction to Kennedy's narration and his evident star quality, Stevenson asked the senator to officially nominate him as the Democratic presidential candidate. Working all night with Sorensen on the nominating speech, Kennedy delivered a ringing defense of Stevenson and the Democratic Party and a forceful critique of his Republican rivals. Referring to President Eisenhower and Vice President Nixon, Kennedy said Stevenson confronted "two tough candidates, one who takes the high road and one who takes the low road." Few missed Kennedy's biting dig at his former colleague, Richard Nixon.[6]

After Stevenson secured the presidential nomination, he decided not to choose his own vice presidential nominee and instead allowed the convention to make the selection. Kennedy plunged into the race and came within a whisker of winning. Battling the heavy favorite, Tennessee senator Estes Kefauver, Kennedy surged ahead on the second ballot and came within 38½ votes of winning the vice presidential nomination. But some delegates switched their votes, and Kefauver ultimately prevailed. Deeply disappointed, Kennedy accepted the convention's decision with public grace and went to the podium at the convention hall to congratulate Kefauver and move to make his vice presidential nomination unanimous.

As the convention ended, there was general agreement that Kennedy had emerged as its golden boy. Newspaper editorials gushed about him, and Kennedy was flooded with letters and telegrams from supporters and new fans. "Everybody likes a loser," he quipped to his secretary, Evelyn Lincoln.[7] But he surely knew he was not viewed as a loser by the delegates in Chicago, the millions watching at home on TV, or the nation's opinion leaders, who were always on the lookout for an exciting new political leader. Writing in the *Boston Herald*, columnist Bill Cunningham said Kennedy "probably rates as the one real victor of the entire convention. His was the one new face that actually shone. His charisma, his dignity, his intellectuality and, in the end, his gracious sportsmanship . . . are undoubtedly what those delegates will remember. So will those who watched it and heard it via TV and radio."[8]

Following a European vacation, Kennedy spent the fall of 1956 as a surrogate for Stevenson. Over the course of five weeks Kennedy traveled 30,000 miles and gave 150 speeches in 24 states, ostensibly campaigning for Stevenson. But he also took the opportunity to showcase his own talents. Kennedy addressed the Los Angeles World Affairs Council that September about the proper role of foreign policy in the presidential campaign. Acknowledging his deep interest in the topic, Kennedy said foreign policy rendered "close to comparative insignificance the so-called pocketbook issues of the campaign. For we shall have no pocketbooks and no campaigns and nothing else if we fail to master these complex and gloomy issues." In his view, large majorities in both parties were in general agreement on the long-range goals of American foreign policy, but the parties differed on their approach to collective security, international trade, foreign aid, and the United Nations. Warning Republicans not to politicize the U.S. struggle against Communism, Kennedy said both parties strongly opposed that system of government. Rather, the challenges that required extensive debate pertained to the Suez Canal, Cyprus, Israel, French North Africa, and the need for the United States to support "surging African-Asian nationalism." Blasting Republicans for having used the stalemate in Korea as a political weapon in the 1952 campaign, Kennedy said politicians should avoid "emotionally loaded but meaningless terms like appeasement or co-existence or slogans that promise everything while promising nothing." He urged candidates to discuss foreign policy in a thoughtful, constructive way. "We cannot afford in 1956 to ignore the real foreign policy issues in this campaign."[9]

Meanwhile, the senator's brother, Robert Kennedy, spent the fall traveling with the Stevenson campaign, though it didn't seem to know what to do with him. So Robert observed and took copious notes on how presidential campaigns should—and should not—be run. "Nobody asked me anything, nobody wanted me to do anything, nobody consulted me. So I had time to watch everything. I filled complete notebooks with notes on how a Presidential campaign should be run," Robert Kennedy told journalist Theodore White.[10]

Stevenson was soundly defeated by Eisenhower in November 1956, but John Kennedy emerged from the election as a rising political force. Just weeks after the presidential votes were cast, Kennedy spent the Thanksgiving holiday at his family's Palm Beach home and made the decision to run for the presidency in 1960. He reflected on his narrow loss of the vice presidential nomination in Chicago and was convinced that with four years of diligent work and careful planning he could capture his party's next presidential nomination. "If I work hard for four years, I ought to be able to pick up all the marbles," he told his aide Dave Powers. But he also knew that he had to continue to improve as a candidate. "I've learned you don't get far in politics until you become a total politician. That means you've got to deal with the party leaders as well as the voters. From now on I'm going to be a total politician."[11]

II

If 1956 was the year that Kennedy's national star started to rise, the following year it continued its dramatic ascent. Kennedy won the Pulitzer Prize in May 1957, and that same month the Kennedy Committee garnered headlines for its project to identify five outstanding senators in American history. Kennedy also participated in several high-profile foreign policy debates in the Senate on Algeria and Eastern Europe.

Speaking invitations poured in from across the country for the newly minted star of the Democratic Party. Kennedy received more than 2,500 invitations in 1957 and delivered nearly 150 speeches in 47 states. He was on the road constantly, meeting with state and local officials and the delegates who would determine his party's next presidential nominee. "Since national politics was only people, the Kennedys set out from 1956 on to learn who the people were; the right people," wrote Theodore White.

Kennedy was compiling "possibly the most complete index ever made of the power structure of any national party," White said. Kennedy and his team assembled files on 50,000 Democratic leaders and party members, keeping contact information on 3-by-5 cards.[12]

Lawrence O'Brien, one of the senator's top campaign aides, traveled frequently with Kennedy and marveled that none of his likely competitors for the Democratic nomination could be found on the campaign trail. "As I look back on my travels, the thing that amazes me is that we had the field almost entirely to ourselves," O'Brien later reflected. "I kept waiting for the opposition to show up, but it never did." He was also stunned that other politicians underestimated Kennedy. "His opponents never discovered just how tough, gutty and ringwise he was until it was too late." O'Brien was intrigued by Kennedy's public persona. The senator, he said, was not a natural politician; he was a reserved and private person, but would force himself to do what was necessary to succeed. "Kennedy had talent and he worked hard to perfect it; above all, he was a proud man who took intense pride in every aspect of his work."[13]

To maintain his national profile, Kennedy's office generated a slew of articles with Kennedy's byline. Sorensen drafted and edited many of the articles, book reviews, guest editorials, and speeches that were published under Kennedy's name. Prominent essays by Kennedy appeared in *Foreign Affairs*, *New York Times Magazine*, *Reader's Digest*, *Life*, and *Look*. Many of them positioned Kennedy as a modern, forward-leaning leader who was well versed in American history. The nation's newspapers and magazines couldn't get enough of Kennedy or his family. In 1957 alone, Kennedy was the subject of major profiles in *McCall's*, the *Saturday Evening Post*, *Catholic Digest*, and *U.S. News and World Report*.[14]

Time ran a cover story on Kennedy in December 1957 that gave him the kind of national exposure that most politicians only dream of. "In his unannounced but unabashed run for the Democratic Party's nomination for President in 1960, Jack Kennedy has left panting politicians and swooning women across a large spread of the U.S.," the article gushed. It noted that as he criss-crossed the country, Kennedy spoke to groups that included the American Gastroenterological Association in Colorado Springs, the Arkansas Bar Association in Hot Springs, the Friendly Sons of St. Patrick in Philadelphia, and the American Jewish Congress in New York City. "Kennedy imparts a remarkable quality of shy, sense making sincerity," the *Time* story said.[15]

In the article Kennedy spoke candidly about the difficulty of moving from the Senate to the presidency. "The Senate is just not the place to run from. No matter how you vote, somebody is made happy and somebody unhappy. If you vote against enough people you are dead politically. If you vote for everybody, in favor of every appropriation but against every tax to pay for it, you might as well be dead politically, because you are useless," he told *Time*. In evaluating his prospects for capturing the Democratic nomination and winning the presidency, the article said Kennedy's chief barriers were his age, his religion, and his position in the Senate, which gave him an important platform but also forced him to cast votes that might pose problems on the campaign trail.

Kennedy also increased his visibility as a regular guest on Washington's Sunday TV news shows, such as NBC's *Meet the Press*, CBS's *Face the Nation*, and ABC's *Issues and Answers*. He narrated two programs that the popular television show *Omnibus* produced on the Middle East. He was becoming the face and voice of the Democratic Party. Jack Gould, a TV critic, called Kennedy "the most telegenic person in public life." Columnist Marquis Childs said Kennedy's political ascent was remarkable. "Seldom in the annals of this political capital has anyone risen as rapidly and as steadily in a presidential sweepstakes as Jack Kennedy."[16]

III

Throughout 1958, Kennedy continued his relentless drive for the 1960 Democratic nomination, working aggressively to build contacts across the country. He also made sure that he won his Senate reelection race with sufficient decisiveness to send a message to national political operatives that he was a force to be reckoned with. He continued to travel widely, delivering more than 200 speeches in 1958 and building a nationwide organization as well as an academic brain trust to develop new policies. Kennedy was aggressive, detailed-oriented, and savvy. Fully aware that his political base was, as Sorensen called it, "tiny New England," Kennedy traveled the nation, seeking supporters at state capitals, state fairs, high school gyms, union halls, armories, and coffee shops. "No one had ever worked so hard and so long, and reached so far into the remote corners of the Republic, in a bid for the nation's highest office," wrote journalist Hugh Sidey.[17]

Kennedy's attention to detail can be gleaned from his preparation for the Gridiron dinner in the spring of 1958. Held at Washington's Statler-Hilton hotel, this annual event is attended by leading journalists and politicians and remains an important political ritual. Kennedy was invited to be the featured speaker and took seriously the challenge of being funny to this distinguished and influential audience. He assembled an informal team to review his remarks and vote on what jokes were most appropriate and amusing. He sent drafts to journalists Marquis Childs and Fletcher Knebel, attorney Clark Clifford, historian Arthur Schlesinger Jr., and his own father, among others. They each made edits and voted on more than 100 possible jokes. "Please feel free to cut any and all, particularly anything you think unfunny, inappropriate to the occasion or my style, or too broad, too mean, or too petty," Kennedy wrote to his chosen reviewers. "If you think a particular line should be kept, but in a different context, please indicate."[18]

His father sent an immediate response, praising the draft but offering blunt advice. "The fact that the entire audience is made up of Washington newsmen is important because the guests will be a little slower on the uptake," Joe Sr. said, revealing his low opinion of journalists. He suggested his son speak slowly and give his audience plenty of time to absorb the joke and then laugh. "You ordinarily tell a story very well, but this is a crowd that can be entertained very easily if you keep smiling whenever you take a crack. I am sure that you have a fine speech here."[19]

Kennedy's meticulous preparation was rewarded. Skilled at self-deprecation, he poked fun at himself, his wealth, and his father—all in his opening lines. "I have just received the following wire from my generous daddy," Kennedy began. " 'Dear Jack, Don't buy a single vote more than is necessary. I'll be damned if I'm going to pay for a landslide.' " He went on to tease Sherman Adams, Eisenhower's chief of staff; Lyndon Johnson; Richard Nixon; the press; and of course his fellow senators. He joked that a recent poll was sent to all 96 senators asking for their presidential preferences. It yielded an unsurprising result, Kennedy quipped. "Ninety-six senators received one vote." Adhering to the recommended format, Kennedy ended his remarks with a serious reflection. "Can a nation organized and governed such as ours endure? Have we got the nerve and the will?" he asked, referring to the United States' Cold War standoff with the Soviet Union. "We are moving ahead along a knife-edged path which requires leadership better equipped than any since Lincoln's day to make clear to our people the vast spectrum of challenges."[20]

Kennedy's performance won rave reviews and solidified his reputation within Washington's political class as a major talent with a limitless future. But Kennedy's meteoric rise prompted several influential journalists to urge him to slow down. *New York Times* reporter and columnist William White criticized him in a column head-lined "Kennedy: Good Man Moving Too Fast." White cited Kennedy's aggressive campaign and questioned the "frankly indelicate pace he is setting for the 1960 Democratic presidential nomination." He said that few politicians and practically no Democrats had ever been treated so well by the press, and this wave of publicity had propelled his candidacy far more than any other Democratic hopeful for 1960. White offered a concise assessment of the rising star from Massachusetts: "Good points: An excellent political mind, one of the best, at least academically in the Senate. A strong sense of fairness and tolerance in public issues. Bad Points: A somewhat spotty voting record that has looked at times unduly expedient. A personal ambition perhaps rising too high and too soon. An inordinate aura of youthfulness that somehow makes him look even younger than he is."[21]

In the final weeks of the year, *Congressional Quarterly Weekly Report*, an important magazine for political insiders, marveled at Kennedy's political surge. "One of the most significant political developments of the past two years has been the largely unreported travel of Senator John F. Kennedy. Kennedy has emerged as the early front runner for the 1960 Democratic Presidential nomination," the article began. The magazine had calculated that Kennedy had spoken in all but two states in the last two years, missing only Tennessee and Rhode Island. He averaged two major speeches a week outside of Massachusetts during this time. The senator received more than 3,000 speaking invitations in the first half of 1958. The article cited a Gallup poll released a few weeks earlier that indicated Kennedy was the third-best-known Democratic politician behind the two men on the party's 1956 ticket: Stevenson and Kefauver. During his travels, Kennedy met with thousands of Democratic Party leaders and rank-and-file members. He also developed contacts in groups outside of the formal party structure. "Winning fame, meeting party workers, identifying himself with local issues, learning of local problems and making friends in labor are all viewed as steps to the main goal—the 1960 Presidential nomination," the article concluded.[22]

While continuing to make a splash across the nation, Kennedy also took care of his reelection campaign in Massachusetts. Although he personally spent only 17 days in Massachusetts from September 1958 until Election Day on November 4, Kennedy's political operation ran like a high-precision machine, and he overwhelmed his hapless opponent, Vincent Celeste. Kennedy received 74 percent of the vote, winning by nearly 875,000 votes.

IV

The Kennedy political operation was firing on all cylinders by 1959. Kennedy assembled his senior campaign advisers, first in April in Palm Beach and then in October in Hyannis Port, to review the national landscape, discuss political leaders and delegates in each state, and chart the campaign's overall strategy. His team was composed of his brothers, Robert and Edward; his brother-in-law Stephen Smith; and advisers Ted Sorensen, Lawrence O'Brien, Ken O'Donnell, Pierre Salinger, John Bailey, and Abe Ribicoff. Kennedy's Senate staff took the lead in drafting policy papers for the campaign. Key staffers included Sorensen, Ted Reardon, Richard Goodwin, Fred Holborn, and Myer Feldman. Kennedy also drew policy ideas from an academic brain trust, many of whom taught in the Boston area: Archibald Cox, Abram Chayes, Kenneth Galbraith, and Arthur Schlesinger Jr. from Harvard; Walter Rostow, Max Millikin, and Paul Samuelson from MIT; and Earl Latham of Amherst all contributed ideas to Kennedy's campaign. Respected pollster Louis Harris and a top advertising firm, the John Dowd Advertising Agency, also were important to Kennedy's operation. The Kennedy campaign set up a ten-room headquarters in the Esso Building, just blocks from the Capitol. Stephen Smith ran the

Washington office, but Kennedy did not spend much time there. The candidate leased a twin-engine turboprop jet, which he called the *Caroline* after his daughter, to travel across the country on his many campaign swings. Cross-country flights, recalled Sorensen, often took eight hours. Kennedy logged 110,000 air miles between 1959 and 1960.[23]

A list of Kennedy's speeches in 1959 shows the range of issues he discussed as he traveled through the United States. He spoke on agriculture and water and steel; on Latin America, India, China, Eastern Europe, the Soviet Union, Israel, and Africa; on American leadership, education, the loyalty oath, nuclear weapons, and the challenges of the 1960s. He discussed broad topics such as civil rights and narrower matters such as farm cooperatives, juvenile delinquency, and unemployment compensation. His remarks were often packed with historical references, and he regaled audiences with stories of America's past. "His campaign, it sometimes seemed, was a transcontinental lecture in American history," wrote Theodore White. "The stories not only entertained but gave a lift to his audiences, making them see their connection with America's past."[24] Kennedy took his audiences back to the beginning of the Republic and the Connecticut legislature of 1789. He loved to quote Colonel Davenport, Connecticut's speaker, who refused to suspend the legislative session for an eclipse of the sun. "The day of judgment is either approaching or it is not," said Davenport. "If it is not, there is no cause for adjournment. But if it is, I choose to be found doing my duty. I wish, therefore, that candles may be brought."[25] This was Kennedy's way of urging the nation to be bold and fearless in confronting its challenges.

On Saturday, January 2, 1960, John Kennedy left his office in Room 362 of what by then was called the Old Senate Office Building and strode down the hall to the historic Senate Caucus Room to officially announce his candidacy for president. He had returned the previous day from a brief Christmas vacation in Jamaica. At 12:30 p.m., after conferring with his staff, Kennedy paced nervously in his office before walking down the hallway to the press conference he had called. His secretary, Evelyn Lincoln, remembers the applause growing in the hall as he made his way toward the caucus room. He met his wife at the door, then entered to make his announcement before 300 friends, supporters, and reporters.[26]

Kennedy said he was ready to be president:

The Presidency is the most powerful office in the Free World. Through its leadership can come a more vital life for our people. In it are centered the hopes of the globe around us for freedom and a more secure life. For it is in the Executive Branch that the most crucial decisions of this century must be made in the next four years: how to end or alter the burdensome arms race—where Soviet gains are already threatening our very existence, how to maintain freedom and order in the newly emerging nations, how to rebuild the stature of American science and education, how to prevent the collapse of our farm economy and the decay of our cities, how to achieve—without further inflation or unemployment—expanded economic growth benefiting all Americans, and how to give direction to our traditional moral purpose, awakening every American to the dangers and opportunities that confront us.[27]

He recalled that in the previous 40 months, he had traveled to every state and had met with Democrats from all walks of life. His candidacy was based on the conviction that he could win both the nomination and the election. He said all candidates should be willing to present their records to primary voters, adding he would soon enter the New Hampshire primary and others as well. Addressing the issue of his experience, Kennedy said he had been a member of Congress for 14 years and had traveled to nearly every continent and had visited many countries. "From all of this, I have developed an image of America as fulfilling a noble and historic role as the defender of freedom in a time of maximum peril; and of the American people as confident, courageous and persevering. It is with this image that I begin this campaign."28

Kennedy's formal entrance into the race attracted considerable attention, but it was hardly a shock to the political world. "Senator John F. Kennedy made it official today," wrote *New York Times* reporter Russell Baker. "Mr. Kennedy has been openly campaigning for the Democratic nomination for months. Thus today's ceremonial announcement came as no surprise." Baker added that Kennedy was the first serious Roman Catholic candidate for president since Al Smith ran in 1928.[29] *New York Times* columnist James Reston said Kennedy was in the race to win and had clearly indicated he would not accept the vice presidential nomination. "This was interpreted by leaders of his party as both a temporary tactical move, and as a threat, and it raised once more the question of his powerful political support among Roman Catholics," Reston wrote.[30]

In a major speech at the National Press Club a few weeks later, Kennedy gave a more detailed explanation of why he was eager to leave the Senate and enter the White House. The presidency, he said, is the "vital center of action" in the American political system. It is where decisions are made and the place he could best make a difference. Perhaps somewhat playfully, he recalled Woodrow Wilson's comment when he was asked if he might run for the Senate in 1920 after two terms in the White House: "Outside of the United States, the Senate does not amount to a damn. And inside the United States the Senate is mostly despised. They haven't had a thought down there in fifty years."[31]

Kennedy was a new kind of presidential candidate. He had spent four years traveling the nation and meeting with the party officials who would choose most of the delegates to the convention. He embraced—and relished—the role of outsider rather than Washington power broker. Kennedy's candidacy was based on a domestic agenda that supported minimum wage, housing, Social Security, and agricultural reforms as part of a broad strategy to revive the economy and get the country moving again. At the core of his campaign was a hard-edged foreign policy that proposed additional defense spending to close a supposed missile gap with the Soviet Union.

Kennedy decided that his only chance of winning the Democratic nomination was to win all the primaries he entered. This, he hoped, would persuade Democratic leaders that he had broad support across the country and could successfully represent the party in the fall campaign. He decided to run actively in seven of the 16 primaries. After winning the New

Hampshire primary in March over nominal opposition, Kennedy defeated Hubert Humphrey in the sharply contested Wisconsin primary in early April and then went on to defeat Humphrey again in the West Virginia primary in May. He also won the Illinois, Pennsylvania, and Massachusetts primaries as a write-in candidate and prevailed in primaries held in Indiana, Maryland, Nebraska, and Oregon.

Just prior to the start of the Democratic National Convention in Los Angeles that July, Lyndon Johnson announced he was now a candidate for the party's nomination for president. He said he was launching his candidacy at that late date because he had been consumed by Senate business. In a clear swipe at Kennedy, Johnson said those who had engaged in active campaigns since January had missed hundreds of important votes in the Senate. "This I could not do—for my country or for my party. Someone has to tend to the store," Johnson said. His surrogates attacked Kennedy directly, raising questions about his health, inexperience, and Senate record.[32]

Kennedy arrived at the Los Angeles convention with about 600 of the 761 delegates he needed to secure the nomination. Once there, he intensified negotiations with party leaders and visited state delegations, seeking their support. In one of the convention's most memorable moments, Kennedy and Johnson made a joint appearance before the

Texas delegation. Standing before a packed room and with TV cameras gazing down on the two senators, Johnson delivered a vigorous defense of his Senate leadership record. Taking a thinly veiled jab at Kennedy, who had been absent for much of the Senate session, Johnson repeated that he had been hard at work while others were busy campaigning. Not missing a beat, Kennedy sarcastically praised the Democratic leader for making the Senate's many procedural votes and said this showed Johnson was indeed a strong candidate—to continue as Senate majority leader. "I want to commend him for a wonderful record answering those quorum calls," Kennedy said.[33]

On July 13, Kennedy was nominated as the Democratic candidate for president on the first ballot with 806 delegates, 45 more than necessary. Surprising many, he chose Johnson to be his running mate. In his acceptance speech, which he chose to make at the 100,000-seat Los Angeles Coliseum, Kennedy said his presidency would make demands of Americans, not just provide them with opportunities. "For the world is changing. The old ways will not do," he said, making the case for the agenda he called the New Frontier. "It is time, in short, for a new generation of leadership; new men to cope with new problems and new opportunities."[34]

The general election campaign unfolded in three phases. First, there was an initial period in the early fall in which both Kennedy and his opponent, Vice President Nixon, tried out themes and explained their programs to voters. Then there were four nationally televised debates. Kennedy famously seized control of the presidential race with his strong performance in the first debate on September 26 in Chicago and fought Nixon to a draw in the other three. Finally, in the campaign's final weeks, Kennedy and Nixon frantically traveled the country to make the case for their candidacies. Kennedy won the election narrowly on November 8, securing 303 electoral votes from 23 states while Nixon won 219 electoral votes from 26 states. Of the 68 million Americans who voted, Kennedy won the popular vote by only 118,000 votes. If 4,500 voters in Illinois and 28,000 in Texas had voted for Nixon rather than Kennedy, Richard Nixon would have been elected president in 1960.[35]

Theodore White, the campaign's most famous chronicler, said Kennedy's bid for the presidency combined soaring rhetoric with a tough, efficient organization. "His speeches, which rove through the corridors of American history, quoting Abraham Lincoln, Uncle Joe Cannon, Will Rogers, and Robert Sherwood's poetry, with an occasional fleck of Dante or T. S. Eliot, have the purity of the scholar's touch and the sweetness of books cherished and remembered," White wrote. But he said the drive and pace of Kennedy's campaign reflected "an entirely different personality—of a man who has mastered the cold grammar of power with a toughness of instinct and clarity of analysis that approach remorseless perfection." White described the campaign as swift, precise, and relentless. "And it is the illusion of omnipresence and omnipotence that Kennedy consciously seeks to create."[36]

VI

Kennedy confounded supporters and critics in his victorious four-year quest for the presidency. He became only the second sitting U.S. senator to win election to the presidency; the first was Warren Harding in 1920. To succeed, Kennedy discovered ways to use the Senate as a platform without getting caught up in its day-to-day operations. This rankled Kennedy's opponents who were senators. "Jack was out kissing babies while I was passing bills, including his bills," Johnson snapped.[37]

There is little doubt that Kennedy set aside his Senate workload to focus on the presidential campaign. For example, having finally secured a seat on the Senate Foreign Relations Committee in 1957, Kennedy was so busy on the campaign trail that he rarely attended the committee's hearings: of 117 meetings in 1959, Kennedy only attended 24. The panel's chairman, William Fulbright, grumbled that when Kennedy did attend a hearing he spent much of the time autographing pictures of himself for his presidential campaign. According to a story circulated in the Senate, when Kennedy was asked to chair the Foreign Relations Committee's subcommittee on Africa, he first asked if it had to meet. Apparently, it convened once.[38]

While he participated in several foreign policy debates and pressed ahead on labor legislation, Kennedy's final years in the Senate were not paragons of legislative activity or productivity. His Senate office basically shut down its legislative functions after 1959. Unlike Humphrey and Johnson, his Senate rivals for the presidency, missing Senate votes when he was on the campaign trail did not trouble Kennedy. "Johnson thinks the campaign is in Washington. It's not. It's out here," Kennedy told Sorensen.[39]

Robert Caro, Johnson's leading biographer, credits Kennedy for grasping what Johnson failed to understand, that the path to winning the presidency in 1960 required him to master the politics of America, not Capitol Hill. "Spending time in the Senate was a drawback, so he [Kennedy] would spend as little time as possible there; that meant not doing the job to which he had been elected," Caro wrote. "He would be criticized for absenteeism, for shirking his duties. But he had calculated that, in terms of his presidential run, such criticisms would be far outweighed by the benefits from campaigning across the country; it was a criticism that would have to be accepted —and he accepted it."[40]

Kennedy was always clear in his own mind that he wanted to use the Senate to propel him to the presidency. Jackie confided that her husband dreamed of winning the presidency "for an awfully long time, long before I even knew." She added, "He never stopped at any plateau. He was always going on to something higher." Kennedy himself put it slightly differently: "If you are in this game go for Number One. You settle for anything else, that's where you end up."[41]

Ten

The High Court of History

I

John F. Kennedy resigned from the Senate on December 22, 1960, shortly after his election had been confirmed by the Electoral College. Following protocol, he submitted his letter of resignation to Massachusetts governor Foster Furcolo and to the president of the Senate, Vice President Richard Nixon, whom he had defeated for the presidency less than two months earlier. Kennedy returned to Massachusetts on January, 9, 1961, less than two weeks before his inauguration, and delivered a farewell address to the Massachusetts legislature. In his speech, Kennedy offered warm reflections about his home state, saying it had long served as an exemplar—a City on a Hill—for the rest of the nation.

The president-elect also ruminated on how public careers will be judged by future generations. "For those to whom much is given, much is required. And when at some future date the High Court of History sits in judgment on each one of us—recording whether in our brief span of service we fulfilled our responsibilities to the state—our success or failure, in whatever office we hold, will be measured by the answers to four questions." Kennedy said the High Court of History would ask if each public official was a person of courage, of sound judgment, of integrity, and of dedication. The answers to these questions would determine the respect and esteem by which they were remembered.[1]

Kennedy never specifically defined what he meant by the High Court of History, but it seems reasonable to surmise that he used the phrase to refer to the settled judgment of history, those assessments carefully rendered after the passions of the day subsided and when objective conclusions are possible. At another time in his career, he referred to the judgment of the "cold eye of history," again suggesting a careful assessment reached by those with the necessary distance, perspective, and standing to offer fair verdicts.

Like any ambitious politician, Kennedy wanted to be viewed as great. Presumably Kennedy hoped the High Court of History would place him among the ranks of those he most respected and admired: Thomas Jefferson, Abraham Lincoln, Franklin Roosevelt, and Winston Churchill.

Kennedy's remarkable political career has held the world's interest for a half a century. Thousands of books and articles have attempted to assess him. Many deal with Kennedy's presidency, some with the full arc of his political career, others with his family, his marriage, and, of course, his tragic death in Dallas on November 22, 1963.

"Here surely was one favored by the gods, one possessed of power, wealth, youth, the aura of manly war heroism, zest for living, personal charm and beauty, glamour, imagination, keen insight, intelligence, immense popularity, the adoring love of family and friends," William Carleton, one of the first scholars to try to understand and explain Kennedy, wrote in 1964. "Great achievements were to his credit, and even greater ones seemed in store. Then, in the fullness of his strength, he was cut down in a flash. History has no more dramatic demonstration of the everlasting insecurity of the human condition."[2]

The High Court of History continues to take its measure of Kennedy, but it has yet to reach a final verdict. Respected historians such as James MacGregor Burns, Robert Dallek, Herbert Parmet, Alan Brinkley, and Michael O'Brien have all described John Kennedy as a man of considerable talent who was killed before his policies could be fully designed, let alone implemented. They have found both the man and his career compelling and mysterious with much to admire and much to criticize. Surveys of scholars and the general public on the greatest presidents in American history differ in their assessments of Kennedy. Scholars tend to give him solid, but not spectacular, marks, while the public tends to place him in the top tier of presidents, just below Lincoln, Washington, and FDR. Arthur Schlesinger Jr.'s 1996 poll of leading historians placed Kennedy in the High Average category, below Dwight Eisenhower and John Adams but above Grover Cleveland, Lyndon Johnson, and James Monroe.[3] *Newsweek* conducted a poll of historians in 2012 asking them to rank the top ten presidents since 1900, and they placed Kennedy at number eight, just below Harry Truman and Bill Clinton and above Ronald Reagan and Barack Obama. The debate about President Kennedy continues.[4]

II

Curiously, the High Court of History has never analyzed Kennedy's nearly eight-year Senate career that ran from January 1953 to December 1960. To be sure, there has been plenty of commentary and discussion regarding his Senate years, but not a full reckoning.

Kennedy's adversaries were always underwhelmed by his Senate career and took delight in criticizing it. Lyndon Johnson was famously dismissive about Kennedy as a senator. "Kennedy was pathetic as a congressman and as a senator," Johnson once said. He often described Kennedy as a man of talent, charm, education, and erudition, but said he had little appetite for the grinding detail work that is necessary to succeed in the Senate. "He's smart enough, but he doesn't like the grunt work," Johnson told his aide Bobby Baker. According to biographer Robert Caro, Johnson saw Kennedy as "little more than a joke: a rich man's son, a 'playboy' . . . always away from Washington because of some illness or another." Johnson's references to Kennedy were often condescending and dismissive. He frequently called him "The Boy" or "Sonny Boy," or "Johnny" or "Johnny Boy." Johnson spoke more respectfully of Kennedy's campaign skills and political toughness after the 1960 campaign, but he never softened his criticisms of Kennedy's Senate record.[5]

Other colleagues offered a decidedly mixed view of Kennedy as a senator. They often described him as intelligent, articulate, ambitious, reserved, slightly distant, and never fully engaged in the life of the Senate. Democrat George Smathers, who was a friend of Kennedy's, said he was "not in the top echelon at all" of the Senate and "was not what you would call a really effective senator." Kennedy had several areas of interest, Smathers noted, but he failed to pass significant legislation. However, Senator Smathers said Kennedy changed during his Senate career. "I have never seen anybody in my life develop like Jack Kennedy did as a personality, a speaker, over the last seven, eight years of his life. It was just a miracle transformation." Congressman Tip O'Neill was also struck by Kennedy's growth, arguing that the confident, disciplined man who won the presidency was fundamentally different than the callow lawmaker who left the House less than a decade earlier.[6]

Senator Paul Douglas said Kennedy was an impressive man, but his Senate effectiveness was limited by extended illnesses and political caution. "He followed the rules of the Senate—did not speak up very much, kept himself in the background and I think was probably not particularly notable up to say 1955 or 1956. He published his book which he wrote while he was ill and, of course, that established him." Douglas said Kennedy participated effectively in the Senate debate on altering the Electoral College in 1956. He did his homework and resisted various proposals with intelligence and determination. Douglas described his colleague as active and impressive during the battle over labor legislation in 1958 and 1959, saying Kennedy's mastery of the nuances of labor law "established him in my mind as a man with a truly first rate intellect."[7]

Senate colleagues have pointed out that Kennedy was very cautious on several critical democratic issues of the 1950s. According to Douglas, "He was not particularly ardent in his advocacy of civil rights." Douglas held periodic caucuses on the topic, which Kennedy declined to attend. Douglas believed Kennedy was determined not to damage his relationships with southern senators by getting out front on civil rights legislation that was particularly controversial in the South. Douglas's summation of Kennedy was that "there was general admiration for the high intellectual level of his work and we also felt that he was on the liberal side." He said the Senate's top leadership, the so-called Inner Club, recognized that Kennedy was "a pretty shrewd politician but I don't think there was any real warmth of affection." Douglas described Kennedy as a cool, self-contained person. "He always seemed to be completely composed and not the slightest degree upset or thrown off balance."[8]

Senator Hubert Humphrey, a rival for the 1960 Democratic presidential nomination, said Kennedy was an impressive man—who enjoyed a very good press. "The one thing I remember about him: everything he did seemed to get attention." Humphrey said that Kennedy did not always participate in the work of the Senate. "I never heard anything disparaging. I maybe heard, for example, that he didn't work as hard as he could. But you never heard that he didn't have it or that he was a phony or that he didn't have the ability or the capacity." Humphrey observed that Kennedy never seemed to view the Senate as his final political destination, the place he would put down roots and grow. He was not one to stick around the Senate cloakroom, chat, or share a meal with colleagues. "There are senators who spend time in the dining room or over in the baths with their colleagues. They are friendly, sociable and their life is in the Senate. John Kennedy never made his life in the Senate, as such. He worked in the Senate. He took care of his committee work. He made speeches. But he had many other activities and, in a very real sense, was not a member of the inner circle of the Senate." Humphrey observed that Kennedy used the Senate to advance his political ambitions and didn't speak often but "did when there were debates on the bills that he was handling. But, basically, his speeches were all designed to be statements of public policy, not necessarily something that was current in the deliberations of the Senate."[9]

Leverett Saltonstall, Kennedy's Republican Senate colleague from Massachusetts, described him as an intelligent, fair-minded senator who was personally compelling. "He was an attractive person, never flustered, quick to understand the pros and cons of a problem, a good administrator of his office, a person who demanded and obtained good advice." Saltonstall cited Kennedy's charm as an important trait. "One of his greatest assets was his ability to meet a person, disarm him by quick repartee and persuade him to do what John Kennedy wanted done. He was always courteous and straightforward and could be counted on to live up to his agreements."[10]

Senator John Sparkman, a Democrat from Alabama, found Kennedy bright, conciliatory, and reasonable. "I often watched him and was amazed at his tremendous grasp of facts in connection with any measure he was handling. I was intrigued by his gentleness in debate, his willingness to listen with patience to the arguments that others might have, to work out differences with reference to legislation. He was an able and effective legislator—serious, conscientious and dedicated."[11]

Neither Harry Truman nor Dwight Eisenhower was impressed by Kennedy's Senate service. Truman, who as president campaigned for Kennedy in his 1952 race, said Kennedy "wasn't so great as a senator." Truman's judgment may have been shaped by his deep dislike of Kennedy's father and a cool relationship with Kennedy himself. Eisenhower, who was president during Kennedy's entire Senate career, recalled that Johnson and House Speaker Sam Rayburn criticized Kennedy's congressional career as heavy on show and light on substance. Eisenhower said both Democratic leaders told him that Kennedy was a "mediocrity in the Senate," a "nobody who had a rich father." In Eisenhower's two-volume, 1,200-page memoir, he mentioned Kennedy only briefly and mostly in the context of being his successor.[12]

Even aides and supporters, who lavished praise on Kennedy's overall political career, usually said little about his Senate accomplishments. "John Kennedy was not one of the Senate's great leaders. Few laws of national importance bear his name," Ted Sorensen wrote. He argued that Kennedy did solid work in his committees, participated in policy debates, helped defeat some bad legislation, and passed amendments that improved bills. But Sorensen acknowledged that after 1958 Kennedy was primarily focused on the 1960 presidential campaign, although he did continue to work on labor legislation and took part in the McClellan Committee deliberations. "Senator Kennedy was never a full-fledged member of the Senate's inner circle, the 'club' whose influence has been exaggerated by both its defenders and detractors," Sorensen concluded.[13]

Arthur Schlesinger Jr. used almost the same formulation when he said that Kennedy did not invest energy "in the laborious process of infiltrating the inner ring of the Senate leadership. He preserved affable relations with the club, but he was not of them."[14] Evelyn Lincoln, his secretary, recalled her boss as removed from the Senate: "Despite his warm friendships with many of the other senators of both parties, Senator Kennedy was a 'loner' and did not belong to any of the so-called cliques within the Senate."[15] In their memoirs, Dave Powers, Kenneth O'Donnell, Lawrence O'Brien, and Harris Wofford all say little about his Senate service, an indirect way of acknowledging that Kennedy never envisioned the Senate as his final political destination.[16]

Most historians and political scientists who have written about Kennedy refer to his Senate years as an interlude. Kennedy himself spoke about the Senate with ambivalence. Recalling its importance throughout American history, Kennedy was fascinated by the giants who once dominated the Senate and shaped American life. He wrote with palpable admiration about the eight courageous senators who were the focus of his book *Profiles in Courage* and referred to the Senate with considerable reverence during his work on the Kennedy Committee. This project became a mini-tutorial in Senate history for him, and he enjoyed weighing the strengths, weaknesses, and overall impact of Senate giants.

But Kennedy was far less enamored with the Senate of which he was a member. He called being a senator "the most corrupting job in the world" and said sordid deal making was prevalent. He once said, facetiously, that Senate pages could assume the jobs of senators and little would be lost for the nation.[17]

Kennedy's self-assessment of his Senate career can be deduced by several campaign documents he released in 1960. He was not guilty of overselling his Senate accomplishments. Kennedy's office, working with the Democratic National Committee (DNC), produced a summary of Kennedy's legislative achievements as a senator. The list is lengthy, but when read carefully, it is also quite modest. There are no sweeping claims of significant involvement in major initiatives. The DNC document credits Kennedy for initiating important foreign policy debates regarding Algeria, Indochina, Africa, and Eastern Europe and supporting important domestic policies on housing, labor reform, the minimum wage, unemployment compensation, and government reorganization. But there are no claims to landmark legislation, large accomplishments, or bold leadership.[18]

III

So how should the High Court of History view John Kennedy's tenure in the Senate? I believe that Kennedy, far more than most of the nearly 2,000 people who have served as U.S. senators, would have appreciated the complexity and difficulty of analyzing his own Senate career. His book *Profiles in Courage* primarily assessed one aspect of Senate service—the display of political courage—but the author also delved into other factors that shaped a senator's historical legacy. He recognized that summing up a senatorial career is challenging and complicated.

Kennedy's work on the committee to identify five outstanding senators in American history required him to think in concrete and practical ways about the question of excellence in the Senate. The Kennedy Committee evaluated senators for acts of statesmanship that transcended state and party lines and decided that statesmanship should include leadership in national thought and constitutional interpretation.

In the essay Kennedy wrote in the *New York Times* about the difficulty of identifying great senators, he observed that some of the most obvious measures of senatorial excellence are often of limited usefulness. He noted that some senators who are credited as the authors of landmark legislation often actually had little to do with writing the law and may have not even understood it. Moreover, actively resisting bad ideas can be as consequential as enacting good ones. Kennedy also said that while the length of service can be an important consideration, many senators have had significant careers that were relatively brief. Finally, he observed that a senator's popularity among his contemporaries is not necessarily a helpful guide as to what history's verdict of the lawmaker will be.[19]

Based on his own reflections on the Senate, it's clear that John F. Kennedy was not a great U.S. senator. His Senate career is not associated with acts of historic statesmanship, novel political thought, or landmark legislation.

One of the main responsibilities of a senator is to write and shape legislation, and in this area Kennedy made modest contributions. He drafted more than 300 bills to assist Massachusetts and New England; some became law and continue to provide assistance to the people of his state and region. He also helped write critical labor legislation in the final years of his Senate career. While the final law differed substantially from Kennedy's original draft, he did help shape the measure. Kennedy also contributed to bills that expanded Social Security and unemployment insurance and provided additional funding for education. In the foreign policy realm, he worked hard to revise statutes that rigidly constrained the allocation of foreign assistance funds.

Kennedy's contribution to the national debate during his years in the Senate was substantial. The senator made thoughtful and often provocative speeches regarding American foreign and defense policy; contemporary challenges in Indochina, Algeria, Poland, India, and China; and immigration, government reorganization, lobbying, and budget reforms. Kennedy's speeches on Algeria, Indochina, and Poland were noteworthy at the time and have withstood the scrutiny of history. His warnings to France about the dangers it faced in Algeria and Indochina were prescient and wise, and his contention that Poland was the weak link in the Soviet Union's control over Eastern Europe was proven true three decades later.

Kennedy contributed to the institutional enhancement of the Senate. His work on the Kennedy Committee to identify the Senate's outstanding senators attracted considerable interest when the report was issued in 1957 and was well received by his colleagues, the public, and the academic community. Historians and other scholars continue to consult it to this day. Senate leaders used the Kennedy Committee's final report in their decision to enlarge the Senate's Hall of Fame to include Arthur Vandenberg of Michigan, Robert Wagner of New York, and Oliver Ellsworth and Roger Sherman, both of Connecticut.

Senator John F. Kennedy had an impact on the Senate, but the upper chamber also had an impact on him. The man who left the Senate in December 1960 was much different from the man who entered it in January 1953. During those nearly eight years, Kennedy grew into a polished, tough, forceful politician. Some of this growth was, no doubt, spurred by his experiences on the campaign trail. But Kennedy used the upper chamber effectively as a policy training ground and a political launching pad. Through reading and writing, travel, debate with colleagues, and briefings with experts, Kennedy became an expert on aspects of domestic and foreign policy. He learned how to delve into problems, frame issues, and craft compromises. And he developed a powerful and compelling political narrative that melded his life story with his policy agenda and his vision for America.

Kennedy never regarded a career in the Senate as an end unto itself. It's interesting to note that when Kennedy's brother Edward was elected to the Senate in 1962, his older brother gave him advice that he himself had not followed. John urged him to attend the Senate's weekly prayer breakfasts as a way to get to know other senators, including the older and important ones.[20] But there is no record that John Kennedy ever attended a prayer breakfast, or sought mentors, or even seriously contemplated how he could become a more effective senator. There is little doubt that Kennedy aspired to be president even before he was elected to the Senate in 1952. This ambition only intensified after his career took a remarkable upward turn in 1956 and he became a leading presidential contender. From that point on, Kennedy's primary focus was winning the 1960 Democratic presidential nomination, and he used the Senate stage effectively to achieve this goal.

As a senator, Kennedy was not willing to patiently wait for legislative opportunities. He was not drawn to the day-to-day challenge of developing and advancing bills. His primary professional focus was never to become the best senator he could become. William White, whose book on the Senate, *Citadel*, Kennedy both read and reviewed, argued that for the best senators, "the Institution is a career in itself and an end in itself." White said becoming a good senator requires patience and a long-term commitment. "The making of a good Senator is in some ways similar to the making of a work of art. There are few short cuts: the longest way round is the surest way home. The career must rest upon what is slowly developing and enduring . . . rather than what is quick and spectacular," he wrote. "This is a body of subtle judgments and the most brilliant of arriving members will find it requires years of learning to be able to be truly Senatorial."[21] Senator John Kennedy was not a patient man and was not inclined to slowly develop into a powerful senator.

Still, it was during his Senate years that Kennedy forged his political identity. He learned how to project himself as a modern, future-oriented politician who was keenly focused on the challenges of the coming decade, the 1960s, while also steeped in America's past. Kennedy's love of history was genuine and frequently noted by friends and colleagues. In some ways, his passion for history helped Kennedy counteract the issue of his youth. It allowed him to project himself as a young man with gravitas. As the author of *Why England Slept*, *Profiles in Courage*, *The Strategy of Peace*, and a slew of impressive articles and speeches, Kennedy clearly embraced the role of statesman-scholar and invited comparisons with Abraham Lincoln or Winston Churchill or Thomas Jefferson. He was more intrigued by the allure of statesmanship than the mechanics of muscling legislation through the Senate.

So much of Kennedy's life and career is subject to "what might have been" conjecture. Two intriguing counterfactuals pertain to Kennedy's Senate career. First, what would have become of Kennedy had he lost the 1960 presidential election to Richard Nixon, the election he so narrowly won? Would he have returned to the Senate and bided his time before making another run for the White House in 1964? Would he have served the rest of this term and then left politics, perhaps to become a full-time writer, publisher, or historian? Or would he have put aside his presidential ambitions and refocused his energies on becoming a great senator? We will never know.

But it's intriguing to recall that a later Senator Kennedy, his brother Edward, ran for the presidency in 1980 and was defeated. He then returned to the Senate, put aside his presidential ambitions, and for the next quarter century devoted himself to becoming a great senator, arguably one of the best of the twentieth century.

Another scenario that is fascinating to contemplate is a world in which John Kennedy had lived and been reelected in 1964 and served as president until January of 1969. Would former President Kennedy have considered running for the Senate again? Paul Fay, one of Kennedy's closest friends, has said he discussed this very scenario with Kennedy, and surprisingly Kennedy said he would seriously consider running for the Senate again. Kennedy told Fay it would not be a comedown for him to return to the Senate and recalled the career of John Quincy Adams, who became a member of the House after leaving the presidency. "If a man came from the White House to Congress, he could give a voice of judgment and authority to the legislative body. No, I think being a Senator after being a President is a good job and important," Kennedy said, according to Fay.[22]

There is no way of knowing if Fay's account is accurate. Jackie Kennedy once said the idea of former President Kennedy running again for the Senate was discussed within the family, but her husband brushed the idea aside because he felt his brother Edward, then serving in the Senate, was uncomfortable with being forced to relinquish the Senate seat he won in 1962.[23] But it's conceivable that a different Senate seat would have opened up and the former president might have run for it and won. After all, Robert Kennedy ran for, and won, a Senate seat in New York.

In *Profiles in Courage*, Kennedy wrote vividly about the decision of John Quincy Adams to run for the House after leaving the presidency. According to Kennedy, Adams agreed to do so under two conditions: first, that he should never be expected to promote himself as a candidate and ask for votes; and second, that if elected, he would pursue a career in the House completely independent of the party and the people who elected him.

"On this basis," Kennedy wrote, "Adams was elected by an overwhelming vote and served in the House until his death. Here he wrote perhaps the brightest chapter of his history, for as 'Old Man Eloquent,' he devoted his remarkable prestige and tireless energies to the struggle against slavery."[24]

So perhaps in a second career in the Senate, John Kennedy might have found a home and an institution in which to fully channel his talents. Perhaps he would have developed a sense of the rhythm of the Senate, perfected the art of crafting alliances with members of both parties, and become a champion of principled compromise. With his presidential ambitions satisfied and with his place in history secure, perhaps he would have directed his formidable political skills, probing intelligence, and impressive historical perspective into becoming a great senator—even one worthy of having his portrait adorn the Senate Reception Room, alongside Daniel Webster, Henry Clay, John Calhoun, Robert LaFollette Sr., and Robert Taft.

Eleven
The Footprints of Senator John F. Kennedy

I

On January 20, 2011, the U.S. Congress held a rare public ceremony in the Capitol Rotunda to commemorate the fiftieth anniversary of John F. Kennedy's inauguration as president of the United States. Vice President Joseph Biden, House Speaker John Boehner, Senate Majority Leader Harry Reid, House Minority Leader Nancy Pelosi, Democratic congressman John Lewis, and then Massachusetts senator John Kerry were the main speakers. All offered glowing tributes to Kennedy.

Standing under the majestic Capitol dome before a packed audience of lawmakers, Kennedy family members, civil rights activists, journalists, and members of the first class of Peace Corps volunteers, the speakers talked about Kennedy's political legacy, which began in Congress and led him to the White House.

Boehner noted that 2011 was the first year since Harry Truman was in the White House that there was not a single Kennedy in Congress. The line of service that began with Congressman and then Senator John F. Kennedy and continued through the Senate careers of his brothers, Robert and Edward, and the House service of his nephews, congressmen Joseph Kennedy and Patrick Kennedy, had come to, if not an end, at least a pause.

Biden recalled that it was Senator John Kennedy who spoke passionately about the idea of a Peace Corps during the final weeks of his 1960 presidential campaign, outlining the idea to thousands of students during a pre-dawn rally in Ann Arbor, Michigan. "His call to service literally, not figuratively, still resounds from generation to generation. What an incredible contribution," Biden said.[1]

Reid, the Senate majority leader, recalled working for Senator Kennedy's 1960 presidential campaign as a student at Utah State University. He told the audience about a thank you note he received from Kennedy just a week before his inauguration. "That letter meant an awful lot to me as a 21-year-old. It still does. Today it hangs in the doorway of my office just down the hall from here—and just paces from the chamber where the three youngest Kennedy boys served as United States senators. It is the first thing you see when you visit my office and the last thing you see before you leave," Reid said.[2]

More than a half century has passed since John

Kennedy walked the halls of Congress, and he remains an icon for both parties. His name, far more than that of any of his contemporaries, is invoked with regularity in congressional debates. Like Ronald Reagan, he has become a bipartisan hero embraced by both parties, but for different reasons. Democrats often portray Kennedy as an idealist with strength and conviction. Republicans depict him as a tough, hardheaded Democrat who bravely supported tax cuts and a strong defense. To be sure, Kennedy's enduring renown is largely the result of his dramatic election to the presidency in 1960, the historic challenges his administration faced, and especially his tragic assassination, seemingly in the prime of his life.

In many histories of the 1940s and 1950s and even in biographies of Kennedy, his six years in the House and his eight years in the Senate are discussed briefly and then discounted. But his congressional service, especially his time in the Senate, was a period of remarkable personal and political growth in which an untested backbencher transformed himself into a man of substance and depth and a victorious presidential candidate. The Senate changed John F. Kennedy in profound ways, and he, in a modest way, changed the Senate. You can still see the footprints of Senator John F. Kennedy in the hallways of the Capitol and feel the lingering influence of his service in the Senate.

II

On the third floor in the Senate wing of the U.S. Capitol, in a hallway that looks out across the East Front to the Supreme Court, hang several dozen black and white photos that are part of the Arthur Scott Collection. Scott, the Senate's official photographer, chronicled Senate life, both formally and informally, for over 40 years.

Perhaps the most striking photo shows a young Senator John Kennedy playing baseball in a Georgetown park on a summer afternoon in the mid-1950s with two other Democratic senators, Mike Mansfield and Scoop Jackson, as several sunbathers gaze at them. The three senators are dressed casually, Kennedy in shorts and Jackson and Mansfield in long pants and T-shirts. In the photograph, Kennedy is the catcher, Mansfield the umpire, and Jackson the batter. Seemingly fun and informal, the photo was staged. Kennedy apparently arrived late in his convertible, joined his Senate colleagues, who had been waiting impatiently for him, posed for the picture, and then hustled off. Apparently, the fast-moving, perpetually overscheduled young senator had another appointment to race off to.

There are two other Scott photos of Kennedy hanging in that hallway. One depicts President-elect Kennedy leading the official entourage through the Capitol Rotunda on Inauguration

Day, heading toward the East Front of the Capitol, about to deliver what would become one of the most memorable inaugural speeches of the twentieth century. The third photo is far more somber. It shows Kennedy's flag-draped casket resting on the Lincoln catafalque under the soaring Capitol dome as two of his former colleagues, Everett Dirksen and Hubert Humphrey, speak in the foreground.

On the second floor, adjacent to the Senate Chamber, is the Senate Reception Room, one of the most richly decorated public rooms in the Capitol. It was designed in 1853 as a place for senators to meet with their constituents. During the nineteenth century the room was unofficially known as the Ladies' Reception Room, then the Senators' Withdrawal Room. During the Civil War, war widows came here to lobby senators for survivors' benefits and jobs; later, lobbyists of all types came here to meet with senators. It was here that the March 1959 ceremony was held to unveil the portraits of five great senators in American history as had been determined by the Kennedy Committee. The portraits of Henry Clay, John Calhoun, Daniel Webster, Robert LaFollette Sr., and Robert Taft still adorn the walls of the Senate Reception Room. Nearly a half century later, the Senate decided to add several members to its Hall of Fame. Senate leaders consulted the Kennedy Committee's lengthy and vivid report and drew from its insights to honor former senators Arthur Vandenberg and Robert Wagner in 2004 and Connecticut senators Roger Sherman and Oliver Ellsworth in 2006. There is speculation that the next senator whose portrait might grace this room is Edward Kennedy of Massachusetts, who served from 1962 to 2009 and became one of the most consequential senators of the twentieth century—a fact that would have, no doubt, both astonished and delighted his older brother.

Just across the hall from the Senate Reception Room is S–210, known as the John Fitzgerald Kennedy Room. Kennedy used this suite from the summer of 1960, after he won the Democratic nomination for president, until December, when he resigned from the Senate several weeks before his inauguration. Senate Majority Leader Lyndon Johnson, Kennedy's running mate, commandeered the suite for his new boss so Kennedy could have a convenient office in the Capitol as he prepared for the fall campaign. After Kennedy was elected president, the suite was taken by Democratic leader Mike Mansfield and is now one of the offices of the Senate Republican leadership.

III

You can also see John F. Kennedy's footprints in the three Senate office buildings alongside the Capitol, even though one was built two decades after he left the Senate. On the second floor of the Hart Office Building, which opened in 1982, is the Senate Historical Office. The institutional memory of the Senate, it maintains extensive biographical and bibliographical information on current and former senators.

In its storeroom of files on former senators arc two brown folders that hold documents about Senator John Kennedy. There is his personal file that includes biographical forms he filled out for the congressional directory during his service, reviews of books about him, a copy of his January 2, 1960, presidential announcement, a 1960 campaign brochure, and a 1957 essay he wrote for the *Georgetown Law Journal* about congressional lobbies. Along with many articles about his assassination, there is a copy of the program for the memorial service held for him on November 24, 1963, at the Capitol, two days after his murder in Dallas. The Senate Historical Office's second folder is composed of documents related to the Kennedy Committee. It includes letters to the panel from senators, correspondence from former presidents Herbert Hoover and Harry Truman, and the committee's 125-page final report.

About a dozen photos of John Kennedy during his Senate career are in the Senate Historical Office's annex on the eighth floor of the Hart building. Here, the photographic unit organizes and preserves about 35,000 photos, slides, negatives, news photographs, and editorial cartoons that document Senate history. Kennedy's official Senate portrait, along with pictures of him reading bills, questioning witnesses during committee hearings, speaking with colleagues, and campaigning for office are included in the collection. The Senate Historical Office also maintains a website that has more than 2,400 references to John F. Kennedy.

IV

The Senate building with the clearest footprints of Kennedy is the Russell Building, which was called the Senate Office Building when Kennedy first entered the Senate in 1953 and the Old Senate Office Building by the time he became president. It was named after his former colleague Richard Russell in 1972.

The Senate Library, in the basement of the Russell Building, has files of nearly every current and former senator. The green folder labeled "Kennedy, John F." is in a steel file case, lodged between Dirk Kempthorne, a Republican senator from Idaho who served from 1993 to 1999, and Kennedy's brother Edward, whose file is much thicker than John's. Curiously, there is no Robert Kennedy file. John Kennedy's folder contains a curious assortment of items: a 1967 essay by Gore Vidal about the Kennedy clan called "The Holy Family"; an essay that Kennedy wrote for the March 11, 1957, edition of *Life* called "Where Democrats Should Go From Here"; a 1976 article called "The Mysterious Murder of JFK's Mistress"; and a letter to Kennedy from Emma Sheehy, a professor of education at Teachers College of Columbia University, asking about a rumor that his book, *Profiles in Courage*, was ghostwritten. Stapled to Sheehy's letter is Kennedy's response, firmly denying the rumor. Finally, there is a copy of the *Atlantic Monthly*'s December 2002 cover story about Kennedy's poor health by historian Robert Dallek. The cover photo shows a vigorous-looking Kennedy tossing stones into the ocean.

Also in the Senate Library is a 1,143-page book, *John Fitzgerald Kennedy: A Compilation of Statements and Speeches Made During His Service in the United States Senate and House of Representatives*. It was prepared by the Legislative Reference Service of the Library of Congress and contains all of Kennedy's speeches that were placed in the Congressional Record from 1947 through 1960. Published in 1964, the preface was written by then Senate leaders Mike Mansfield and Everett Dirksen. They wrote that Kennedy's years in Congress can be viewed as his "years of emergence," in which he developed the ideals and policies that he was later to pursue "in his all too brief tenure in the Presidency."[3] The Senate Library has more than 100 books and reports in its stacks about Kennedy, many pertaining to his assassination.

Perhaps the most tangible reminder of Senator John F. Kennedy can be found in Room 394 of the Senate's Russell Building, the suite that he occupied during his eight years of service. In the 1950s it was designated as Room 362. The office numbers in the Russell Building have been changed several times since then, and Kennedy's old suite was redesignated as Room 394 in 1983.

This three-room suite has been in high demand since Kennedy vacated it to move to the White House. It was occupied by Senator Philip Hart, a Democrat from Michigan, from 1961 to 1966; George McGovern, a Democrat from South Dakota, from 1967 to 1973; Albert Gore, a Democrat from Tennessee, from 1985 to 1992; and Judd Gregg, a Republican from New Hampshire, from 1993 to 2009. On a brown plaque with gold trim next to the door is a simple inscription: "The Senate office once occupied by John F. Kennedy, U.S. Senator, Massachusetts, 1953–1960, U.S. President, 1961–1963."

Senator Robert Casey, a Democrat from Pennsylvania, moved into the office in 2009. He specifically sought it out because of its Kennedy heritage. Photos of Senator Kennedy borrowed from the Kennedy Presidential Library hang on the wall, and Casey has placed his desk near where Kennedy's was, close to the fireplace. Casey says that he often thinks about Kennedy, who is one of his political heroes. "There is history here. It's a great privilege to be in this office. When I was growing up the Kennedys were an inspirational political family."[4] Casey recalls stories he was told of Kennedy's presidential campaign, including his visit to Scranton. Casey's father, then a young man who later became governor of Pennsylvania, waited for hours near the town square, trying to get a glimpse of the candidate.

Just down the hall from Kennedy's old office is the Senate Caucus Room, which was renamed the Kennedy Caucus Room in 2009 to commemorate all three Kennedy brothers who served as U.S. senators: John, Robert, and Edward. It is one of the most majestic, stately, and historic rooms in the entire Capitol complex. Visitors are riveted by its marble walls and columns, 35-foot-high gilded ceiling, large crystal chandeliers, and three oversized windows. In this historic space, storied Senate hearings have been held on the sinking of the *Titanic*, the Teapot Dome scandal, the attack on Pearl Harbor, the Vietnam War, and Watergate. It has been the venue for the confirmation hearings of several Supreme Court justices and was used in 1962 in the film *Advise and Consent*. It was also the place where a number of senators chose to declare their candidacies for president: George McGovern of South Dakota and Scoop Jackson of Washington in 1971, Lloyd Bentsen of Texas in 1975, Hubert Humphrey of Minnesota in 1976, and Howard Baker of Tennessee in 1979. Robert Kennedy, then a senator from New York, announced his run for the presidency in this room in the spring of 1968.

And it was here on January 2, 1960, that a junior senator from Massachusetts declared his candidacy for the presidency. Senator John F. Kennedy took the one-minute walk from his Senate office to the Caucus Room that Saturday afternoon, the next critical steps on his path to the presidency.

Since he took that journey from the Senate to the White House more than a half century ago, many senators have tried to replicate his success. So far only one, Barack Obama, has succeeded. Kennedy proved that an ambitious but untested young politician can use the Senate as a forum, a platform, and, finally, as a launching pad to win the presidency. Others in the future, no doubt, will try to find and follow that same path.

Notes

Chapter One: The Unveiling

1. *Proceedings at the Unveiling of the Portraits of Five Outstanding Senators, March 12, 1959* (Washington, D.C.: Government Printing Office, 1959), 14.
2. Ibid., 9, 10.
3. Ibid., 13.
4. Ibid.
5. Ibid., 12.
6. Ibid.
7. Ibid., 11.
8. Ibid., 12.
9. James MacGregor Burns, *John F. Kennedy: A Political Profile* (New York: Harcourt, Brace & World, 1961), 281.
10. Harry McPherson, *A Political Education: A Washington Memoir* (Austin: University of Texas Press, 1972), 42.
11. Thomas O'Neill with William Novak, *Man of the House: The Life and Political Memoirs of Speaker Tip O'Neill* (New York: Random House, 1987), 86.
12. Ted Widmer, *Listening In: The Secret White House Recordings of John F. Kennedy* (New York: Hyperion, 2012), 49.

Chapter Two: Congressman Kennedy

1. Kenneth O'Donnell and David F. Powers with Joe McCarthy, *Johnny, We Hardly Knew Ye: Memoirs of John Fitzgerald Kennedy* (Boston: Little, Brown, 1970), 76.
2. Thomas Whalen, *Kennedy Versus Lodge: The 1952 Massachusetts Senate Race* (Boston: Northeastern University Press, 2000), 21.
3. William Carleton, "Kennedy in History: An Early Appraisal," *Antioch Review* 24, no. 3 (Autumn 1964): 282.
4. Herbert Parmet, *Jack: The Struggles of John F. Kennedy* (New York: Dial Press, 1980), 111.
5. Ibid., 110.
6. Whalen, *Kennedy Versus Lodge*, 22; Alan Brinkley, *John F. Kennedy* (New York: Times Books, 2012), 22.
7. Widmer, *Listening In*, 43–44.
8. Ibid., 46–47.
9. John F. Kennedy, 1946 congressional campaign brochure, undated document, John F. Kennedy Library.
10. Ibid.
11. John F. Kennedy, 1946 campaign platform statement, undated document, JFKL.
12. Parmet, *Jack*, 152.
13. O'Donnell and Powers, *Johnny, We Hardly Knew Ye*, 53.

14. Ibid., 59.
15. Whalen, *Kennedy Versus Lodge*, 64.
16. Nigel Hamilton, *JFK: Reckless Youth* (New York: Random House, 1992), 755.
17. Ibid., 753.
18. Ibid., 758.
19. Parmet, *Jack*, 152.
20. Hamilton, *JFK*, 793.
21. Parmet, *Jack*, 164–165.
22. Joan and Clay Blair, *The Search for JFK* (New York: Berkeley, 1976), 539.
23. James T. Patterson, *Mr. Republican: A Biography of Robert A. Taft* (Boston: Houghton Mifflin, 1972), 315.
24. Blair and Blair, *The Search for JFK*, 565.
25. John F. Kennedy, *John Fitzgerald Kennedy: A Compilation of Statements and Speeches Made During His Service in the United States Senate and House of Representatives* (Washington, D.C.: U.S. Government Printing Office, 1964), 10.
26. Ibid., 10–11.
27. O'Donnell and Powers, *Johnny, We Hardly Knew Ye*, 75.
28. John F. Kennedy, *Statements and Speeches*, 48.
29. Patterson, *Mr. Republican*, 355.
30. Ibid.
31. John F. Kennedy, *Statements and Speeches*, 4.
32. Ibid., 5.

33. Christopher Matthews, *Kennedy and Nixon: The Rivalry That Shaped Post War America* (New York: Simon & Schuster, 1996), 52.
34. Parmet, *Jack*, 181.
35. Ibid., 216.
36. John F. Kennedy, *Statements and Speeches*, 971–972.
37. Ibid., 41–42.
38. *CQ Almanac 1960* (Washington, D.C.: Congressional Quarterly Press, 1960), 836.
39. Burns, *John F. Kennedy*, 93.
40. O'Neill, *Man of the House*, 85.
41. Robert Dallek, *An Unfinished Life, John F. Kennedy, 1917–1963* (Boston: Little, Brown, 2003), 152–153.
42. Mark Dalton, oral history, JFKL.
43. Parmet, *Jack*, 165.
44. Blair and Blair, *The Search for JFK*, 547.
45. Mary Davis, oral history, JFKL.
46. Michael O'Brien, *John F. Kennedy: A Biography* (New York: Thomas Dunne Books, 2005), 219.
47. Dallek, *An Unfinished Life*, 136.
48. Widmer, *Listening In*, 48–49.

Chapter Three: The 1952 Campaign

1. O'Neill, *Man of the House*, 87.
2. O'Donnell and Powers, *Johnny, We Hardly Knew Ye*, 78.
3. Ibid.

4. Ibid.
5. Lawrence O'Brien, *No Final Victories: A Life in Politics—from John F. Kennedy to Watergate* (Garden City, NY: Doubleday, 1974), 26.
6. Whalen, *Kennedy Versus Lodge*, 29.
7. O'Neill, *Man of the House*, 105.
8. O'Donnell and Powers, *Johnny, We Hardly Knew Ye*, 82.
9. John F. Kennedy, announcement statement, April 7, 1952, JFKL.
10. Ibid.
11. John F. Kennedy, campaign biography, April 7, 1952, JFKL.
12. Ibid.
13. John F. Kennedy, 1952 campaign document, undated, JFKL.
14. Ibid.
15. Ibid.
16. Ibid.
17. Ibid.
18. Ibid.
19. O'Donnell and Powers, *Johnny, We Hardly Knew Ye*, 85.
20. Lawrence O'Brien, *No Final Victories*, 30.
21. O'Donnell and Powers, *Johnny, We Hardly Knew Ye*, 90.
22. Cabell Phillips, "Case Study of a Senate Race," *New York Times Magazine*, October 25, 1952.

23. Whalen, *Kennedy Versus Lodge*, 7.
24. Ibid., 30.
25. Ibid., 46.
26. Ibid., 116.
27. Ibid., 71–72.
28. Ibid., 69.
29. Henry Cabot Lodge, 1952 campaign brochure, undated, JFKL.
30. Phillips, "Case Study of a Senate Race."
31. Parmet, *Jack*, 253; Leo Damore, *The Cape Cod Years of John Fitzgerald Kennedy* (Englewood Cliffs, NJ: Prentice Hall, 1967), 115.
32. Parmet, *Jack*, 211–214.
33. Whalen, *Kennedy Versus Lodge*, 130.
34. Parmet, *Jack*, 255.
35. O'Brien, *No Final Victories*, 31.
36. Whalen, *Kennedy Versus Lodge*, 157.
37. Lawrence O'Brien, *No Final Victories*, 27.
38. John F. Kennedy interview, *Meet the Press* transcript, November 11, 1952, JFKL.
39. O'Neill, *Man of the House*, 118.

Chapter Four: The Senate of the 1950s

1. Stephen Ambrose, "Dwight Eisenhower," in *Dictionary of American Biography* (New York: Charles Scribner's Sons, 1980), 374–379.
2. Ibid.

3. Fred Greenstein, *The Presidential Difference: Leadership from FDR to Clinton* (New York: Free Press, 2000), 46.
4. Herbert Parmet, *Eisenhower and the American Crusades* (New York: Transaction, 1999), 578.
5. James T. Patterson, *Grand Expectations: The United States, 1945–1974* (New York: Oxford University Press, 1996), 244.
6. Parmet, *Eisenhower*, 105.
7. Patterson, *Grand Expectations*, 389.
8. George C. Herring, *From Colony to Superpower: U.S. Foreign Relations Since 1776* (New York: Oxford University Press, 2008), 700.
9. Ibid., 662.
10. David Halberstam, *The Fifties* (New York: Villard Books, 1993), 243.
11. Widmer, *Listening In*, 49.
12. Rowland Evans and Robert Novak, *Lyndon B. Johnson: The Exercise of Power* (New York: Signet Books, 1966), 34.
13. Ibid., 105.
14. Robert Caro, *Master of the Senate: The Years of Lyndon Johnson* (New York: Alfred A. Knopf, 2002), xx.
15. Doris Kearns, *Lyndon Johnson and the American Dream* (New York: Signet Books, 1976), 125.
16. Howard Shuman, "Lyndon B. Johnson: The

Senate's Powerful Persuader," in *First Among Equals: Outstanding Senate Leaders of the 20th Century*, ed. Roger Davidson and Richard Baker (Washington, D.C.: Congressional Quarterly Press, 1991), 201.

17. Kearns, *Lyndon Johnson*, 162.
18. Evans and Novak, *Lyndon B. Johnson*, 166.
19. Caro, *Passage of Power*, 9.
20. Harry McPherson, *A Political Education: A Washington Memoir* (Austin: University of Texas Press, 1972), 159.
21. Ibid., 42.
22. Evans and Novak, *Lyndon B. Johnson*, 44.
23. "The Senate's Most Valuable Ten," *Time*, April 3, 1950.
24. Parmet, *Jack*, 242.
25. Donald Matthews, *U.S. Senators and Their World* (Chapel Hill: University of North Carolina Press, 1961), 148–152.
26. William White, Citadel: *The Story of the U.S. Senate* (New York: Harper & Row, 1957), 72.
27. Ibid., 88–89.
28. Donald Matthews, *U.S. Senators*, 110.
29. Ibid., 72.
30. Jacqueline Kennedy, *Historic Conversations on Life with John. F. Kennedy* (New York: Hyperion, 2011), 45.
31. Donald Matthews, *U.S. Senators*, 89.

32. Dwight Griswold, "A Freshman Senator Makes His Report," *New York Times*, May 8, 1953.
33. Richard Neuberger, "Mistakes of a Freshman Senator," *The American Magazine*, June 1956.
34. Donald Matthews, *U.S. Senators*, 91.
35. Ibid., 76.

Chapter Five:
Senator Kennedy and the Home Front

1. Paul Douglas, oral history, JFKL.
2. Burns, *John F. Kennedy*, 204.
3. Theodore Sorensen, *Counselor: A Life at the Edge of History* (New York: HarperCollins, 2008), 250.
4. John F. Kennedy, speech, Massachusetts State CIO convention, October 5, 1952, JFKL.
5. Ibid.
6. John F. Kennedy, May 18, 1953, *Congressional Record*, 83rd Cong., 1st sess., 5054–5055.
7. Ibid., 5055.
8. Ibid., 5056.
9. Ibid., 5055.
10. John F. Kennedy, May 25, 1953, *Congressional Record*, 83rd Cong., 1st sess., 5466.

11. John F. Kennedy, May 20, 1953, *Congressional Record*, 83rd Cong., 1st sess., 5236.

12. John F. Kennedy, May 18, 1953, *Congressional Record*, 83rd Cong., 1st sess., 5070.

13. John F. Kennedy, "What's the Matter with New England," *New York Times Magazine*, November 8, 1953.

14. John F. Kennedy, "New England and the South," *Atlantic Monthly*, January 1954.

15. John F. Kennedy, office memo, December 1957, JFKL.

16. Parmet, *Jack*, 258.

17. Evelyn Lincoln, *My Twelve Years with John F. Kennedy* (New York: David McKay, 1965), 17–19.

18. Theodore Sorensen, *Kennedy* (New York: Konecky & Konecky, 1965), 43.

19. George Smathers, oral history, U.S. Senate Historical Office.

20. Lincoln, *My Twelve Years*, 5–6.

21. Ibid., 31.

22. Harris Wofford, interview with author, July 2012.

23. Lincoln, *My Twelve Years*, 53.

24. *CQ Almanac 1954* (Washington, D.C.: Congressional Quarterly Press, 1954), 491.

25. Ibid.

26. John F. Kennedy, letter, February 13, 1953, JFKL.
27. John F. Kennedy, letter, March 9, 1953, JFKL.
28. Sorensen memo to John F. Kennedy, January 4, 1954, JFKL.
29. John F. Kennedy, January 14, 1954, *Congressional Record*, 83rd Cong., 2nd sess., 238–240.
30. Ibid., 240.
31. *CQ Almanac 1954*, 490.
32. "Senate Votes St. Lawrence Seaway," *Wall Street Journal*, January 21, 1954.
33. Parmet, *Jack*, 272.
34. "Kennedy's Seaway Stand," *Everett Leader-Herald and News Gazette*, January 22, 1954.
35. "National Affairs," *Time*, January 25, 1954.
36. Stephen Benedict, letter to John Kennedy, February 2, 1954, JFKL.
37. O'Neill, *Man of the House*, 90.
38. Chris Matthews, *Kennedy and Nixon*, 45.
39. Patterson, *Grand Expectations*, 43.
40. *CQ Almanac 1957* (Washington, D.C.: Congressional Quarterly Press, 1957), 191–197.
41. *CQ Almanac 1958* (Washington, D.C.: Congressional Quarterly Press, 1958), 75.
42. Ibid.
43. John F. Kennedy, August 22, 1958,

Congressional Record, 85th Cong., 2nd sess., 19032.

44. Ibid.
45. Ibid., 19034.
46. Ibid.
47. *CQ Almanac 1959* (Washington, D.C.: Congressional Quarterly Press, 1959), 156–172.
48. John F. Kennedy, September 3, 1959, *Congressional Record*, 86th Cong., 2nd sess., 17901.
49. John F. Kennedy, "Labor Reform Bill," undated statement, 1959, JFKL.
50. Ibid.
51. Paul Douglas, oral history, JFKL.
52. Herbert Humphrey, oral history, JFKL.
53. Sorensen, *Kennedy*, 54.

Chapter Six:
The High Realm of Foreign Affairs

1. John F. Kennedy, February 15, 1951, *Congressional Record*, 82nd Cong., 1st sess., 1301.
2. Ibid., 1301–1302.
3. Ibid., 1302.
4. John F. Kennedy speech, November 14, 1951, JFKL.
5. Ibid.
6. Ibid.

7. Ibid.
8. Wofford, interview with author, July 2012.
9. Herring, *From Colony to Superpower*, 656.
10. Fredrik Logevall, *Embers of War: The Fall of an Empire and the Making of America's Vietnam* (New York: Random House, 2012), xii.
11. John F. Kennedy speech, November 14, 1951, JFKL.
12. John F. Kennedy, June 30, 1953, *Congressional Record*, 83rd Cong., 1st sess.,7624.
13. Ibid., 7623.
14. Ibid., 7625.
15. Patterson, *Grand Expectations*, 296–297.
16. John F. Kennedy, April 6, 1954, *Congressional Record*, 83rd Cong., 2nd sess.,4672.
17. Ibid.
18. Ibid., 4673.
19. Ibid., 4674.
20. Ibid., 4674–4681.
21. Ibid., 4678.
22. John F. Kennedy, *Statements and Speeches*, 1001.
23. Ibid.
24. John F. Kennedy, *Strategy of Peace* (New York: Popular Library, 1960), 91.
25. Logevall, *Embers of War*, 663–666.
26. John F. Kennedy, *Strategy of Peace*, 91.

27. Ibid., 94.
28. Ibid.
29. Logevall, *Embers of War*, 666.
30. John F. Kennedy, *Strategy of Peace*, 91.
31. John F. Kennedy, July 2, 1957, *Congressional Record*, 85th Cong., 1st sess.,10780.
32. Ibid., 10784.
33. Ibid., 10787.
34. Ibid.
35. Burns, *John F. Kennedy*, 195–96.
36. John F. Kennedy, July 8, 1957, *Congressional Record*, 85th Cong., 1st sess.,10966.
37. John F. Kennedy, "The Algerian Crisis," *America*, October 5, 1957, 15.
38. Ibid., 16.
39. Ibid., 17.
40. Ibid.
41. Ibid.
42. John F. Kennedy, *NANA Special*, March 29, 1958, JFKL.
43. "Algeria," in *The New Encyclopedia Britannica*, 15th ed., vol. 24, 975.
44. John F. Kennedy, letter, March 12, 1957, JFKL.
45. John F. Kennedy, August 21, 1957, *Congressional Record*, 85th Cong., 1st sess., 15446.
46. Ibid., 15449.

47. John F. Kennedy, April 14, 1959, *Congressional Record*, 86th Cong., 1st sess., 5902.
48. Ibid.
49. Ibid.
50. John Kennedy, "A Democrat Looks at Foreign Policy," *Foreign Affairs*, October 1957, 59.
51. John F. Kennedy, *Statements and Speeches*, 583.
52. Ibid., 705.
53. Ibid.
54. Ibid.
55. John F. Kennedy, *Strategy of Peace*, 235–241.
56. John F. Kennedy, *Statements and Speeches*, 928.
57. Ibid., 929.
58. Ibid., 934.

Chapter Seven: The Scholarly Senator

1. Hamilton, *JFK*, 279–282.
2. Ibid., 321–322.
3. John F. Kennedy, *Why England Slept* (New York: Wilfred Funk, 1940), 183.
4. Ibid., 211.
5. Ibid., 230.
6. Ibid., xvi.
7. S. T. Williamson, review of *Why England*

Slept, New York Times, August 11, 1940.

8. R. J. Cruikshank, review of *Why England Slept, The Star*, excerpted in "News and Views of Literary London," *New York Times*, November 24, 1940.

9. Ole Lexau, review of *Why England Slept, Atlanta Constitution*, August 25, 1940.

10. Hamilton, *JFK*, 377–378.

11. Ibid., 333.

12. Richard Tofel, *Sounding The Trumpet: The Making of John F. Kennedy's Inaugural Address* (Chicago: Ivan R. Dee, 2005), 86–87.

13. Thurston Clarke, *Ask Not: The Inauguration of John F. Kennedy and the Speech That Changed America* (New York: Henry Holt, 2004), 72.

14. Ibid., 52.

15. Sorensen, *Kennedy*, 105.

16. Jacqueline Kennedy, *Historic Conversations*, 44.

17. William Manchester, *Portrait of a President: John F. Kennedy in Profile* (Boston: Little, Brown, 1962), 92.

18. Arthur Schlesinger Jr., *A Thousand Days: John F. Kennedy in the White House* (Boston: Houghton Mifflin, 1965), 105; Gretchen Rubin, *Forty Ways to Look at JFK* (New York: Ballantine Books, 2005), 62.

19. Schlesinger, *A Thousand Days*, 105.

20. Sorensen, *Kennedy*, 4.
21. John F. Kennedy, speech, Mississippi Valley Historical Association, April 28, 1958, JFKL.
22. Alan Brinkley, *John F. Kennedy* (New York: Times Books, 2012), 107.
23. John F. Kennedy, "The Heritage of Andrew Jackson," speech, Tennessee, January 24, 1959, JFKL.
24. Gretchen Rubin, *Forty Ways to Think About JFK* (New York: Ballantine Books, 2005), 206.
25. Sorensen, *Counselor*, 234.
26. Ibid., 236.
27. John F. Kennedy, *Profiles in Courage* (New York: Harper & Brothers, 1956), 4.
28. Ibid., 7–8.
29. Ibid., 16.
30. Ibid., 225.
31. John F. Kennedy, "The Challenge of Political Courage," *New York Times Magazine*, December 18, 1955.
32. Cabell Phillips, "Men Who Dared to Stand Alone," *New York Times*, January 1, 1956.
33. Charles Poore, review of *Profiles in Courage*, *New York Times*, January 7, 1956.
34. Chris Matthews, *Kennedy and Nixon*, 199.
35. Parmet, *Jack*, 395–396.
36. John F. Kennedy, *Profiles in Courage* file, JFKL.

37. Ibid.
38. Ibid.
39. Ibid.
40. Ibid.
41. Ibid.
42. Ibid.
43. Ibid.
44. Gilbert Seldes, "The Lively Arts," *Village Voice*, May 15, 1957.
45. Emma Sheehy, letter to John Kennedy, July 17, 1957, John F. Kennedy file, U.S. Senate Library.
46. John F. Kennedy, letter to Emma Sheehy, July 23, 1957, John F. Kennedy file, U.S. Senate Library.
47. Sorensen, *Counselor*, 240.
48. Ibid., 242.
49. Parmet, *Jack*, 333.
50. Sorensen, *Counselor*, 245.
51. John F. Kennedy, keynote speech, National Book Award banquet, February 7, 1956, JFKL.
52. John F. Kennedy, speech, Harvard Commencement, June 15, 1956, JFKL.
53. Parmet, *Jack*, 355.
54. John F. Kennedy, "The Education of an American Politician," speech, American Association of School Administrators and National School Board Associations, March 19, 1957, JFKL.

55. Ibid.
56. John F. Kennedy, *Strategy of Peace*, 60.
57. Ibid., 73.
58. Henry Kissinger, letter to Kennedy, May 6, 1960, JFKL.
59. Michael O'Brien, *John F. Kennedy: A Biography* (New York: Thomas Dunne Books, 2005), 379.
60. Caro, *Passage of Power*, 14–15.

Chapter Eight: The Kennedy Committee

1. William Knowland and Earle Clements, August 2, 1955, *Congressional Record*, 84th Cong., 1st sess., 12859.
2. Lyndon B. Johnson, statement, summer 1955, Lyndon B. Johnson Library.
3. William Kittrell, memo, August 17, 1955, LBJL.
4. Richard Baker, "Historical Minute" remarks, March 24, 2009, Senate Historical Office.
5. John F. Kennedy, memo, June 1, 1956, JFKL.
6. John F. Kennedy, letter, February 11, 1957, JFKL.
7. Report of Special Senate Committee on Senate Reception Room, May 1, 1957, 85th Cong., 1st sess., Report No. 279.
8. Ibid.

9. Kennedy Committee file, U.S. Senate Historical Office.
10. Ibid.
11. Ibid.
12. Ibid.
13. Ibid.
14. Gilbert Fite, *Richard B Russell, Jr., Senator From Georgia* (Chapel Hill: University of North Carolina Press, 1991).
15. Ibid., 501.
16. Edward Kennedy, *True Compass: A Memoir* (New York: Twelve, 2009), 203.
17. Ross Baker, "Mike Mansfield and the Birth of the Modern Senate," in *First Among Equals*, ed. Roger Davidson and Ross Baker (Washington, D.C.: Congressional Quarterly Press, 1991), 265.
18. Ibid., 267.
19. Don Oberdorfer, *Senator Mansfield: The Extraordinary Life of a Great American Statesman and Diplomat* (Washington, D.C.: Smithsonian Books, 2003), 146.
20. James Kiepper, *Styles Bridges: Yankee Senator* (Sugar Hill, NH: Phoenix, 2001), 64.
21. Ibid., xi.
22. Richard Russell, remarks, Memorial Services for Henry S. Bridges, January 17, 1962.
23. Richard Davies, *Defender of the Old*

Guard: John Bricker and American Politics (Columbus: Ohio State University Press, 1993), 141.

24. Ibid., 155.
25. Ibid., 126–127.
26. Arthur Schlesinger, letter to John Kennedy, April 10, 1957, JFKL.
27. Sorensen, *Kennedy*, 74.
28. John F. Kennedy, "Search for the Five Greatest Senators," *New York Times*, April 14, 1957.
29. Ibid.
30. Ibid.
31. Ibid.
32. Ibid.
33. John F. Kennedy, May 1, 1957, *Congressional Record*, 85th Cong., 1st sess., 6206.
34. Ibid., 6208.
35. Ibid.
36. "The Immortals of the United States Senate," *Life*, May 6, 1957.
37. "The Senate Judges Its Past," *New York Herald Tribune*, May 2, 1957.
38. "The Five Are Picked," *Wilmington Evening Journal*, May 1, 1957.
39. "A Hard Task Well Done," *New Bedford Standard-Times*, May 2, 1957.
40. "Worse Than a Baby Contest," *Bethlehem Globe Times*, May 3, 1957.

41. *Washington Post* editorial, April 14, 1957.
42. John F. Kennedy, letter to *Washington Post*, April 17, 1957, JFKL.
43. "What Makes These Senators Great," *Christian Century*, May 15, 1957.
44. Holmes Alexander, *The Famous Five*, foreword by John F. Kennedy (New York: Bookmailer, 1958), n.p.
45. John F. Kennedy, speech, 51st annual meeting, Mississippi Valley Historical Association, April 25, 1958, JFKL.
46. Ibid.
47. Ibid.
48. Ibid.
49. Ibid.

Chapter Nine: The Total Politician

1. Parmet, *Jack*, 361.
2. Ibid., 359.
3. Ibid., 357.
4. John F. Kennedy, "The Pursuit of Happiness," transcript, August 14, 1956, JFKL.
5. Parmet, *Jack*, 367.
6. Ibid., 372.
7. Lincoln, *My Twelve Years*, 89.
8. Parmet, *Jack*, 382.
9. John F. Kennedy, "The Proper Role of Foreign Policy in the 1956 Campaign," speech to the Los Angeles World Affairs

Conference, September 21, 1956, JFKL.

10. Theodore White, *The Making of the President, 1960* (New York: Atheneum, 1961), 246.

11. O'Donnell and Powers, *Johnny, We Hardly Knew Ye*, 126–128.

12. Theodore White, *Making of the President*, 137.

13. Lawrence O'Brien, *No Final Victories*, 61.

14. John F. Kennedy, office memo, March 31, 1958, JFKL.

15. "Senator John Kennedy: Man Out Front," *Time*, December 2, 1957.

16. Caro, *Passage of Power*, 53.

17. Hugh Sidey, *Remembering Jack: Intimate and Unseen Photographs of the Kennedys* (Boston: Bulfinch Press, 2003), 86.

18. John F. Kennedy, letter, March 5, 1958, JFKL.

19. Joseph Kennedy, letter to John F. Kennedy, March 7, 1958, JFKL.

20. John F. Kennedy, remarks at Gridiron Dinner, March 15, 1958, JFKL.

21. William White, "Good Man Moving Too Fast," syndicated column, May 12, 1958.

22. "Kennedy: Man in Motion," *CQ Weekly*, December 19, 1958, 1553.

23. Sorensen, *Kennedy*, 100.

24. Theodore White, *Making of the President*, 491–492.

25. Ibid.

26. Lincoln, *My Twelve Years*, 127–129.
27. Theodore Sorensen, *Let the Word Go Forth: The Speeches, Statements and Writings of John F. Kennedy, 1947–63* (New York: Laurel, 1988), 89.
28. Ibid., 90.
29. Russell Baker, "Kennedy in Race," *New York Times*, January 3, 1960.
30. James Reston, "Party's Debate on Kennedy Takes Note of Catholic Vote," *New York Times*, January 3, 1960.
31. Sorensen, *Let the Word Go Forth*, 17.
32. Evans and Novak, *Lyndon B. Johnson*, 282.
33. Ibid., 290–291.
34. Sorensen, *Let the Word Go Forth*, 98–99.
35. Theodore White, *Making of the President*, 350.
36. Theodore White, "Perspective/1960," *Saturday Review*, January 1960.
37. Caro, *Passage of Power*, 95.
38. Ibid., 33.
39. Ibid., 49.
40. Ibid.
41. Sidey, *Remembering Jack*, 60.

Chapter Ten: The High Court of History

1. Sorensen, *Let the Word Go Forth*, 57–58.
2. William Carleton, "Kennedy in History: An Early Appraisal," *Antioch Review* 24, no. 3 (1964): 298–299.

3. Arthur Schlesinger Jr., "Rating the Presidents: From Washington to Clinton," *Political Science Quarterly* 112, no. 2 (1997): 179–190.

4. *Newsweek*, commemorative edition, summer 2012.

5. Bobby Baker with Larry L. King, *Wheeling and Dealing* (New York: W.W. Norton, 1978), 45; Caro, *Passage of Power*, 14–15.

6. George Smathers, oral history, JFKL and Senate Historical Office.

7. Paul Douglas, oral history, JFKL.

8. Ibid.

9. Hubert Humphrey, oral history, JFKL.

10. Leverett Saltonstall, *Congressional Record*, December 11, 1963, 88th Cong., 1st sess., 24104.

11. John Sparkman, *Congressional Record*, December 11, 1963, 88th Cong., 1st sess., 24107.

12. Dwight Eisenhower, *Mandate for Change* (Garden City, NY: Doubleday, 1963); Dwight Eisenhower, *Waging Peace* (Garden City, NY: Doubleday, 1963).

13. Sorensen, *Kennedy*, 43.

14. Schlesinger, *A Thousand Days*, 99.

15. Lincoln, *My Twelve Years*, 53.

16. O'Donnell and Powers, *Johnny, We Hardly Knew Ye*; Lawrence O'Brien, *No Final Victories*; Harris Wofford, *Of Kennedys and*

Kings: Making Sense of the Sixties
(Pittsburgh: University of Pittsburgh Press, 1980).

17. Burns, *John F. Kennedy*, 177.
18. Democratic National Committee document, fall 1960, Senate Historical Office.
19. John F. Kennedy, "Search for the Five Greatest Senators," *New York Times*, April 14, 1957.
20. Edward Kennedy, *True Compass*, 190.
21. William White, *Citadel*, 107-108.
22. Paul Fay, *The Pleasure of His Company* (New York: Popular Library, 1966), 260.
23. Jacqueline Kennedy, *Historic Conversations*, 127; Fay, *Pleasure of His Company*, 260.
24. John F. Kennedy, *Profiles in Courage*, 47–48.

Chapter Eleven: The Footprints of Senator John F. Kennedy

1. Congressional Ceremony in Honor of the 50th Anniversary of John F. Kennedy's Inauguration Speech, C-SPAN.org, January 20, 2011.
2. Ibid.
3. John F. Kennedy, *Statements and Speeches*, v.
4. Senator Robert Casey, interview with author, January 3, 2013.

Bibliography

Alexander, Holmes. *The Famous Five.* New York: Bookmailer, 1958.

Alsop, Joseph W. with Adam Platt. *I've Seen the Best of It: Memoirs.* Mount Jackson, VA: Axios, 1992.

Baker, Bobby with Larry L. King. *Wheeling and Dealing.* New York: W.W. Norton, 1978.

Blair, Joan and Clay Blair. *The Search for JFK.* New York: Berkley, 1976.

Brinkley, Alan. *John F. Kennedy.* New York: Times Books, 2012.

Brown, Thomas. *JFK: History of an Image.* Bloomington: Indiana University Press, 1988.

Burns, James MacGregor. *John F. Kennedy: A Political Profile.* New York: Harcourt, Brace & World, 1961.

———. *Running Alone: Presidential Leadership, JFK to Bush II.* New York: Basic Books, 2006.

Byrd, Robert C. *The Senate, 1789–1989: Addresses on the History of the United States Senate.* Washington, D.C.: U.S. Government Printing Office, 1989.

Caro, Robert. *Master of the Senate: The Years of Lyndon Johnson.* New York: Alfred A. Knopf, 2002.

————. *The Passage of Power: The Years of Lyndon Johnson.* New York: Alfred A. Knopf, 2012.

Clarke, Thurston. *Ask Not: The Inauguration of John F. Kennedy and the Speech That Changed America.* New York: Henry Holt, 2004.

Clymer, Adam. *Edward M. Kennedy: A Biography.* New York: William Morrow, 1999.

Dallek, Robert. *Harry S. Truman.* New York: Times Books, 2008.

————. *John F. Kennedy.* New York: Oxford University Press, 2011.

————. *An Unfinished Life: John F. Kennedy, 1917–1963.* Boston: Little, Brown, 2003.

Damore, Leo. *The Cape Cod Years of John Fitzgerald Kennedy.* Englewood Cliffs, NJ: Prentice-Hall, 1967.

Davidson, Roger H. and Richard Baker, eds. *First Among Equals: Outstanding Senate Leaders of the 20th Century.* Washington, D.C.: Congressional Quarterly Press, 1991.

Davies, Richard. *Defender of the Old Guard: John Bricker and American Politics.* Columbus: Ohio State University Press, 1993.

Douglas, Paul H. *In the Fullness of Time.* New York: Harcourt Brace Jovanovich, 1971.

Drury, Allen. *Advise and Consent.* Garden City, NY: Doubleday, 1959.

Evans, Rowland and Robert Novak. *Lyndon B. Johnson: The Exercise of Power.* New York: Signet Books, 1966.

Fay, Paul. *The Pleasure of His Company.* New York: Popular Library, 1966.

Fetner, Gerald. *Immersed in Great Affairs: Allan Nevins and the Heroic Age of American History.* Albany: State University of New York Press, 2004.

Fite, Gilbert C. *Richard B. Russell, Jr., Senator from Georgia.* Chapel Hill: University of North Carolina Press, 1991.

Goldsmith, John A. *Colleagues: Richard B. Russell and His Apprentice Lyndon B. Johnson.* Macon, GA: Mercer University Press, 1998.

Greenstein, Fred I. *The Presidential Difference: Leadership from FDR to Clinton.* New York: Free Press, 2000.

Halberstam, David. *The Fifties.* New York: Villard Books, 1993.

Hamilton, Nigel. *JFK: Reckless Youth.* New York: Random House, 1992.

Herring, George C. *From Colony to Superpower: U.S. Foreign Relations since 1776.* New York: Oxford University Press, 2008.

Kaufman, Robert G. *Henry M. Jackson: A Life in Politics.* Seattle: University of Washington Press, 2000.

Kearns, Doris. *Lyndon Johnson and the*

American Dream. New York: Signet Books, 1976.

Kennedy, Edward. *True Compass: A Memoir.* New York: Twelve, 2009.

Kennedy, Jacqueline. *Historic Conversations on Life with John. F. Kennedy.* New York: Hyperion, 2011.

Kennedy, John F. *Profiles in Courage.* New York: Harper & Brothers, 1956.

———. *The Strategy of Peace.* New York: Popular Library, 1960.

———. *Why England Slept.* New York: Wilfred Funk, 1940.

Kennedy, Robert. *The Enemy Within: The McClellan Committee's Crusade Against Jimmy Hoffa and Corrupt Labor Unions.* New York: Da Capo Press, 1960.

Kiepper, James J. *Styles Bridges: Yankee Senator.* Sugar Hill, NH: Phoenix, 2001.

Krock, Arthur. *Memoirs.* New York: Funk & Wagnalls, 1968.

Lasky, Victor. *JFK: The Man and the Myth.* New York: Macmillan, 1963.

Leaming, Barbara. *Jack Kennedy: The Education of a Statesman.* New York: W.W. Norton, 2006.

Lincoln, Evelyn. *My Twelve Years with John F. Kennedy.* New York: David McKay, 1965.

Logevall, Fredrik. *Embers of War: The Fall of an Empire and the Making of America's*

Vietnam. New York: Random House, 2012.

Loomis, Burdett A., ed. *The U.S. Senate: From Deliberation to Dysfunction.* Washington, D.C.: CQ Press, 2012.

Manchester, William. *Portrait of a President: John F. Kennedy in Profile.* Boston: Little, Brown, 1962.

Matthews, Christopher. *Kennedy and Nixon: The Rivalry That Shaped Post War America.* New York: Simon & Schuster, 1996.

Matthews, Chris. *Jack Kennedy: Elusive Hero.* New York: Simon & Schuster, 2011.

Matthews, Donald. *U.S. Senators and Their World.* Chapel Hill: University of North Carolina Press, 1961.

McPherson, Harry. *A Political Education: A Washington Memoir.* Austin: University of Texas Press, 1972.

Nasaw, David: *The Patriarch: The Remarkable Life and Turbulent Times of Joseph P. Kennedy.* New York: Penguin Press, 2012.

Newton, Jim. *Eisenhower: The White House Years.* New York: Random House, 2012.

Oberdorfer, Don. *Senator Mansfield: The Extraordinary Life of a Great American Statesman and Diplomat.* Washington, D.C.: Smithsonian Books, 2003.

O'Brien, Lawrence. *No Final Victories: A Life in Politics—from John F. Kennedy to Watergate.* Garden City, NY: Doubleday & Co., 1974.

O'Brien, Michael. *John F. Kennedy:A Biography.* New York: Thomas Dunne Books, 2005.

———. *Rethinking Kennedy: An Interpretive Biography.* Chicago: Ivan R. Dee, 2009.

O'Donnell, Kenneth P. and David F. Powers with Joe McCarthy. *Johnny, We Hardly Knew Ye: Memoirs of John Fitzgerald Kennedy.* Boston: Little, Brown, 1970.

O'Neill, Thomas P. with William Novak. *Man of the House: The Life and Political Memoirs of Speaker Tip O'Neill.* New York: Random House, 1987.

Parmet, Herbert S. *Eisenhower and the American Crusades.* New York: Transaction, 1972.

———. *Jack: The Struggles of John F. Kennedy.* New York: Dial Press, 1980.

Patterson, James T. *Grand Expectations: The United States, 1945–1974.* New York: Oxford University Press, 1996.

———. *Mr. Republican: A Biography of Robert A. Taft.* Boston: Houghton Mifflin, 1972.

Pietrusza, David. *1960: The Epic Campaign that Forged Three Presidencies.* New York: Union Square Press, 2008.

Reeves, Richard. *President Kennedy: Profile of Power.* New York: Touchstone, 1993.

Riedel, Richard Langham. *Halls of the Mighty: My 47 Years at the Senate.* New York: Robert R. Luce, 1969.

Rubin, Gretchen. *Forty Ways to Look at JFK.* New York: Ballantine Books, 2005.

Schlesinger, Arthur M., Jr. *A Thousand Days: John F. Kennedy in the White House.* Boston: Houghton Mifflin, 1965.

Sorensen, Theodore. *Counselor: A Life at the Edge of History.* New York: Harper-Collins, 2008.

———. *Kennedy.* New York: Konecky & Konecky, 1965.

———. *Let the Word Go Forth: The Speeches, Statements and Writings of John F. Kennedy, 1947–63.* New York: Laurel, 1988.

Steel, Ronald. *In Love with Night: The American Romance with Robert Kennedy.* New York: Simon and Schuster, 2000.

Tofel, Richard J. *Sounding the Trumpet: The Making of John F. Kennedy's Inaugural Address.* Chicago: Ivan R. Dee, 2005.

Whalen, Thomas J. *Kennedy Versus Lodge: The 1952 Massachusetts Senate Race.* Boston: Northeastern University Press, 2000.

White, Theodore. *In Search of History: A Personal Adventure.* New York: Warner Books, 1978.

———. *The Making of the President 1960.* New York: Atheneum, 1961.

White, William S. *Citadel: The Story of the U.S. Senate.* New York: Harper & Row Publishers, 1957.

Wicker, Tom. *Dwight D. Eisenhower.* New York: Times Books, 2002.

———. *Kennedy Without Tears: The Man Behind the Myth.* New York: William Morrow, 1964.

Widmer, Ted, ed. *Listening In: The Secret White House Recordings of John F. Kennedy.* New York: Hyperion, 2012.

Wofford, Harris. *Of Kennedys and Kings: Making Sense of the Sixties.* Pittsburgh: University of Pittsburgh Press, 1980.